SOUTHAMPTON RECORDS SERIES

General Editor:
T.B. James: C.P.S. Platt: J.G. Rule

VOLUME XXXIX

THE FRENCH-SPEAKING REFORMED COMMUNITY AND THEIR CHURCH IN SOUTHAMPTON, 1567–*c.*1620

The French-speaking Reformed Community and their Church in Southampton, 1567–*c*.1620

ANDREW SPICER

© Andrew Spicer 1997

ISBN 0 85432 647 2

For Mum and Dad

Produced by Sutton Publishing Limited, Stroud, Gloucestershire
Printed in Great Britain by Bookcraft, Midsomer Norton, Somerset

CONTENTS

ACKNOWLEDGEMENTS

This volume is a revised version of a doctoral thesis which was submitted to the University of Southampton in 1994. I was fortunate enough to be helped by a number of people in completing the thesis and this book. I am particularly grateful for the financial support which I received from the University of Southampton, the ERASMUS scheme and the Trustees of the French Church of London. The publication of this volume was made possible by a grant from the Scouloudi Foundation in association with the Institute of Historical Research.

My research took me to a number of record repositories in this country and on the continent, and I am grateful for the assistance that I received. In particular I would like to thank the archivists of Southampton Record Office – Miss Thomson, Mrs Woolgar and Mr George – for their generous assistance and interest in my research. The staff at the Hartley Library has been helpful, in particular the librarians of the Cope Collection and the Inter-Library Loans Office.

A number of friends and colleagues have freely shared with me their knowledge of exile communities, Calvinism and the Dutch Revolt, in particular the late Dr Marcel Backhouse, Dr Raingard Esser, Ms Lien Luu, Dr Darryl Ogier, Dr Andrew Pettegree and Dr Paul Regan. Dr David Seward provided invaluable advice about the textile industry in the early modern period. The European Reformation Research Group provided an important forum in which to discuss ideas and present papers. However, my greatest debt is to my supervisors Dr Tom James and Dr Alastair Duke. I am grateful for their enthusiasm and interest in the subject as well as their sound advice, respectively, on sixteenth-century Southampton and the Revolt of the Netherlands. I was fortunate to have such generous supervisors whose assistance and advice has continued up to the publication of this volume.

I would like to thank my friends at Stonyhurst, particularly Eddie, as well as the curious members of various Playrooms, for their encouragement in completing this volume. John Trappes-Lomax kindly read the entire typescript with his customary efficiency and attention to detail. Finally I would like to thank my parents for all their encouragement and support and to them this book is dedicated.

AS
Stonyhurst, December 1996

A NOTE ON SPELLING AND STYLE

The spelling of the names of refugees who settled in Southampton varies considerably in the archives. I have attempted to standardise the spelling of names by using the most common version of an individual's name which appears in the records, rather than attempting to Anglicise names or to standardise all the variants of a single Christian name.

The Old Style has been used throughout the book but dates have been standardised so that each year is assumed to commence on 1 January. It should however be noted that some of the local records and the Port Books during the sixteenth century, run from Michaelmas to Michaelmas.

The term 'French-speaking' has been used to refer to the whole exile community in Southampton and includes Walloons and Channel Islanders, as well as exiles from France. The terms 'exile' and 'refugee' have also been used to describe these settlers from the continent.

ABBREVIATIONS

Actes du Consistoire, I	*Actes du Consistoire de l'Eglise Française de Threadneedle Street, Londres, Vol. I, 1560–1565*, ed. E. Johnston, (HSQS, 38, 1937).
Actes du Consistoire, II	*Actes du Consistoire de l'Eglise Française de Threadneedle Street, Londres. Vol. II, 1571–1577*, ed. A.M. Oakley, (HSQS, 48, 1969).
Acts of the Privy Council	*Acts of the Privy Council of England*, ed. J.R. Dasent, 32 vols. (London, 1890–93).
ADN	Archives du Nord, Lille
ADS-M	Archives Départementales de la Seine-Maritime, Rouen
AGR	Archives Générales de Royaume, Brussels
Assembly Books	*The Assembly Books of Southampton*, ed. J. W. Horrocks, 4 vols. (PSRS, 19, 21, 24, 25; 1917, 1920, 1924–25).
BL	British Library, London
BSHPF	*Bulletin de la Société de l'Histoire du Protestantisme Français*
CDRO	City and Diocesan Record Office, Canterbury
Court Leet Records	*Court Leet Records*, ed. F.J.C. Hearnshaw & D.M. Hearnshaw, (PSRS, 1, 2, 4; 1905–7).
CPR Elizabeth	*Calendar of Patent Rolls, preserved in the Public Record Office, Elizabeth*, (London, 1939–).
D.N.B.	*Dictionary of National Biography*, ed. L. Stephen & S. Lee, 21 vols. (Oxford, 1917).
Ec.H.R.	*Economic History Review*
HCA	High Court of Admiralty
HRO	Hampshire Record Office, Winchester
HLL	Huguenot Library, London
HSP	*Proceedings of the Huguenot Society*
HSQS	Huguenot Society Quarto Series
PCC	Prerogative Court of Canterbury
PHFC	*Proceedings of the Hampshire Field Club*
PRO	Public Record Office, London
PSRS	Publications of the Southampton Record Society
Registre	*Registre des Baptesmes, Mariages & Mortz, et Jeusnes de l'Eglise Wallonne . . . étable à Southampton*, ed. H.M. Godfray, (HSQS, 4, 1890).

Returns of Aliens	*Returns of Aliens dwelling in the City and Suburbs of London*, ed. R.E.G. Kirk & E.F. Kirk, 4 Parts, (HSQS, 10, 1900–8).
SA	Stadsarchief Antwerpen
SP	State Papers
SRO	Southampton Record Office, Southampton
SRS	Southampton Records Series
The Third Book of Remembrance	*The Third Book of Remembrance of Southampton, 1514– 1602*, ed. A.L. Merson, *et al.*, 4 vols. (SRS, 2, 3, 8, 22; 1952, 1955, 1965, 1979).

TABLES

INTRODUCTION

The religious and political policies of Philip II of Spain during the 1560s precipitated the Dutch Revolt and gave rise to an exodus of religious dissidents from the Southern Netherlands. According to recent estimates about one hundred and fifty thousand fled from these provinces – about five percent of the total population – amongst them some of the wealthiest and most highly educated and skilled members of society. These exiles sought refuge in Germany where new communities congregated in the Lower Rhine, the Palatinate and Frankfurt-am-Main. In the case of Emden the Netherlanders became members of the local Reformed church which they came to dominate. Refugees also settled in England; stranger communities were founded in London, Sandwich, Norwich, Southampton and Canterbury. These communities grew further as exiles from the French Wars of Religion sought refuge in England, especially in the wake of the Massacre of St. Bartholomew's Day, 1572.

The Calvinist Netherlanders who settled in Southampton in 1567 were only the latest in a series of foreign influxes. In the thirteenth century the English wool trade and Gascon wine trade had drawn Flemish, French and Spanish merchants to the town. During the fourteenth and fifteenth centuries Southampton had become the English entrepôt for Italian merchants importing spices and luxury goods and dyes for the cloth industry. There were also settlers from the Low Countries in the town in the fifteenth century. Descendants of some of these aliens were still in Southampton when the Walloons arrived.

Certain characteristics, such as residential segregation and a degree of informal self-help, might be considered typical of any alien settlement. During the Middle Ages the Hanse and the Italian merchants had developed highly sophisticated organisations. The community of French-speaking refugees which was established in Southampton provides a marked contrast with these earlier alien settlements. Those aliens had settled in Southampton for commercial reasons but the exile community founded in 1567 was different. It was essentially a 'planted' community which was admitted on certain conditions; in particular it was required to introduce and transfer the innovative skills used in the 'new draperies'. Unlike the previous settlers, the Calvinist refugees were not looked on as a mercantile colony; they were expected to revive the flagging local economy. Furthermore one other very important distinction needs to be made between the refugee community and earlier alien settlements. Religion, which in the case of the Italians served to unite them with their host community, set the French-speaking refugees apart from the townspeople. These fundamental differences from the previous foreign communities in Southampton need to be borne in mind when considering the refugee community established in 1567.

THE FRENCH-SPEAKING REFORMED COMMUNITY
AND THEIR CHURCH IN SOUTHAMPTON, 1567–*c*.1620

THE EXILES AND THEIR ANTECEDENTS

On the 21 December 1567 a group of about fifty men and women gathered in the chapel of St. Julien, a part of the medieval hospital of God's House. They met together to celebrate the Lord's Supper; the names of those who received the sacrament were carefully recorded. This was the first service of the newly established French-speaking Reformed church in Southampton.

The survival of the register of the French church from the very beginnings of the community has provided a unique opportunity to analyse the origins of the initial settlers and to establish their motives for migrating to Southampton. The names of 166 settlers are recorded in the *Registre* between 21 December 1567 and 2 January 1569, and the origins of 66 per cent can be firmly established. Sixteen were either English or Channel Islanders and ten came from France, but the majority came from the Southern Netherlands: Antwerp (7), Armentières area (10), Bruges (1), Liège (1), Tournai (13) and Valenciennes (51).[1]

Almost a third of the initial settlers came from Valenciennes, a town now in Northern France but which in the sixteenth century was in the Southern Netherlands under the jurisdiction of the Habsburgs. This group of settlers also included those who were to be the most prominent members of the community during the first twenty years of its history: Mathieu Sohier, Arnoul le Clercq and Jean de Beaulieu. While close family relationships and business connections might be expected to develop within a refugee community, in the case of the Southampton community those links had already been forged before the strangers had been forced to leave the Southern Netherlands. At least twenty-six of the fifty-one people who originated from Valenciennes came from two families, the Sohiers and their distant relatives the de Beaulieus. A further six people were described as servants of these families.

Mathieu Sohier and his brother Jehan were among those present at the first celebration of the Lord's Supper held in December 1567. Also in the congregation were their sister Wauldrue Sohier with her husband (Guillaume Coppin) and family, their cousin Jehan le Mesureur and his family, and also Arnoul le Clercq (another cousin of Mathieu Sohier) with his family. Mathieu Sohier's niece, Catherine des Plus, and his widowed mother Jehanne de Caig-noncle, also joined the Church within the first twelve months of its establishment.[2] Other members of Mathieu Sohier's immediate family joined other exile

---

[1]   A. Spicer, 'The French-speaking Reformed community and their Church in Southampton, 1567–*c*.1620', (unpublished Ph.D. thesis, University of Southampton, 1994), pp. 18–20.

[2]   *Registre*, pp. 3–4.

communities. His brothers Pierre and Claude Sohier both became members of the French church in London while Cornille Sohier and his sister Marie Sohier with her husband, Christopher de Faloise, settled in Rye.[3]

The Sohiers were a prosperous Valenciennes family headed by Mathieu Sohier *père* and his wife Jehanne de Caignoncle. Although Mathieu Sohier described himself as a merchant, he had begun to invest in the countryside. His will, drawn up in 1557, referred to property and manorial rights in the seigneurie of Bailloel and the fief of Haussy, as well as *rentes* on rural properties and in Valenciennes itself.[4] These interests later appear in the records of the *Conseil des Troubles*.[5] Even as late as 1593, the Sohier lands at Haussy were referred to by Mathieu Sohier's son and namesake in his will.[6] The family also had a limited interest in the public *rentes* issued by the city of Valenciennes although they proved a less lucrative investment than trade and so did not attract many merchants.[7] Such investment in seigneuries, land and *rentes* not only provided a financial return but it also opened the route for possible social advancement.[8] However the Sohiers' holdings do not match those belonging to the wealthy Calvinist merchants such as Vincent Resteau and the wealthy wine merchant Michel Herlin, whose properties and interests were scattered throughout Hainaut.[9]

A further gauge of the family's economic standing can be obtained from the value of the property that was confiscated from the Sohiers and their relatives by the *Conseil des Troubles*. The household goods of Jean le Thieullier, the cousin of Jehanne de Caignoncle, realised 527 *livres tournois* 3s 3d.[10] Guillaume Coppin's household goods may only have realised 83 *livres tournois* 2s, yet in a will drawn up in 1566, he made bequests in excess of 4,100 *livres tournois*.[11]

The Sohiers were distantly related to the ancient Sohier de Vermandois family of Mons who had held several positions of local prominence in Valenciennes

---

[3] *Returns of Aliens dwelling in the City and Suburbs of London*, ed. R.E.G. Kirk & E.F. Kirk, 4 parts, (HSQS, 10, 1900–8), I, p. 397; HMC, *The Manuscripts of Rye and Hereford Corporations; Capt. Loder-Symonds, Mr. E.R. Wodehouse, M.P., and others*, (London, 1892), pp. 6, 24, 25, 59, 62; W.J. Hardy, 'Foreign Refugees at Rye', *HSP*, 2 (1887–88), 568, 570; G. Mayhew, *Tudor Rye*, (Hove, 1987), pp. 88–89, 254, 258, 295–96.

[4] ADN, B20115 (Matières généalogiques 1355–1564) 22472 Mathieu Sohier & Jehanne de Caignoncle, 1557.

[5] ADN, Chambre des Comptes B12700, ff. 12, 19, 21v, 40v.

[6] PRO, PCC Prob. 11/106 Mathieu Sohier.

[7] Archives Communales de Valenciennes, CC146I Comptes des Massards 1565–66, ff. 45, 115, 141, 186, 193v.

[8] G.W. Clark, 'An Urban Study during the Revolt of the Netherlands: Valenciennes, 1540–1570', (unpublished Ph.D. thesis, Columbia University, 1972), pp. 71–72, 73, 74, 117; F. Barbier, 'L'imprimerie, la Réforme et l'Allemagne: Le cas de Nicolas Bassé, Valenciennois', *Valentiana*, 12 (1993), 11.

[9] Clark, 'An Urban Study', pp. 72, 74.

[10] ADN, Chambre des Comptes B12701, f. 12.

[11] ADN, Chambre des Comptes B12701, ff. 11v–12; PRO, PCC Prob. 11/55 Guillaume Coppin.

in the past.[12] This may have served to enhance the social standing of the Sohiers; the family certainly possessed the wealth and status to marry into the leading families of the town. Mathieu Sohier had married Jehanne de Caignoncle, the sister-in-law of Jacques le Clercq and the sister of Nicolas de Caignoncle, another prominent Valenciennes merchant. Their children also made advantageous marriages, some into *échevinale* families: Pierre married Anne de la Fontaine dit Wicart; Mathieu married Catherine Resteau, the daughter of François Resteau and Anne Godin.[13]

The family's economic status and marriage alliances therefore placed them amongst the mercantile élite of Valenciennes. While the government of the city rested in the hands of a tight oligarchy of *échevinale* families who dominated the *Magistrat*, the merchant families controlled the *Conseil Particulier* which served as an important adjunct to the *Magistrat*. Some *bourgeois* families such as the de Caignoncles and the le Mesureurs did serve for short periods on the *Magistrat* but other wealthy merchants such as Michel Herlin and Vincent Resteau were excluded.[14] The Sohiers were probably represented on the *Conseil Particulier*. Although there are no lists of those who served on the *Conseil Particulier*, the membership usually included the constables of the bourgeois militia. Arnoul le Clercq and Guillaume Coppin were both constables in 1553 while Jehan le Mesureur and Jehan Sohier were amongst those appointed to act as the captains of the Town Watch at the bungled execution of the *Maubruslez* in 1562.[15]

For all their economic success and social status, the Sohiers did not assume a prominent rôle in Valenciennes. Lacking the wealth of the Herlins and the prestige of such established families as the le Boucqs, they do not appear frequently in the political life of the city. They may in fact have chosen to direct their energies towards commerce rather than becoming involved in civic affairs. The family might also have been 'disqualified' on account of suspicions about their religious orthodoxy. In 1544, Jacques Sohier, probably the nephew of Mathieu Sohier, had been arrested in the company of '*dogmatiseurs*'.[16] There is however stronger evidence to link the Sohiers with heresy in Valenciennes.

---

[12]   For example, Florence Sohier was the Abbesse des Dames de Beaumont at Valenciennes at the end of the fifteenth century. In 1531, Guillaume Sohier was *Chartreux* at Valenciennes. J.B. le Carpentier, *La Véritable origine de la très-ancienne et très-illustre maison de Sohier*, (Leiden, 1661), p. 9; *Armorial Général de France de d'Hozier. Complément. Notice Généalogique sur la famille Sohier de Vermandois*, (Paris, 1879), pp. 7–8, 9.

[13]   Bibliothèque Municipale de Valenciennes, Manuscrits 809–818 Casimir de Sars, livres généalogiques, III, p. 19, IX, p. 601.

[14]   Clark, 'An Urban Study', pp. 72, 74, 114, 116.

[15]   C. Paillard, *Histoire des Troubles religieux de Valenciennes 1560–1567*, 4 vols. (Brussels, 1874–76), II, pp. 176–85, III, pp. 413, 416. For the *Maubruslez*, see below p. 6.

[16]   ADN, B20115 (Matières généalogiques 1355–1564) 22472, Mathieu Sohier & Jehanne de Caignoncle, 1557; C. Paillard, *Une page de l'histoire religieuse des Pays-Bas. Le procès de Pierre Brully*, (1878), p. 148; C. Rahlenbeck, 'Les chanteries de Valenciennes. Episodes de l'histoire du seizième siècle', *Bulletin de la Commission de l'Histoire des Eglises Wallonnes*, First Series, 3 (1888), 124–25.

By the late 1540s the Reformed movement had begun to recover from the fierce bout of persecution which had followed the arrest and execution of Pierre Brully in 1545.[17] The hostility towards the religious policy of Brussels among the magistrates of Valenciennes was particularly conducive to such a recovery. The civic authorities resented in particular the jurisdiction of the special commission set up by central government to try cases in the wake of Brully's preaching and alleged that it contravened their privileges. Furthermore, the torture of suspected heretics and the confiscation of their property was contrary to the privileges of Valenciennes.[18] A *placard* issued on 20 November 1549 upheld Charles V's claim to the confiscated property in the case of heretics and initiated a long-running dispute between the government and the Valenciennes authorities.[19] The *placard* seems to have coincided with the execution of Michelle de Caignoncle, the widow of the *bourgeois* Jacques le Clercq, and the confiscation of her goods.[20] This no doubt heightened the concern of the Valenciennes authorities about the issue of confiscated property.

Michelle de Caignoncle was the sister of Jehanne de Caignoncle and so was closely related to the Sohiers. The accounts of the confiscation of her property reveal that amongst those who received payments from her estate were Georges des Plus and Mathieu Sohier. The sale of her moveable goods raised 1212 *livres tournois* 4s 12d, a sizeable sum.[21] Although the privileges of the citizens of Valenciennes did not protect the widow of a *bourgeois*, such as Michelle de Caignoncle, her execution revealed that this class was not exempt from the powers of the Inquisition. She was in fact the only member of a merchant family to be executed in Valenciennes during Charles V's reign and merited inclusion in Jean Crespin's martyrology.[22]

---

[17] For a recent article on early Protestantism in Valenciennes, see D. Courbet, 'Les Protestants à Valenciennes entre 1520 et 1545', *Valentiana*, 12 (1993), 17–24.

[18] See Paillard, *Histoire des Troubles*, IV, pp. 35–69.

[19] The *placard* upheld the Emperor's claim to confiscated property, in the case of heretics '*nonobstant coustumes, privileges et usances pretendues ou contraires par aulcuns ville ou pays*'. *Receuil des Ordonnances des Pays-Bas (Deuxième série – 1506–1700)*, ed. C. Laurent et al., (Brussels, 1893–), V, pp. 575–78. See A.C. Duke, *Reformation and Revolt in the Low Countries*, (London, 1990), p. 164; Paillard, *Histoire des Troubles*, IV, pp. 42–69, 248–62.

[20] The actual date of Michelle de Caignoncle's execution has been fiercely contested by historians. Jean Crespin's martyrology dates the execution to 1551 but Paillard attempted to disprove this and other possible dates, concluding that the execution took place in 1549, probably later than 2 April. The most likely date of the execution, according to Hodeigne's thorough examination of the sources, was between 15 September and 1 December 1549. J. Crespin, *Histoire des Martyrs persecutez et mis à mort pour la verite de l'Evangile, depuis le temps des apostres iusques à present (1619)*, ed. D. Benoit, 3 vols. (Toulouse, 1885–89), I, p. 558; C. Paillard, 'Note sur Michielle de Caignoncle', *BSHPF*, 26 (1877), 554–58; M. Hodeigne, 'Le protestantisme à Valenciennes jusqu'à la veille de la Révolution des Pays-Bas', (unpublished mémoire de licence, Université de Liège, 1966–67), pp. 97–102.

[21] ADN, Chambre de Comptes B12696. Extracts were published in Paillard, 'Note sur Michielle de Caignoncle', 559–61.

[22] Crespin, *Histoire des Martyrs*, I, p. 558.

The Calvinist movement grew in strength during the 1550s and the Sohiers continued to be actively involved. Jehan le Mesureur, a cousin of Jehanne de Caignoncle and later a refugee in Southampton, assumed an important role in the emerging church. He was a member of an informal group of wealthy Calvinists which predated the first formal Calvinist consistory in Valenciennes organised by Ambroise Wille of Tournai in 1563.[23] Jehan le Mesureur examined Paul Chevalier prior to his appointment as the Calvinist minister in December 1561.[24] He may also have helped to organise the psalm-singing demonstrations, the *chanteries*, in the autumn of 1561.[25]

The power of the Calvinists in Valenciennes was vividly demonstrated in 1562 in the *Maubruslez* affair. Following the arrest of two deacons, Maillart and Fauveau, the Calvinists put pressure on the *Magistrat* and reminded them of their responsibilities as godly magistrates, while also threatening civil disorder.[26] On the other side the Regent demanded action against Maillart and Fauveau as she believed that the spread of heresy in the city was due to the failure of the civic authorities to deal effectively with the problem. After vacillating the *Magistrat* solved its dilemma by appointing a Town Watch to supervise the execution and to maintain order, which included thirty loyal Catholics and thirty suspected Calvinists. These included Michel Herlin and Jehan de Lattre, as well as Jehan le Mesureur and Jehan Sohier.[27] The release of the *Maubruslez* by the crowd in Valenciennes revealed the extent to which the Calvinists had undermined the authority of the *Magistrat*.

The Regent blamed the *Magistrat* for the *Maubruslez* affair and attempted to ensure that office-holding in Valenciennes was restricted to loyal Catholics.[28] The appointment to the *Magistrat* of suspected Calvinists, such as Michel Herlin, Bertrand Gruel and also Guillaume Coppin in July 1562 and Jehan le Mesureur in July 1563, demonstrates the failure of this policy.[29] Margaret of Parma also appointed her '*conseiller et maistre d'hostel*' to supervise the implementation of the *placards* in Valenciennes.[30] Still the Calvinists continued to defy the government and in the spring of 1563 they held a series of open-air sermons.[31] The central government punished Valenciennes by imposing a garrison on the town in May 1563 and in September a further *placard* was issued

---

[23]   P. Beuzart, *La répression à Valenciennes après les troubles religieux de 1566*, (Paris, 1930), pp. 118–19.

[24]   L-E. Halkin & G. Moreau, 'Le procès de Paul Chevalier à Lille et Tournai en 1564', *Bulletin de la Commission Royale d'Histoire*, 131 (1965), 9.

[25]   On le Mesureur's involvement with the Reformed cause, see AGR, Conseil des Troubles 88, f. 80. A transcription of this confession is published in L.A. van Langeraad, *Guido de Bray. Zijn leven en werken*, (Zierikzee, 1884), pp. LXXVII–LXXVIII.

[26]   Paillard, *Histoire des Troubles*, II, pp. 144–45.

[27]   Paillard, *Histoire des Troubles*, II, pp. 176–85.

[28]   Paillard, *Histoire des Troubles*, II, pp. 308, 311; P.J. le Boucq, *Histoire des Troubles advenues à Valenciennes à cause des hérésies 1562–1579*, ed. A-P-L. de Robaulx de Soumoy, (Brussels, 1864), p. 7.

[29]   Le Boucq, *Histoire des Troubles*, pp. 5, 8.

[30]   Paillard, *Histoire des Troubles*, II, pp. 362–66.

[31]   Paillard, *Histoire des Troubles*, III, pp. 246–48.

to deal with the city.[32] This *placard* reiterated an earlier *placard* of 1561 which imposed harsh penalties upon suspected Calvinists or their sympathisers. This development alarmed the *Magistrat*. In particular, they resented the require-ment that clerics provide certificates of religious orthodoxy for people who travelled between parishes and the need for newcomers to the city to bring such certificates with them.[33] Such restrictions were seen to threaten not merely Valenciennes' trade but also the cloth industry which depended upon workers coming in from the surrounding villages. The city authorities protested to the Regent that such restrictions contravened the privileges Philip had sworn to uphold and threatened '*la ruyne et depopulation de la ville et de l'entrecours de la marchandise*'.[34] Furthermore the garrison placed a heavy financial burden upon the city which served further to disrupt the trading life of the city. The repression caused some Calvinists to leave Valenciennes. Jehan le Mesureur had gone by the end of June, having migrated to Sedan in the Ardennes, later to be joined by his wife and household.[35] A *marchand de laine*, Jacques de Leau, was summoned to appear before the Inquisition in November 1564 for not going to church and having attended the *presches*. Since de Leau had already left Valenciennes with his household without permission from the *Magistrat*, he was banished from the town and his property was confiscated.[36]

There was in fact a general emigration from the Walloon towns after 1562. Some chose exile and migrated either to France or to the emerging stranger communities in England. There was also a clear movement towards Antwerp from the Walloon towns. As one lay preacher commented in 1558: 'Antwerp is a world of its own; one can hide away there without having to flee'.[37] The city authorities were not prepared to jeopardise Antwerp's position as an inter-national trading centre or to alienate the foreign merchants there by rigorously enforcing the *placards*. Fifteen Valenciennes merchants became citizens of Antwerp between 1542 and 1566, compared with only one since 1533 and eight merchants between 1567 and 1585.[38] Unfortunately there is no indication as to the religious beliefs of these merchants. However migration was not solely motivated by religion but also by commercial reasons, although in some instances it would be difficult to distinguish between the two motives. (Jean de Beaulieu seems to have migrated from Valenciennes for commercial reasons

---

[32] Paillard, *Histoire des Troubles*, III, pp. 303, 428–43.
[33] Paillard, *Histoire des Troubles*, III, pp. 428–43.
[34] Paillard, *Histoire des Troubles*, III, pp. 460–61, 465–68.
[35] Le Boucq, *Histoire des Troubles*, p. 8.
[36] ADN, Chambre de Comptes B12704, ff. 66v-67; Paillard, *Histoire des Troubles*, IV, pp. 103–4, 383–84, 426–27. It seems likely that this was the Jacques de Leau who died in Southampton in December 1567. *Registre*, p. 100.
[37] J. Decavele, *De Dageraad van de Reformatie in Vlaanderen (1520–1565)*, 2 vols. (Brussels, 1975), I, p. 586.
[38] E. Coornaert, *Les Français et le commerce international à Anvers. Fin du XVᵉ – XVIᵉ siècle*, 2 vols. (Paris, 1961), I, p. 184.

and became a citizen as early as 1558.)[39] Indeed the close commercial links between the Walloon towns and Antwerp may suggest that in many cases this migration was merely a transfer of business location.

The Sohiers and de Beaulieus were actively involved in Antwerp's overseas trade and became part of the city's merchant community, in which Calvinists were particularly well-represented. The Walloons formed a close knit group in Antwerp, living in the same area of the city and forming close business and personal ties.[40] This strengthened existing relationships and new links were established. In 1564 Cornille Sohier married Marie, the daughter of François Cocquiel dit le Merchier one of the leading and wealthiest Tournai Calvinists.[41] Other later settlers in Southampton may have been part of this Walloon community: Anthoine Jurion had moved to Antwerp from Hainaut by 1558 and the van Santuoort family may have been related to the prominent Antwerp Calvinists of that name.[42]

The government used spies to identify the leading Calvinists in Antwerp. One of these was a merchant, Philippe Dauxy, who sent a list to Margaret of Parma of the leading Calvinists from the Walloon towns.[43] On the list of Valenciennes Calvinists he identified:

> *Jehan de Beaulieu, beaufils de Jan van Hof leur rabby, et Nicolas de Beaulieu, beaufils de Sͬ Caerle Cocquel, et tous leurs freres compaignons dont Jan Damman est lung.*[44]

Dauxy also produced *Les moyens pour remedier au desastre d'Anvers* which gives further details about the Calvinists. Adrien de la Barre, an associate of Jan Damman and '*compaignon de Jan de Beaulieu, pres les freres mineurs*' appears in this second memorandum.[45] It also suggested that Jan van Hof and Jean de Beaulieu were members of the consistory in Antwerp.[46] A further report from another spy, Geronimo de Curiel denounced the company of Jan Damman (i.e. including Jean de Beaulieu and Adrien de la Barre).[47] From these spy reports, it appears that de Beaulieu was a significant figure within Antwerp's Reformed community.

---

[39]   Stadsarchief Antwerpen, *Antwerpse Poortersboeken 1533–1608*, 3 vols. (Antwerp, 1977), 6 May 1558.

[40]   G. Marnef, *Antwerp in the Age of Reformation. Underground Protestantism in a Commercial Metropolis, 1550–1577*, (London, 1996), pp. 92–93, 95–97.

[41]   See below pp. 9, 12.

[42]   SA, Certificatieboek 13, f. 181v; HRO, Wills 1578/B/53; *Registre*, p. 39; L. van der Essen, 'Le progrès du Luthéranisme et du Calvinisme dans le monde commercial d'Anvers et l'espionage politique du marchand Philippe Dauxy, agent secret de Marguerite de Parme, en 1566–1567', *Vierteljahrschrift für Sozial- und Wirtschaftgeschichte*, 12 (1914), 220; L. van der Essen, 'Episodes de l'histoire religieuse et commerciale d'Anvers dans la seconde moitié du XVIᵉ siècle', *Bulletin de la Commission Royale d'Histoire*, 80 (1911), 355–56.

[43]   Van der Essen, 'Le progrès du Luthéranisme', 152–234.

[44]   Van der Essen, 'Le progrès du Luthéranisme', 215.

[45]   Van der Essen, 'Le progrès du Luthéranisme', 225.

[46]   Van der Essen, 'Le progrès du Luthéranisme', 221.

[47]   Van der Essen, 'Episodes de l'histoire religieuse', 358–59, 360.

Although none of these reports refer to the Sohiers, the family was associated with the Antwerp Calvinists. The contract of marriage between Cornille Sohier and Marie Cocquiel dit le Merchier, was witnessed by Denis des Maistres, a prominent Calvinist who had fled from Tournai to Antwerp and was denounced by Dauxy. Furthermore Nicolas du Vivier, a leading member of the Antwerp church acted on behalf of the Sohiers.[48] Mathieu Sohier and his wife Catherine Resteau seem to have been closely linked to the Calvinist cause in Antwerp and were cited to appear before the *Conseil des Troubles* for having sheltered a Calvinist minister in their home.[49]

During 1566, Antwerp like other parts of the Southern Netherlands experienced the wave of hedge-preaching and then the Iconoclastic Fury of the *Wonderjaar*. An agreement was quickly reached between Orange and the Reformed in Antwerp which granted them three places of worship within the city. Consequently the Reformed community assumed a more public role during the remainder of 1566. They were involved in formulating the Three Million Guilders Request. Ostensibly an attempt to purchase religious freedom from Philip II, this was in reality intended to finance troops to defend the Reformed churches should the Request fail.[50] Mathieu, Cornille and Claude Sohier and Arnoul le Clercq all contributed to the Three Million Guilders Request, though de Beaulieu's name is surprisingly absent.[51] Brederode agreed at a meeting in Antwerp in February 1567 to protect the Reformed churches, if they financed the necessary military forces. Arnoul le Clercq was one of the two people appointed to collect the 20,000 florins that had been apportioned to the Valenciennes church.[52] While the Reformed community in Antwerp played a prominent part in 1566–1567, the Calvinists there were spared the traumas and persecutions experienced by their coreligionists in the Walloon towns of Valenciennes and Tournai. Consequently many of the Protestants, who were later cited to appear before the *Conseil des Troubles* or whose property was to be confiscated, had been able to escape from the city and to dispose of their property.[53]

A number of Calvinist sympathisers, who were to become refugees in Southampton, had remained at Valenciennes after the imposition of the garrison in

---

[48] SA, Certificatieboek 22, ff. 156–58. On Denis des Maistres, see G. Moreau, *Histoire du Protestantisme à Tournai jusqu'à la veille de la Révolution des Pays-Bas*, (Paris, 1962), pp. 245, 330–31; van der Essen, 'Le progrès du Luthéranisme', 216, 220. On Nicholas du Vivier, see Moreau, *Histoire du Protestantisme*, pp. 295–96; G. Marnef, 'Antwerpen in Reformatietijd. Ondergrondse protestantisme in een internationale handelsmetropool 1550–1577', (unpublished thesis, Katholieke Universiteit Leuven, 1991), II, p. 283.

[49] AGR, Chambre de Comptes 111, f. 11v.

[50] A. Pettegree, 'The Exile Churches and the Churches "Under the Cross": Antwerp and Emden during the Dutch Revolt', *Journal of Ecclesiastical History*, 38 (1987), 200–3.

[51] R. van Roosbroeck, *Het Wonderjaar te Antwerpen 1566–67. Inleiding tot de studie der godsdienstonlusten te Antwerpen van 1566 tot 1585*, (Antwerp, 1930), pp. 502–3.

[52] Beuzart, *La répression à Valenciennes*, p. 134.

[53] This seems to have been the case with Mathieu Sohier and his wife. AGR, Chambre des Comptes 18312, f. 10.

1563 in spite of the damaging economic consequences that it had upon the town.[54] The Reformed movement there was suppressed until April 1566 when Margaret of Parma was forced to mitigate the effects of the heresy legislation and the powers of the Inquisition, in response to the presentation of the Request by the lesser nobility or *Gueux*. After the earlier repression of the Calvinists, the Reformed seized the opportunity of this more tolerant atmosphere to reassert their faith. A wave of hedge-preaching broke out in the Southern Netherlands and exiles began to return to the the area. Around Tournai and Valenciennes, the *presches* suspended since 1563, started again in June 1566 with encouragement from the Antwerp consistory. This wave of hedge-preaching was on a much larger scale than the earlier *presches*, which also included Reformed baptisms and marriages, and was closely watched by authorities who employed spies to report on the meetings.[55] Prominent Valenciennes Calvinists such as Michel Herlin and Vincent Resteau attended, as well as relatives of the *échevinale* family, de la Fontaine dit Wicart.[56] Government spies also noted Guillaume Coppin, a member of the Valenciennes consistory and later an exile in Southampton, and members of his extended family among those present at the *presches* during the summer.[57]

The wave of hedge-preaching gave way in August 1566 to the Iconoclastic Fury, with the violent destruction of religious images. In Valenciennes itself this was more of a deliberate act for the religious images were removed from the parish churches by the Calvinists so that the buildings would be fit for Reformed worship. The *Magistrat* felt unable to oppose the destruction, in view of the suspected Reformed sympathies of the civic militia and so acquiesced in the Calvinists' demands.[58] Margaret of Parma saw this as a violation of the recently agreed Accord, in which concessions had been granted in return for noble assistance in restoring order to the Netherlands. The Calvinists were given permission to worship freely in the places where their religion had already been established. Furthermore the Regent viewed the iconoclasm not only as a violation of the Accord but also as further evidence of the ineffectiveness of the *Magistrat* in Valenciennes.[59] She attempted to impose a garrison upon Valenciennes in order to secure the city against a perceived threat from France.[60] When the city refused to accept the garrison the central government declared on 14 December 1566 that Valenciennes was in a state of rebellion because the Calvinists had seized the parish churches in contravention of the Accord and had refused to admit the garrison.[61]

---

[54] On the impact of the garrison, see Clark, 'An Urban Study', pp. 248–60.

[55] Rahlenbeck, 'Les chanteries de Valenciennes', 168, 184.

[56] Rahlenbeck, 'Les chanteries de Valenciennes', 163, 167, 168, 171, 175, 177 179, 181, 182.

[57] Rahlenbeck, 'Les chanteries de Valenciennes', 164, 167, 168, 172, 173, 179, 183; Beuzart, *La répression à Valenciennes*, p. 119.

[58] Beuzart, *La répression à Valenciennes*, pp. 117–18.

[59] C. Paillard, (ed.), 'Papiers d'état & documents inédits pour servir à l'histoire de Valenciennes pendant les années 1566 et 1567', *Mémoires Historiques sur l'arrondissement de Valenciennes*, 6 (1879), 6–9, 297–300.

[60] Paillard, 'Papiers d'état & documents inédits', 40–41, 239–40.

[61] Van Langeraad, *Guido de Bray*, pp. XCIII-XCVI.

Within Valenciennes power had effectively passed to the *Conseil Particulier* in which the leading Calvinists such as Michel Herlin assumed a prominent role. Though the consistory itself did not have any formal role within the city during the rebellion, several of its members exerted a powerful influence on the *Conseil Extraordinaire*.[62] With the establishment of rebel Calvinist government in the city, many decided to leave Valenciennes though some like Jehan le Mesureur returned from exile. He later confessed that he had left his wife and eight children in order to return and fight so that he could live with a free conscience.[63] There were three main problems that the town faced during the rebellion: poverty and unemployment, provisions and defence. Even before the town had been declared rebel, the *Général Aumosne* had begun to provide poor relief for both Calvinists and Catholics. In the face of protests from the Governor, Noircarmes, the *Conseil Extraordinaire* appointed Jehan le Mesureur, Jehan le Thieullier and several other members of the consistory as the administrators and supervisors of the *Général Aumosne*.[64] Three *bourgeois* companies were organised for the defence of the town as well as a largely artisan force known as the *soldats à deux patars*.[65] Jehan le Mesureur took part in sorties from the town and was involved in collecting money to finance the *soldats à deux patars*.[66] This artisan army was financed by a levy imposed on the town, for which Georges des Plus, served as a collector.[67] The town surrendered only on 23 March 1567, by which time the government had regained control of the situation: the Calvinist forces had been defeated at Wattrelos, Lannoy and Oosterweel, and the relieving forces assembled by Brederode were in disarray in Holland.

The leading participants in the rebellion were arrested in the wake of the town's surrender and interrogated. These included Jehan le Thieullier and Jehan le Mesureur; Guillaume Coppin appears to have avoided arrest. The executions began on 31 May 1567, when the two ministers, Peregrin de la Grange and Guy de Brès were hanged and the Michel Herlins (father and son) and Jean Mahieu were beheaded. Jehan le Thieullier was beheaded on 28 March 1568.[68] Jehan le Mesureur, however, managed to escape from Michel Herlin's house where he had been imprisoned and fled to Southampton, in spite of a reward being offered for his capture.[69]

---

[62] Clark, 'An Urban Study', pp. 344–47.

[63] AGR, Conseil des Troubles 88, f. 80.

[64] Beuzart, *La répression à Valenciennes*, p. 125.

[65] Several later exiles in Southampton and their relations can be identified amongst the members of the *bourgeois* companies: François de le Becq, Marc le Blanc, Jacques le Clercq, Jehan Coppin *le jeusne*, Nicholas Dorville, Georges des Plus, Pierre Sohier. AGR, Conseil des Troubles 104, pp. 87, 88, 90, 93, 96. On the military organisation of Valenciennes during the seige, see Clark, 'An Urban Study', pp. 373–80.

[66] Beuzart, *La répression à Valenciennes*, p. 130.

[67] Beuzart, *La répression à Valenciennes*, p. 129. Several later exiles in Southampton were amongst those who contributed: Arnoul le Clercq, Guillaume Coppin, Jehan Coppin and Gilles Seulin. AGR, Conseil des Troubles 104, pp. 102–3.

[68] Le Boucq, *Histoire des Troubles*, pp. 25–26, 30.

[69] AGR, Conseil des Troubles 88, f. 80; le Boucq, *Histoire des Troubles*, pp. 27–28.

Many of those who had fled from Valenciennes during the Troubles, were summoned to appear before the *Conseil des Troubles* in order to explain their absence. Those who failed to attend after the third summons were banished and had their property confiscated. Some of these people had played a prominent role in the Calvinist church, such as Guillaume Coppin and Jehan le Mesureur.[70] The list of those summoned includes the names of people who became members of the Southampton community but whose role during the Troubles is unknown, such as Bon Rapareiller and Gilles Seulin.[71] Many fled to Southampton with their families and some of the confiscations made by *Conseil des Troubles* refer to the property left behind by their relations who were not directly involved in the events of 1566.[72] Others who settled in Southampton seem to have gone unnoticed by the *Conseil*.

The events at Valenciennes should not be seen in isolation; Tournai, with its strong commercial and Reformed links with France, had emerged as another major centre of Walloon Calvinism. Although the refugees from Tournai formed a much smaller and less cohesive group than the exiles from Valenciennes, they too had shown a longstanding commitment to the Reformed cause. François Cocquiel dit le Merchier attended a conventicle at which Guy de Brès preached and when the royal commissioners arrived in Tournai, he took refuge in Rouen, where he met Paul Chevalier.[73] Merchier returned briefly to Tournai in 1562 before migrating to Antwerp.[74] One of the founder members of the Southampton community, Roland Petit was the son of a prosperous merchant and *échevin*, Nicaise Petit, who had been arrested in the wake of the *chanteries*.[75] Another merchant and later exile, Louis de Callonne, was fined 100 *livres* for his involvement in the *presches* of 1563.[76] The Calvinist community in Tournai like that of Valenciennes had been repressed, but the Reformed reasserted themselves during the *Wonderjaar*. Petit and de Callonne were reported as frequently being in the company of the Reformed ministers, in the autumn of 1566.[77] They also participated in the Iconoclastic Fury and were amongst those

[70] Beuzart, *La répression à Valenciennes*, p. 119.

[71] AGR, Conseil des Troubles 315A, ff.189v-90; le Boucq, *Histoire des Troubles*, p. 48.

[72] For example, Anne le Mesureur, sister of Jehan le Mesureur and widow of Philippe Dorville: AGR, Conseil des Troubles 315A, f. 143v; ADN, Chambre des Comptes 12704, ff.123v-24v, 12705, f. 82v. Wauldrue Malapert, widow of Vincent de Beaulieu: AGR, Chambre des Comptes 19082, ff.113v-14; ADN, Chambre des Comptes 12704, ff. 142v–43, 12705, f. 52v.

[73] Moreau, *Histoire du Protestantisme*, pp. 332–34; Halkin & Moreau, 'Le procès de Paul Chevalier', 8.

[74] Moreau, *Histoire du Protestantisme*, pp. 332–33. Following the Troubles, Merchier migrated to Rye. He was the father of Jean le Mercier who later settled in Southampton. Spicer, 'The French-speaking Reformed community', p. 38.

[75] SA, Certificatieboek 23, f. 3; *Registre*, p. 3; Moreau, *Histoire du Protestantisme*, p. 340.

[76] Moreau, *Histoire du Protestantisme*, pp. 232, 362.

[77] A. Hocquet, *Tournai et le Tournaisis au XVIᵉ siècle au point de vue politique et social*, (Brussels, 1906), pp. 385–86.

who directed the sack of the church of St. Brice.[78] They were banished and their property confiscated by the *Conseil des Troubles*.[79]

A second and much smaller wave of settlers arrived from the Southern Netherlands after the establishment of the Southampton community. Like many of their co-religionists from Valenciennes they were implicated in the events of 1566 and formed a relatively cohesive group. They originated from Armentières and were the largest group to settle in Southampton after those from Valenciennes and Tournai. Although one family, the du Beffroys, and some individuals from nearby villages arrived in Southampton at the time of the community's establishment, the majority settled in the town after 1569.[80] These exiles initially took refuge at Sandwich before moving to Southampton.[81] In January 1569 Eloy Bacquelier and Jan Seneschal were recorded as collecting alms amongst the Walloon community in Sandwich. Several later members of the Southampton church were in receipt of poor relief there: Charles Face received 6*d* in October 1568; in October 1569, 4*d* was given to Nicolas Seuery and in June 1571 the church paid 3*s* for the wife of Gilles le Plus of Armentières to travel to Southampton.[82]

Like the families from Valenciennes, the refugees from Armentières were also closely related although the precise ties are harder to determine. Eloy Bacquelier was admitted to Communion on 1 January 1570 with his wife Jane Seneschal; his son André was admitted in 1574 and in 1575 Marguerite and Marie Bacquelier were admitted. Andrieu Bacquelier, probably Eloy's brother, had been admitted with his wife in October 1569.[83] The family was also associated with Pierre le Gay, and another refugee, Jan Seneschal, was related to Eloy's wife.[84] The de Seuerys were also related to several Armentières families that settled in Southampton.[85]

The antecedents of these refugees are less certain than of those from Valenciennes. Eloy was probably related to the Bacqueliers of Armentières who had

78 Moreau, *Histoire du Protestantisme*, p. 362; E. Soil de Moriamé, 'L'église de Saint-Brice à Tournai', *Annales de la Société historique et archéologique de Tournai*, nouvelle série, 13 (1908), 228, 378–79.

79 Louis de Callonne: ADN, Chambre des Comptes B13190, f. 161; AGR, Chambre des Comptes 1203, ff. 282v-84. Roland Petit: ADN, Chambre des Comptes B13190, f. 1; AGR, Chambre des Comptes 1203, ff. 246–51.

80 *Registre*, p. 4. Tibaut d'Armentières seems likely to be the same person as Tiebault du Beffroy whose wife and daughter were admitted in July 1568.

81 P. Beuzart, 'La Réforme dans les environs de Lille, spécialement à Armentières, en 1566 d'après un document inédit', *BSHPF*, 78 (1929), 52.

82 HLL, MS/J 27, pp. 6, 12, 47, 122.

83 *Registre*, pp. 5, 10, 11; A.L.E. Verheyden, 'Une correspondance inédite adressée par des familles protestantes des Pays-Bas à leurs coreligionnaires d'Angleterre (11 novembre 1569–25 février 1570)', *Bulletin de la Commission Royale d'Histoire*, 120 (1955), 194–95.

84 *Registre*, p. 5, 43; Verheyden, 'Une correspondance inédite', 195. It is possible that le Gay was also related by marriage to Balthasar des Maistres who was married to Martine le Gay, *Registre*, p. 10.

85 *Registre*, pp. 6, 11, 43, 84, 87.

extensive commercial interests, retaining factors at Antwerp and Lille.[86] Eloy and André Bacquelier were among the thirty-six people prosecuted in 1565 for irregularities concerning their cloth; Balthasar des Maistres was prosecuted in August 1567 for similar reasons.[87] In 1565 des Maistres, François Ghemart and Anthoine Flayel from nearby Erquinghem sur la Lys had contributed to the purchase of grain for the use of the poor, to ease the economic crisis.[88]

The exiles had played an important part in the development of the Reformed faith in Armentières. The movement had grown quickly during the 1560s and a church was organised. The Calvinists of Armentières benefited from the growing strength of the faith in the Pays de l'Alleu, with *presches* and the services of itinerant ministers. During 1566 these *presches* became more audacious and violent, eventually exploding in the Iconoclastic Fury. In Armentières these attacks were concentrated on the town church and on the convent of the Grey Sisters with its church and hospital. There were also attacks on the religious houses and churches in the surrounding area. This destruction culminated in the occupation of the church by the Calvinists in Armentières and an attempt to establish a Genevan style of church government. Gradually however Catholicism and the authority of central government was restored through the intervention of the provincial governor Egmont who was also '*Seigneur-propriétaire de la ville*'. In early September 1566, Egmont visited Armentières and granted concessions to the Calvinists in the town, allowing them to build a temple outside the town and to retain a minister.[89]

The activities of several of the Southampton exiles came to the attention of the *Conseil des Troubles*. One Andrieu Bacquelier, an *échevin* of Armentières, was accused of having sympathised with and attended the *presches* but he had died by September 1567.[90] Andrieu Bacquelier *fils*, Michel du Jardin, Eloy Bacquelier and his wife were all banished and had their goods confiscated for '*avoir frequenté les presches des sectaires et eulx demonstré favorisans aux troubles et désordres passez*'.[91] François Ghemart was a member of the Armentières consistory and had been involved in the construction of a Protestant temple.[92] Anthoine Flayel was accused of having participated in the iconoclasm at Erquinghem and Armentières as well as fighting for the Calvinists at Lannoy as also did Jan Seneschal.[93] These men had all fled from Armentières by September 1567 and were banished in their absence.[94]

---

[86] SA, Certficatieboeken 14, f. 129, 15, ff. 543–45v, 17, ff.8–9, 18, f. 462, 20, f. 74v, 21, ff. 115v, 135, 167, 169.

[87] Archives Communales d'Armentières, FF40, ff. 189v, 323v, 328.

[88] Archives Communales d'Armentières, HH1, ff. 1–6v.

[89] J-M. Regnault & P. Vermander, 'Armentières au temps des troubles religieux du XVIᵉ siècle, 1545–1574', (unpublished mémoire de maîtrise, Université de Lille III, 1972), pp. 21, 159–90.

[90] Beuzart, 'La Réforme dans les environs de Lille', 53.

[91] AGR, Conseil des Troubles 6, f. 119v.

[92] Beuzart, 'La Réforme dans les environs de Lille', 54–55.

[93] Beuzart, 'La Réforme dans les environs de Lille', 55, 56.

[94] AGR, Conseil des Troubles 6, ff. 118–19v; Beuzart, 'La Réforme dans les environs de Lille', 52, 55, 56.

Some members of the Calvinist community in Armentières were conciliatory in the wake of the Troubles. In January 1567, 134 confessed Calvinists petitioned for the suspension of the *presches* for six months in order to avoid the possibility of having troops billeted upon them. The signatories included Andrieu Bacquelier *fils* and Balthasar des Maistres.[95] The latter was not banished nor does he seem to have been prosecuted by the *Conseil des Troubles*; in fact he was still in Armentières as late as August 1567.[96] He does not appear in the Southampton records before 1574.[97]

The exiles from Armentières did not form such a cohesive group as the refugees from Valenciennes. However Armentières and Valenciennes were very different communities, the former was a sizeable village which had expanded rapidly with the growth of the cloth industry whereas the latter was a well-established city with significant local authority. In spite of these differences, the migrants had links which predated their exodus in their commitment to the Reformed faith and their involvement in the events of 1566–67.

Southampton's geographical location meant that it inevitably became a focus for migration from Northern France. Although the migration from France became considerable, it was significantly different from the exodus from the Southern Netherlands. The migrants from the Southern Netherlands, who settled in Southampton, mostly arrived in the wake of the Troubles of 1566 and Alva's régime in the Netherlands. The migration from France took place over a longer period of time. A few migrants from France had settled in Southampton before 1572 but the significant influx only began in the wake of the Massacre of St. Bartholomew's Day. The French refugees gradually came to dominate the Southampton church for, as the situation in France deteriorated with the continuing civil war, more refugees sought safety in Southampton. For example, sixty-four people were admitted to the Lord's Supper in the wake of the Treaty of Nemours of 1585 which resulted in renewed persecution of the Huguenots.[98] Southampton continued to be an important refuge for French Huguenots into the seventeenth century with exiles arriving from the Ile de Ré in 1628.[99]

The French migrants were drawn from a much wider area than the exiles from the Southern Netherlands. These settlers came from a number of different towns and villages in Northern France; many came directly across the Channel from the Pays de Caux. This rural area lies between the Channel coast, as far as Dieppe to the north and the river Seine to the south. The area forms part of the rural hinterland of Rouen and includes the ports of Le Havre,

---

[95] Archives Communales d'Armentières, FF84, ff. 60–61v.
[96] Archives Communales d'Armentières, FF40, ff. 323v, 328. Proceedings were taken against des Maistres in August 1567 relating to cloth production.
[97] *Registre*, p. 10.
[98] *Registre*, pp. 19–20. They were admitted between October 1585 and January 1586.
[99] *Registre*, pp. 35–36.

Fécamp and Dieppe which had strong commercial links with Southampton.[100] Generally these exiles do not seem to have been such a cohesive group as those from the Southern Netherlands, with often only individuals or families being drawn from the villages of the Pays de Caux, the only significant exception being the group which migrated from Dieppe in the wake of the Massacre of St. Bartholomew's Day.[101] These migrants seem to have been members of the same congregation and to have familial ties which predated their migration.[102]

The St. Bartholomew's Day Massacre caused widespread migration from France to the exile communities in England as well as to the Channel Islands. The scale of this migration can be seen from a census of the French community in Rye made in November 1572. This listed 395 refugees from Dieppe, 173 from Rouen and 5 from Lillebonne who had all arrived in Rye since the end of August. While the census was being compiled a further eighteen people arrived in the port for religious reasons on 4 November, and a further thirty-nine Frenchmen were noted on the ships that arrived in the following few days.[103] Many of the refugees dispersed beyond Rye and a number of them joined the Southampton community such as the Miffant family. Jacques Miffant with his wife and three children had arrived in Rye on 1 September, but they were admitted to the French church in Southampton in July 1573.[104] The influx of French refugees to Southampton is noticeable in the numbers who were admitted to the Lord's Supper. In July 1572, only five people were admitted including two Channel Islanders who were merely passing through the town, and in October, thirteen were admitted of whom nine were described as *françois*. There was a significant increase in admissions in 1573: thirty-nine were admitted in January, thirty-nine in April, fifty-four in July and twenty in October. The arrival of so many refugees from France alarmed the authorities in Southampton who feared that the community might also harbour spies and so from July 1573, they required those who were admitted to the church to produce testimonials as proof of their beliefs.[105]

The dislocation and personal anguish caused by the Massacre can be clearly seen in several instances. A family from Armentières, the du Beffroys, had fled from the Southern Netherlands to Southampton in the wake of the Troubles

---

[100] P. Benedict, *Rouen during the Wars of Religion*, (Cambridge, 1981), pp. 18–19; P. Benedict, 'Rouen's Foreign Trade during the Era of the Religious Wars (1560–1600)', *The Journal of European Economic History*, 13 (1984), 31–32; J.L. Thomas (née Wiggs), 'The Seaborne Trade of Southampton in the second half of the sixteenth century', (unpublished M.A. thesis, University of Southampton, 1955), pp. 83–84.

[101] On the development of Protestantism in this area, see E. Lesens, *Le Protestantisme dans le Pays de Caux*, ed. V. Madelaine, (Paris, 1906).

[102] *Registre*, pp. 8–9. Members of the community testified on each other's behalf as they were admitted to the Lord's Supper. Nicolas Gobelot may have been an elder of the church.

[103] Hardy, 'Foreign Refugees at Rye', 569–75. N.B. The figures exclude anyone who is noted as having been in Rye for a longer period.

[104] Hardy, 'Foreign Refugees at Rye', 574; *Registre*, p. 8.

[105] *Registre*, pp. 7–9.

and then had migrated to Fécamp in 1571. They were forced to return to Southampton in the wake of the Massacre.[106] A number of those who fled from France had attended Mass before their departure, probably in an attempt to prove their Catholic beliefs, and were obliged to acknowledge publicly their fault before they were admitted to the Lord's Supper.[107]

Generally it is difficult to identify the antecedents of these French migrants and the circumstances which caused them to seek exile because of the disparate character of the French refugees. Nevertheless it is possible to identify some of the more prominent migrants. Ministers, being subject to sudden reverses in the Reformed cause, were particularly conspicuous exiles.[108] For example, four of the five ministers admitted to the Lord's Supper in April 1573 in the wake of the St. Bartholomew's Day Massacre, can easily be identified.[109] M. des Moulins, alias Richard le Molere, had been the minister at Carentan in the Cotentin where his preaching had come to the attention of the Norman gentleman, Gilles de Gouberville.[110] The second minister M. de la Vigne was probably Mathieu de la Faye, dit de la Vigne, a correspondent of Calvin who had links with the leading Huguenots. He had been a minister at St. Lô during the Huguenot occupation of the town and he finally returned there in 1591. He had been forced into exile on Jersey, in the wake of the Edict of St. Maur in 1568.[111] The third minister, Jean Louveau Sieur de la Porte, had been a prominent preacher in the Orléanais as well as in Brittany. He had been arrested in October 1572 but escaped in a canoe in a journey which took ten days. He eventually left France from Morlaix and was admitted to the Southampton church with his wife.[112] The fourth minister, M. Boisel, was probably Jean de Boisseul, formerly the minister at Guérande.[113] All of these ministers were accompanied by their wives and families when they came to Southampton.

A second prominent group can be identified amongst the refugees from France, they were from the Huguenot nobility and the *officier* class. The

---

[106] See above p. 13; *Registre*, pp. 4, 9, 84.

[107] See below p. 107.

[108] A. Spicer, ' "A Faythful Pastor in the Churches": ministers in the French and Walloon communities in England, 1560–1620', in A. Pettegree, (ed.), *The Reformation of the Parishes. The ministry and the Reformation in town and country*, (Manchester, 1993), p. 196.

[109] *Registre*, p. 8.

[110] M. Cauvin, 'Le Protestantisme dans le Cotentin, XVIᵉ, XVIIᵉ, XVIIIᵉ, XIXᵉ & XXᵉ siècles', *BSHPF*, 116 (1970), 60, 72–73; Gilles de Gouberville, *Le journal du Sire de Gouberville*, ed. Abbé Tollemer, (Société des Antiquaires de Normandie, Caen, 1892), p. 783.

[111] Cauvin, 'Le Protestantisme dans le Cotentin', *BSHPF*, 117 (1971), 73; J. Pannier, 'Les Montgommery et leurs Eglises de Lorges et de Ducey (1562–1682)', *BSHPF*, 90 (1941), 293; F. Delteil, (ed.), 'Lettres de l'Eglise de Saint-Lo', *BSHPF*, 117 (1971), 87; F. de Schickler, *Les Eglises du Refuge en Angleterre*, 3 vols. (Paris, 1892), I, p. 200, II, pp. 385, 423, 426, 431, 444, III, p. 104; J.A. Messervy, 'Listes des Recteurs de l'île de Jersey', *Société Jersiaise. Bulletin Annual*, 7 (1910–14), 86–87.

[112] De Schickler, *Les Eglises du Refuge*, I, p. 200.

[113] S. Stelling-Michaud, (ed.), *Le Livre du Recteur de l'Académie de Genève (1559–1878)*, 6 vols. (Geneva, 1959–80), II, p. 242; de Schickler, *Les Eglises du Refuge*, I, p. 200.

entourage of the Comte de Montgommery's widow, Elisabeth de la Touche, was admitted to the Lord's Supper on 3 April 1575.[114] The Comte de Montgommery was a key figure in the Huguenot aristocracy and had played a prominent role in the French Wars of Religion. However his attempted invasion of Normandy for the Protestant cause resulted in his defeat and his execution in June 1574.[115] His widow had also supported the Reformed cause being one of an important group of female patrons.[116] She was accompanied to Southampton by her son and by her daughter Charlotte whose husband, Christophe de Chateaubriand, Sieur de Beaufort, had been killed at the battle of Jarnac in 1568.[117] However the Comtesse and her entourage were only passing through Southampton, although her minister, Michel de la Forest, did remain.[118]

Jan le Noble, the '*Contrerolleur*', from Dieppe and '*le Lieutenant Criminel de Rouen*' were sufficiently prominent to attract the attention of the French ambassador. They were both admitted to the Lord's Supper in July, 1573.[119] The latter figure was Vincent le Tellier, the *Lieutenant Criminel du Bailli de Rouen*, who had been deprived of office by the *Parlement de Rouen* for being a Huguenot.[120] Another refugee from Rouen was Damoiselle Claude Auber, the daughter of Guillaume III Auber, Sieur de la Haye et du Mesnil Varin, who had been *conseiller au Parlement de Rouen* from 1537 to 1554.[121]

Not all of the Frenchmen who were admitted to the Lord's Supper were religious exiles; some seem to have been visiting Southampton for commercial reasons. This seems to have been the case with three Rouennais – René le Nud, Richard le Nud and Maillart *libraire* – who were admitted to the Lord's Supper in April 1569.[122] It is not possible to identify 'Maillart *libraire*' certainly as there were several *libraires* in sixteenth century Rouen with that surname.[123] Richard le Nud was a Rouen merchant who frequently acted as a factor for merchants from the Devon port of Totnes but he had died around 1559.[124]

114 *Registre*, p. 11.
115 Pannier, 'Les Montgommery', 293–95. See below pp. 132–33.
116 J.H.M. Salmon, *Society in Crisis. France in the Sixteenth Century*, (London, 1975), p. 120.
117 De Schickler, *Les Eglises du Refuge*, I, p. 330.
118 *Registre*, p. 85; de Schickler, *Les Eglises du Refuge*, III, p. 372.
119 *Registre*, pp. 9, 42; Bertrand de la Mothe-Fénélon, *Correspondance diplomatique de Bertrand de Salignac de la Mothe-Fénélon, Ambassadeur de France en Angleterre de 1568 à 1575*, ed. A. Teulet, 7 vols. (Paris-London, 1838–40), V, p. 155.
120 ADS-M, ANC/1B0615, Arrêts de Parlement, December 1568-June 1569; *Recveil des Lettres & Mandemens du Roy, enuoyées en sa Court de Parlement de Rouen*, (Paris, 1569); H. de Frondeville, *Les conseillers du Parlement de Normandie au seizième siècle (1499–1594)*, (Paris-Rouen, 1960), p. 245; Benedict, *Rouen during the Wars of Religion*, pp. 76–78.
121 A transcript of her marriage contract with Michel de la Forest reveals that she was also related to the Miffant family of Rouen. *Registre*, p. 8; de Schickler, *Les Eglises du Refuge*, III, pp. 370–73; Frondeville, *Les conseillers du Parlement de Normandie*, p. 276.
122 *Registre*, p. 5.
123 Spicer, 'The French-speaking Reformed community', pp. 53–54.
124 ADS-M, G6479 St. Etienne des Tonneliers, Easter 1557–1560; M. le Parquier, 'Le commerce maritime de Rouen dans la seconde moitié du XVIe siècle', *Bulletin de la Société libre d'Emulation du commerce et de l'industrie de la Seine-Inférieure*, (1926–27), 96.

However his widow continued actively to be involved in Rouen's foreign trade. The reference in the *Registre* may have been to either a relative of the late Richard le Nud or to his widow. René le Nud was also involved in the commercial life of Rouen but does not seem to have been associated with the Reformed church.[125] It therefore seems likely that these men were not religious exiles but were admitted to the Lord's Supper while in Southampton on business.

The Protestants from France therefore comprised a very diverse group. Prominent figures and merchants passed through the town and were admitted to the Lord's Supper. Some humbler figures such as the Deserts, the Hersents, the Heslins and the le Pages settled in Southampton. While some of them did come to hold office in the French church in Southampton, they were also actively involved in the town's overseas trade, particularly with Northern France.

The third element in the composition of the exile community were the Channel Islanders, usually described in the *Registre* as '*Anglois*'. The long-standing commercial links between Southampton and the Islands, as well as a favourable rate of custom between 1515 and 1553, had led some Channel Islanders to settle in the town for commercial reasons, before the establishment of the refugee community. Some of these settlers married into local families and became burgesses of the town and several became members of the newly founded French church.[126] Cornelis Poingdextre, Hugh Darvall and Peter Janverain were all admitted to the first celebration of the Lord's Supper in 1567; Lawrence Williams and Richard Etuer were both admitted before 1570.[127]

Southampton continued to attract settlers from the Channel Islands in the second half of the sixteenth century. They settled in the town for commercial reasons and were admitted to the Lord's Supper in the French church, for example, Isaac Herevill and John Clungeon.[128] Other Channel Islanders came to the town in search of employment or to be apprenticed in Southampton.[129] These settlers were less welcome in the town, and the Corporation ordered several shipmasters from the Islands in 1575, not to 'bring any maner of men women or children over unto this town of Southampton to remayne here or inhabit other than such as are merchants such as passeth too and froo about theyre affairs'.[130]

The continued commercial links brought a more transient population of Channel Islanders to Southampton, who were sometimes noted in the *Registre*,

[125] Archives Communales de Rouen, B2, ff. 200, 259v, 264, B3, f. 14v; Spicer, 'The French-speaking Reformed community', pp. 54–55.
[126] See T.B. James, 'The Geographical Origins and Mobility of the Inhabitants of Southampton, 1400–1600', (unpublished Ph.D. thesis, University of St. Andrews, 1977), pp. 368–410; see below pp. 146–47.
[127] *Registre*, pp. 3, 5.
[128] See below p. 147; *Registre*, pp. 16, 17.
[129] On the apprenticeship of Channel Islanders, see below p. 114; James, 'Geographical Origins and Mobility', pp. 404, 407–9.
[130] SRO, SC9/3/2.

as '*passant*'.[131] It is difficult to identify many of these Channel Islanders, some of whom were presumably sailors or traders visiting the port. The death of Thomas de la Court from Guernsey was recorded in the *Registre* in 1573, with the comment '*qui estoit venu en ceste ville de Hamptone pour sa marchandise ... passant*'.[132] There is no reference to de la Court being admitted to the Lord's Supper. The death of another Channel Islands merchant, Thomas de Lecq of St. Brelade, Jersey, was not recorded in the community's register although he did make a bequest to the poor of the French church.[133] In some cases people appear to have been readmitted to the Lord's Supper on their return to Southampton.[134]

Links between the Calvinist church of the Channel Islands and the diocese of Winchester and the French church, resulted in other transient visitors being admitted, such as '*monsieur le doien*', the Dean of Guernsey, John After, in 1569.[135] Adrian Saravia had originated from the Southern Netherlands but had lived in exile on Guernsey before migrating to Southampton. Two of his students, Nicollas Effard and Nicollas Carye, may have accompanied him from Guernsey; they were admitted to the Lord's Supper in April 1572.[136]

The Channel Islanders therefore represent a different element in the French-speaking community in Southampton. Their motivation for coming to Southampton was purely economic; they continued to settle in the town after 1567, just as they had before that date. However a French-speaking church with a Reformed service naturally attracted the Channel Islanders while they were in the town.

In London, some prominent English Puritans were attracted to the services in the French church.[137] The situation there was however exceptional, but even in Southampton on rare occasions Englishmen were admitted to the Lord's Supper. Some of Adrian Saravia's students became members of the French church; Edward Reynolds was admitted in April 1577. Reynolds later rose to

---

[131]   In some cases men had actually left the town in the period between being given permission to attend the Lord's Supper and the service. *Registre*, pp. 4, 7, 14, 16.

[132]   *Registre*, p. 101.

[133]   The inventory of de Lecq's goods suggests that he was only visiting Southampton on business, and had not settled in the town. HRO, Wills 1578/B/31.

[134]   Nicolas Samarais was admitted on Easter Sunday, 1568. He may be the same person as the Nicolas Samares from Guernsey who was admitted on 3 July 1569. Another person who may have been admitted twice was Nicolas Poiteuin. He was probably the Nicolas le Pot Vin admitted in 1569. *Registre*, pp. 3, 4, 5.

[135]   *Registre*, p. 8.

[136]   *Registre*, p. 7. It seems likely that these were the two students for whom the Governor of Guernsey, Sir Thomas Leighton, sought to obtain places at either Oxford or Cambridge, to allow them to train for the ministry. I am indebted to Dr. Ogier for this reference. PRO, SP15/19/26.

[137]   P. Collinson, 'The Elizabethan Puritans and the Foreign Reformed Churches in London', in *idem, Godly People. Essays on English Protestantism and Puritanism*, (London, 1983), pp. 262–63, 269–70; A. Pettegree, *Foreign Protestant Communities in Sixteenth-Century London*, (Oxford, 1986), pp. 212, 273–75.

prominence through his service to the Earl of Essex.[138] The Queen's physician, Dr. John James, was admitted in July 1579. A skilled linguist, he served under Leicester in the Netherlands where he corresponded with Saravia.[139]

These admissions to the Lord's Supper were exceptional. Occasionally the Mayor and Corporation attended the French church, in 1567 to hear the first sermon preached to the congregation and in 1617 to attend the funeral of Philippe de la Motte.[140] Other Englishmen stood as sponsors to children baptised in the French church.[141]

The refugees from the Southern Netherlands were the most important element in the newly-established French community in Southampton. Furthermore these exiles predominantly came from three centres – Valenciennes, Tournai, Armentières. The dominance of refugees from particular towns can also be seen in the exile communities which were established in Wesel and Frankfurt. In Norwich, many settlers originated from Ieper. The settlers in Southampton were members of extensive cohesive groups bound together by commercial and familial ties. In most cases these exiles also revealed a strong commitment to the Reformed cause.

Although a few refugees from the Southern Netherlands continued to appear in Southampton, the majority had arrived in the town in the wake of 1566 and Alva's regime. The dominance of the Walloon exiles in Southampton was gradually diluted by the settlement of other French-speaking groups in the town. These settlers were generally not members of a large cohesive group; the exiles from France were drawn from a very wide area and arrived in Southampton over a longer period of time. Many refugees fled from France in the wake of the Massacre of St. Bartholomew's Day and subsequent reverses in the fortunes of the Huguenot cause in France brought further exiles during the remainder of the century. Some of these settlers may have been religious exiles but others may have come to Southampton for commercial reasons. The Channel Islanders who attended the French church had settled in Southampton for economic motives, just as they had done before 1567. Although the Walloon exiles long dominated the French-speaking community in Southampton, the character of the community slowly changed as these more disparate elements settled in the town.

---

[138] *Registre*, p. 13; C.F. Russell, *A History of King Edward VI School, Southampton*, (Cambridge, 1940), pp. 55–66; P.W. Hasler, (ed.), *The History of Parliament. House of Commons 1558–1603*, 3 vols. (London, 1981), III, pp. 286–88.
[139] *Registre*, p. 13; J.H. Hessels, (ed.), *Ecclesiae Londino-Batavae Archivum*, 3 vols. (Cambridge, 1887–97), II, pp. 790–91, 796–97, 798–802, 814–15, 817–18, 820–31; Hasler, *House of Commons*, II, p. 374. A further link with Southampton is suggested in a letter sent to James by Saravia, in June 1586, in which Arnoul le Clercq sent greetings to the doctor. Hessels, *Ecclesiae Londino-Batavae Archivum*, II, pp. 799–800.
[140] Hessels, *Ecclesiae Londino-Batavae Archivum*, III, pp. 2555–56; *Registre*, pp. 111–12.
[141] The links between the host community and the church are discussed more fully in Chapter 8. See below, p. 148.

THE FOUNDATION OF THE COMMUNITY

According to a long-standing tradition the French church was established by letters patent granted by Edward VI. Indeed this claim was subsequently inscribed in the *Registre* and was mentioned in legal opinions in the eighteenth and nineteenth centuries, as the French church sought to defend their right to use God's House Chapel.[1] There seems to have been an assumption that because letters patent existed for other stranger communities, they should also survive for Southampton. Yet not all stranger communities received letters patent, that at Canterbury being a particularly good example of a settlement that did not do so. In fact, letters patent only survive for the Dutch/Flemish communities: London (1550), Sandwich (1561), Norwich (1565), Maidstone (1567). There is no evidence of letters patent being granted for the establishment of the Southampton community in either Edward VI's or Elizabeth's reign. It would seem that the Southampton Church was referring to the letters patent granted for the settlement of foreign Protestants in England by Edward VI in 1550 and their subsequent reaffirmation by Charles II.[2] By appealing to these privileges, the foreign Protestants came to assume that they also sanctioned the community in Southampton.[3]

While the French-speaking community was not formally established in Southampton until 1567, aliens from Northern Europe had settled in the town before that date. There were groups of alien craftsmen and a few aliens even managed to achieve burgess status. However these aliens did not form any sizeable community.[4] Of greater significance was the settlement of merchants from the Channel Islands, such as the Darvalls, the Janverains, the Majors and Lawrence Williams as well as other less prominent figures. Some Channel Islanders achieved municipal office, they married into local families and were quickly assimilated.[5] Although the Reformation had progressed more rapidly in the Channel Islands, these settlers worshipped in the local parish churches; Richard Etuer and Lawrence Williams both became churchwardens of St. Lawrence's church.[6]

---

[1] SRO, D/FC3/8/10b. Attempts were also made during this dispute to discover the letters patent. SRO, D/FC3/8/3–4.
[2] *The Minute Book of the French Church at Southampton, 1702–1939*, ed. E. Welch, (SRS, 23, 1979), p. 3.
[3] *The Minute Book of the French Church*, p. 107.
[4] James, 'Geographical Origins and Mobility', pp. 339–44.
[5] James, 'Geographical Origins and Mobility', pp. 379–410.
[6] SRO, PR4/2/1, ff. 13, 15.

There is no evidence that the refugees had settled in Southampton before negotiations to obtain official permission for the establishment of the community began, as had happened at Sandwich.[7] Claims that Anthoine Jurion, a founder member of the French church, was living in Southampton as early as 1560 lack substance.[8] The refugees arrived in Southampton during the summer of 1567; de Beaulieu referred to being in Southampton in June 1567 and Jurion's name appears in the muster list drawn up in August 1567.[9] The first entry in the *Registre* records the burial of Jean Rapareiller in the town's cemetery on 21 September and the first celebration of the Lord's Supper was on 21 December 1567.[10]

Provincial communities of refugees had already been established by 1567 in Sandwich and Norwich, with the assistance of the exile churches in London. Sir William Cecil was keen to exploit the economic opportunities offered by the refugees for introducing new industries which had the combined advantage of reducing England's dependence on foreign powers and reducing the flow of currency overseas. The Privy Council had become worried during the 1560s that the value of luxuries being imported to England could not be met by the value of the country's exports. Sir William Cecil had begun to assess the value of England's overseas trade; in 1559–61 an assessment was made on the figures for London's overseas trade, and a document for the year ending Michaelmas 1565 revealed the details of the value and form of all English exports. He attacked the import of superfluous luxuries and attempted to encourage domestic production of goods to offset the damaging adverse balance of trade.[11] Cecil showed a particular interest in granting patents and monopolies for innovative projects put forward by foreigners.[12] As secretary to Protector Somerset, he had also witnessed the community established at Glastonbury in order to produce continental-style worsteds, and as a result may have been encouraged to sanction the creation of alien communities with innovative skills in provincial towns.[13]

The town council of Sandwich was granted letters patent in July 1561 allowing the creation of an exile community. Permission was given for twenty-five households to go to Sandwich who had been selected for their skills in the

---

[7] M.F. Backhouse, 'The Strangers at Work in Sandwich: Native Envy of an Industrious Minority 1561–1603', *Immigrants and Minorities*, 10 (1991), 74.

[8] James, 'Geographical Origins and Mobility', p. 347. Jurion is recorded as paying 'stall & art' dues in the parish of Holy Rood in a Leet Estreat roll which has been dated *c.* 1560. However the document is probably much later. Jurion's name does not appear in the surviving 'stall & art' lists for 1558, 1559, 1565 and 1566. The same estreat list includes the names of other refugees who also do not appear in the surviving pre-1567 'stall & art' lists. The document is therefore more likely to date from after the establishment of the French community. SRO, SC6/1/3–6, SC6/2/2.

[9] PRO, SP12/43/20; SRO, SC13/2/3.

[10] *Registre*, pp. 3, 100.

[11] L. Stone, 'Elizabethan Overseas Trade', *Ec.H.R.*, Second Series, 2 (1949–50), 32–37, 43–44.

[12] Pettegree, *Foreign Protestant Communities*, pp. 139–42.

[13] Pettegree, *Foreign Protestant Communities*, pp. 140–41; see below pp. 71, 94.

'new draperies' by the ministers of the Dutch church in London. The households also had to receive letters of attestation from the Archbishop of Canterbury, the Bishop of London and the Lord Warden of the Cinque Ports, Lord Cobham.[14] In 1565 the Norwich authorities approached the Duke of Norfolk at his palace about the possibility of establishing an alien community in the city, similar to those that had been developed in London and Sandwich. Looking back to the prosperity of the earlier settlement of Netherlanders and their contribution to the cloth industry, the Norwich authorities sought to benefit from the sixteenth century diaspora.[15] The duke already had contacts with a leading figure in the Dutch community, Jan Utenhove. Permission was granted for the settlement by the Privy Council, and the London churches assisted in the migration of thirty households, mainly from Sandwich, to Norwich.[16]

There is no surviving evidence that the Southampton Corporation directly petitioned for permission for an alien community, but like Norwich the town seems to have traditionally associated prosperity with alien communities of French and Italians.[17] The establishment of the refugee community in the town has been seen as an attempt to revive Southampton's prosperity. While the Corporation was experiencing financial difficulties at this time, these difficulties should be seen as being distinct from the condition of the town's economy. A decline in the Corporation's finances did not necessarily mean that the town's trade had declined; in fact in some cases the Corporation painted an excessively bleak picture in order to gain concessions for the town. The town was not suffering from economic stagnation; in fact the period 1561 to 1579 seems to have been one of renewed prosperity. The Corporation was however prone to take advantage of any financial opportunites which emerged.[18]

The Southampton Corporation lacked the opportunity provided to Norwich by the residence of the local magnate. The Earl of Southampton was a minor and his Southampton residence, Bull Hall in Bugle Street, was not purchased until 1568.[19] However the Earl of Pembroke, at one time the Earl's guardian, did have an interest in the town for he had leased the Friary site after the Dissolution of the religious houses and later bought the adjoining property.[20] It was no doubt the Earl's interest in the town and his membership of the Privy

14 *CPR, Elizabeth*, II, p. 336; Pettegree, *Foreign Protestant Communities*, pp. 141–42; Backhouse, 'The Strangers at Work in Sandwich', 74–75.
15 W.J.C. Moens, *The Walloons and their Church at Norwich. Their History and Registers, 1565–1832*, (HSQS, 1, 1887–88), pp. 17–18.
16 *CPR, Elizabeth*, IV, pp. 209–10; Pettegree, *Foreign Protestant Communities*, p. 263.
17 This prosperity was referred to in 1552 when the town's fee farm was lowered. J.S. Davies, *A History of Southampton*, (Southampton, 1883), pp. 157–58.
18 Thomas, 'The Seaborne Trade of Southampton', pp. 4–7, 9. See below, p. 36.
19 *D.N.B.* entry on Henry Wriothesley, 2nd Earl of Southampton; A. Bartlett, 'Beaulieu in Tudor and Stuart Times. The End of the Abbey: The Wriothesleys 1500–1673', pp. 53–54. There is a copy of this unpublished typescript in the Cope Collection, Hartley Library, University of Southampton.
20 *D.N.B.* entry on Henry Wriothesley, 2nd Earl of Southampton; Bartlett, 'Beaulieu in Tudor and Stuart Times', pp. 53–54; C. Platt, *Medieval Southampton. The port and trading community, AD 1000–1600*, (London, 1973), p. 211.

Council which made him the recipient of regular gifts from the Corporation.[21] During 1566, the Earl of Pembroke arbitrated in the town's dispute with Benedict Spinola over the sweet wine monopoly.[22]

During this dispute the town's affairs in London were handled by John Caplin, a wealthy and prominent burgess and the town's representative in the 1563 Parliament.[23] His accounts for the session of Parliament at the end of 1566 show that he had access to the Earl of Pembroke, providing him with a New Year's gift and making payments to his secretary.[24] It is conceivable that some informal approaches may have been made by Caplin on behalf of the Corporation concerning the establishment of an alien community in the town during Pembroke's arbitration over the sweet wine monopoly. Pembroke certainly seems to have been involved in the negotiations for the establishment of the French community because one of the letters sent by the refugees was directed to Pembroke, as well as to Sir William Cecil.[25]

Besides having access to the Earl of Pembroke at this time, Caplin also had close links with another local magnate, Robert Horne, Bishop of Winchester. Horne attempted to build up a Protestant party in Hampshire, centred around the Kingsmill and Gifford families, as a counterbalance to the conservative Paulet faction.[26] Caplin himself seems to have had Reformed sympathies; he may have been the John Caplin who appeared before the Winchester Consistory Court in 1529 for importing Protestant works. Caplin was also the commissioner who surveyed the remaining church goods in the town in 1552–53.[27] While in London during the autumn of 1566 Caplin had made payments for services to a Mr. Kingsmill.[28] The Caplin family had more direct links with the Bishop; John Caplin leased land from him at Bitterne and in 1572 Horne urged the town corporation of Winchester to elect Caplin's son and namesake as their Member of Parliament.[29]

Caplin's precise role in the negotiations for the establishment of a stranger community is unclear. It is possible that he mediated between the town corporation and the government. In the surviving letters, there is a reference to earlier

[21] SRO, SC5/3/5, SC5/3/1, f. 120.
[22] *The Third Book of Remembrance*, III, pp. 70–71.
[23] Hasler, *The History of Parliament*, I, p. 535; PRO, PCC Prob. 11/52 John Caplin.
[24] SRO, SC5/3/5.
[25] PRO, SP12/43/30.
[26] R.H. Fritze, 'The role of the family and religion in the local politics of Early Elizabethan England: The case of Hampshire in the 1560s', *The Historical Journal*, 25 (1982), 267–87; R.H. Fritze, ' "A Rare Example of Godlyness Amongst Gentlemen": The role of the Kingsmill and Gifford Families in promoting the Reformation in Hampshire', in P. Lake & M. Dowling, (ed.), *Protestantism and the National Church in Sixteenth Century England*, (London, 1987), pp. 144–61.
[27] R.A. Houlbrooke, *Church Courts and the People during the English Reformation, 1520–1570*, (Oxford, 1979), p. 227; 'Church Goods in Hampshire, A.D. 1549', trans. T. Craib, *PHFC*, 9 (1921–25), 96.
[28] SRO, SC5/3/5.
[29] PRO, PCC Prob. 11/52 John Caplin; HRO, W/K5/4, p. 56. It is interesting to note that by 1568 Caplin had also purchased the Friary site from the Earl of Pembroke.

Table I – Correspondence relating to the establishment of the French Church

Date	Correspondence	Content of Letters	Reference
16 May 1567	Request presented to the Queen of England by the refugees of the Low Countries.		PRO, SP12/43/29
16 May 1567	Refugees of the Low Countries to Cecil.		PRO, SP12/43/29
29 May 1567	Mayor and Corporation of Southampton to Cecil.	Response to letters sent to John Caplin by Bishop Horne which express the Corporation's willingness to admit refugees skilled in the 'new draperies'.	PRO, SP12/42/71
Undated	'A Copy of the Straungers sute for the inhabiting in the Towne of Southampton.'	A copy of the original petition sent by the refugees to the Mayor and Corporation of Southampton, complete with its preamble and conclusion, making a number of requests concerning their settlement.	British Library, Cottonian MSS. Vesp. FIX f. 230.
Undated	'Abstract of a petition of certain strangers of the Low Countries to the Mayor and Corporation of Southampton; with answers thereto.'	A copy of the strangers petition with the Corporation's responses to the requests made by the refugees with further notes and answers added by Sir William Cecil.	PRO, SP15/13/80

Table I (*cont.*)

Date	Correspondence	Content of Letters	Reference
Undated	'Low Country aliens to the Bishop of Winchester.'	Response to the objections to their petition made by the Corporation.	PRO, SP15/13/ 81
Undated	Answer to certain petitions made by the town of Southampton.	Permission granted for the settlement of twenty families, ten servants per household and the payment of half strangers' customs.	PRO, SP15/13/ 82
June 1567	'Petition of John de Beaulieu, for himself and other foreigners at Southampton, to Cecil.'	A letter largely concerned with the payment of customs duties.	PRO, SP12/43/ 20
30 June 1567	The Bishop of Winchester to Cecil.	He recommends the case of the refugees who wish to settle in Southampton.	PRO, SP12/43/ 16
22 July 1567	The Bishop of London to Sir William Cecil.	Grindal commented on Cecil's notes on the original petition. There are further notes made on this letter by Cecil concerning the numbers to be allowed to settle and customs duties. The two letters of the 16 May 1567 were enclosed with this letter.	PRO, SP12/43/ 29
22 July 1567	The refugees of the Low Countries to the Earl of Pembroke and Sir William Cecil.	The letter concerns the number of servants to be permitted, customs duties and the raw materials required for the 'new draperies'.	PRO, SP12/43/ 30
19 Sept. 1567	The Bishop of Winchester to Cecil.	An assurance by the Bishop that the refugees were not sectaries.	PRO, SP12/44/8

correspondence between Caplin and Horne concerning the establishment of the refugee community.[30] These links with Bishop Horne may partly explain the following enigmatic entry which appears in the Mayor's Account Book for Michaelmas 1567 to Michaelmas 1568:

> Itm. for charges at mr John Capelins when the too bysshopes dined there as apperethe by a bill . . . . iij*li* xij*s* x*d*[31]

As the town corporation reimbursed Caplin for the cost of entertaining these two bishops, it is likely that Caplin was attending to the Corporation's business which may have been related to the establishment of a stranger community. Besides Horne, the entry may refer to Edmund Grindal, Bishop of London, who was also involved in the negotiations over the settlement.

The two bishops had both been religious refugees during Mary's reign; Horne allegedly left England in the company of John à Lasco, the first Superintendent of the London stranger churches. Horne had been the pastor of the English church at Frankfurt where he also came into contact not only with à Lasco but also with Valerand Poullain who had been the pastor of the short-lived Walloon community at Glastonbury.[32] Both bishops retained a close interest in continental affairs after their return from exile and regularly corresponded with the continental reformers.[33] Edmund Grindal, as Bishop of London, was the Superintendent of the newly reconstituted stranger churches in London and was actively involved in their affairs, as well as playing an important role in the establishment of the Sandwich community.[34]

Unfortunately the Southampton strangers remain largely anonymous during the course of the negotiations; only Jean de Beaulieu is mentioned by name, in a petition which he sent to the government concerning customs duties.[35] In view of the detailed knowledge that de Beaulieu had about the negotiations and his prominence in the early years of the community, it seems likely that he played a pivotal role. The other refugees were actively involved in the negotiations, commenting on the various proposals made about the size of their settlement, the production of the 'new draperies' etc.[36] The

---

[30] PRO, SP12/42/71.

[31] SRO, SC5/3/1, f. 122v.

[32] C.H. Garrett, *The Marian Exiles. A Study in the Origins of Elizabethan Puritanism*, (Cambridge, 1938), pp. 188–90; P. Denis, *Les Eglises d'étrangers en Pays Rhénans (1538–1564)*, (Paris, 1984), pp. 60, 344, 346, 349, 356–58. On Grindal, see P. Collinson, *Archbishop Grindal, 1519–1583. The Struggle for a Reformed Church*, (London, 1979).

[33] See *The Zurich Letters*, ed. H. Robinson, (Cambridge, 1842); *The Zurich Letters, (Second Series)*, ed. H. Robinson, (Cambridge, 1845).

[34] Pettegree, *Foreign Protestant Communities*, pp. 137–38, 142, 146, 150–51, 154, 157, 161–63, 171–72, 178–79, 245–49, 271.

[35] PRO, SP12/43/20.

[36] The refugees' views were expressed in various correspondence but the following letters were actually sent by the refugees themselves. PRO, SP12/43/20, SP12/43/30, SP15/13/81.

role of the French Church in London during the negotiations is largely unknown due to a *lacuna* in the consistory records but their role may have been greater than has been previously assumed. In the refugees' petition to the Queen they stated that each had a certificate from the French church in London regarding '*leur religion, conduicte, fame et renommée*'.[37] The Dutch Church in London had selected suitable exiles to settle in Sandwich when the community was established in 1561.[38] Whether Threadneedle Street was involved to the same extent in directing the refugees to Southampton is unclear but it is interesting to note that a few of those recorded as attending the first celebration of the Lord's Supper in Southampton in December 1567, were recorded in 1568 as living in London or as being members of the French church there.[39] These refugees may have been directed to Southampton by the Threadneedle Street church but had soon returned to the capital.

On 16 May 1567, a letter was sent to Sir William Cecil by refugees from the Low Countries which emphasised the Queen's kindness in the past to strangers who sought refuge in England and begged permission to present a petition, which was enclosed, to the Queen. Neither of these documents contains the names of any of the petitioners nor states from which towns in the Low Countries they originated. They do however seem to relate to the Southampton settlers as both letters were later enclosed with a letter in which Bishop Grindal discussed the establishment of this community.[40]

The refugees' petition bewailed the situation in the Low Countries and provided a vivid account of the events of 1566. This told of the enthusiasm and confidence of the Reformed following the suspension of the *placards* and the Inquisition but also of their stunned reaction to the subsequent repression of the movement. They went on to describe the persecution which had forced them to flee from their natural country. The refugees therefore petitioned the Queen for permission to settle in England and requested that she

> ... *donner grâce et licence à tous gentilhommes, bourgeois, marchants et artisans des Pais-Bas de povoir librement venir en cestuy vostre royaume et soy retirer ès villes lesqueles il vous plaira dénommer et désigner à cest effect, èsqueles il leur soit permis de librement demeurer, négotier et exercer toutes sortes de stiles et mestiers, chascun selon sa sorte et qualité ou quelque aultre qu'il estimera plus convenable, eu regard aux particulières commodités des lieux ...*[41]

[37]   PRO, SP12/43/29.

[38]   See above pp. 23–24.

[39]   Jehan Castelain, François Cruel, Pasque Gosseau were all described in 1568 as being members of the French church and natives of the lands of Philip II. Gilles du Mortier and Bon Rapareiller were also recorded as living in London in 1568. All of these men were admitted to the first celebration of the Lord's Supper in Southampton. *Returns of Aliens*, I, pp. 395, 396, 397, III, pp. 331–32, 416; *Registre*, p. 3.

[40]   PRO, SP12/43/29.

[41]   PRO, SP12/43/29.

The refugees were directed to Southampton by the Queen.[42] The government was no doubt responding to the informal approaches which had been made by the Corporation concerning the establishment of an alien community.

Southampton was probably not completely unknown to the strangers. There were long-established trading links between Rouen and Southampton, and the de Beaulieu family had factors in Rouen and Dieppe for the trade with Valenciennes and Antwerp.[43] There were also connections between the Calvinist communities in Rouen and the Walloon towns.[44] Furthermore a branch of the Sohier family had emigrated to the Channel Islands from Mons in the early sixteenth century. There were strong trading links between Southampton and the Channel Islands and the Sohiers also visited the port.[45]

The Corporation's opinion about the establishment of the community had already been canvassed in a letter sent by Bishop Horne to John Caplin. This letter has not survived but the Corporation's response to it has. The Corporation's letter is dated 29 May, only two weeks after the refugees' initial petition. They wrote that since 'certayne persons being destitute of dwelling places for them and there family wysheth to have abode in the Towne of Southampton' and if 'theye wilbe quiet persons there cane but do good amongest us ... and thinke we maye and shalbe hable well to have a hundreth or more of them'.[46]

The refugees then wrote to the Mayor and Corporation of Southampton concerning the establishment of a community and their plight. They claimed that they could not

'endure and abide our consciences to be burdened and in especiall to beare the intolerable clogge of the Spanish Inquisicon: Wee have determined with our selves without regard either of the losse of our goodes or native Contrey to seeke out an other place of habitacon where it may be lawfull for us to live more quietly and Christian like'.[47]

The surviving records of the negotiations about the Southampton community are concerned with the conditions for the settlement after the Queen 'appointed us [the strangers] unto this your Towne, where wee should freely & peaceably make our abode and quietly exercise marchandizyng'.[48]

[42] BL, Cotton MS Vespasian F.IX, f. 230.

[43] SA, Certificatieboek 26, f. 436.

[44] Halkin & Moreau, 'Le procès de Paul Chevalier', 8–10; Moreau, *Histoire du Protestantisme*, pp. 166–67; J.F. Gilmont, 'Premières éditions françaises de la *Confessio belgica* (1561–1562)', *Quaerendo*, 2 (1972), 173–81.

[45] *Armorial Général de France de d'Hozier. Complément. Notice Généalogique sur la famille Sohier de Vermandois*, (Paris, 1879), pp. 9–10, 29–32. The will of Andrew Booke was witnessed by Philip Sohier in 1568. HRO, Wills 1569/B/22.

[46] PRO, SP12/42/71.

[47] BL, Cott. MS Vesp. F.IX, f. 230.

[48] BL, Cott. MS Vesp. F.IX, f. 230.

Some of these requests were settled quickly during the negotiations. For example the refugees requested that 'wee shall deale with landlordes and owners for taking of howses, noe more yearly rent to be required of us than was used to be paid theise two yeares last past'.[49] The Corporation readily agreed to this demand stating that 'they shall fynd theyr landlords reasonable'.[50]

However there was more prolonged discussion which focussed on three main areas: the size of the community to be established, the rate of customs duties to be paid, and their religious practices. On the first issue, the size of the community, the refugees requested that 'wee may have in our houses soe many men, servants and maidens of our Country folke as wee shall thincke needfull for the doeing and finishing of this our syrvices'. They claimed that if they were forced to take on inexpert help they would be unable to produce the new draperies adequately. They also sought some form of accommodation for any artisans such as shoemakers, tailors, etc.[51] The decision on this latter point was ultimately left to the town corporation.[52] The town corporation enthusiastically welcomed the possibility of establishing a stranger community by stating that they would 'have a hundreth or more of them' but Cecil was concerned to limit the size of the community.[53] He commented on the Corporation's response to the strangers' petition to the effect that they should be allowed six servants for the first two years.[54]

The strangers protested to Bishop Horne that they needed servants for the manufacture of the 'new draperies' and that the employment of unskilled Englishmen could be damaging.[55] The Privy Council relented and granted permission for 'twenty families or households of stranngers born in the Low Countries' to settle in Southampton and in every household there should be ten menservants besides any children under twelve.[56] After a year there should be two English apprentices in every household and after seven years one English apprentice should be taken for every two strangers, in order to instruct Englishmen in the skills of the 'new draperies'.[57] The refugees appealed to the Earl of Pembroke and Sir William Cecil that they initially needed their own servants rather than Englishmen who would be inexperienced in the new techniques but they were prepared, in time, to train Englishmen.[58]

---

[49] BL, Cott. MS Vesp. F.IX, f. 230v.
[50] PRO, SP15/13/80.
[51] BL, Cott. MS Vesp. F.IX, f. 230v.
[52] PRO, SP12/43/29. See below pp. 92–93.
[53] PRO, SP12/42/71, SP15/13/80.
[54] PRO, SP15/13/80.
[55] PRO, SP15/13/81.
[56] For a discussion of household sizes, see below pp. 79–80, 160.
[57] PRO, SP15/13/82.
[58] PRO, SP12/43/30.

The size of the community seems to have been finally settled in July 1567 when Sir William Cecil made some notes on a letter from Edmund Grindal, Bishop of London, concerning the settlement. Here Cecil stated that the community should be brought to a 'competent nomber' within three years. There were not to be more than twelve strangers per household and no more than forty households were to be permitted. Cecil also waived the suggestion that the refugees should settle in Salisbury and Winchester and not be confined to Southampton.[59] The Southampton community was therefore potentially much larger than the Sandwich community which was restricted to twenty-five households and the Norwich community which was restricted to thirty households.[60] It was also potentially larger than has been assumed by earlier historians.[61]

The exiles in their initial petition to the Queen pledged to pay '*toutes contributions, tailles, subsides, imposts, charges ordinaires et extraordinaires*' and promised the Southampton Corporation that they would be 'readie at all times with our goodes for habilitie to pay such taxes & talents and other Imposicons for the maintenance of your Towne'.[62] In spite of these promises the payment of the strangers' rate of customs duties became an important area of discussion. Merchant strangers were liable to pay higher taxes and dues than native merchants.[63] The refugees in their original petition had requested that they should have a favourable rate of custom for a twenty year period, after which it could be raised according to the Queen's pleasure, on goods which were made in Southampton and exported overseas.[64] The Mayor and Corporation referred this issue to the Privy Council, and according to Cecil's notes on the petition the refugees were not to be granted a favourable rate of custom.[65] Again the refugees protested against the decision to the Bishop of Winchester, stating that the introduction of the 'new draperies' would result in some risk and expense for the refugees themselves. The 'new draperies' would be innovative as well as providing employment and prosperity. Therefore the refugees requested that they should pay only half the usual strangers' customs.[66]

Jean de Beaulieu protested directly to the Privy Council concerning the decision that the refugees should continue to pay the strangers' rate of customs. He complained that the refugees would have to bear the cost and expense of introducing 'the art and science of many handycraftes'. However

---

[59] PRO, SP12/43/29.

[60] *CPR, Elizabeth*, II, p. 336, III, pp. 209–10.

[61] Davies, *A History of Southampton*, pp. 404–5; W.J.C. Moens, 'The Walloon Settlement and French Church at Southampton', *HSP*, 3 (1881–91), 59.

[62] PRO, SP12/43/29; BL, Cott. MS Vesp. F.IX, f. 231.

[63] *Returns of Strangers in the Metropolis 1593, 1627, 1635, 1639. A Study of an Active Minority*, ed. I. Scouloudi, (HSQS, 57, 1985), pp. 29–30.

[64] BL, Cott. MS Vesp. F.IX, f. 230v.

[65] PRO, SP15/13/80.

[66] PRO, SP15/13/81.

having established and shared their knowledge with native Englishmen, they would be at a disadvantage due to the higher rate of duties.[67]

The Privy Council did accede to the refugees's request. They stated 'that during the space of seven yeres, the said stranngers shall paye but half such custome and subsydye as stranngers do or ought to paye, for any maner of wares which the sayd stranngers shall make in the sayd town of Southampton and that hath not ben usually made heretofore in this Realm'.[68] In spite of this concession the refugees protested to Cecil and the Earl of Pembroke that the customs they paid on goods produced in Southampton should be moderated so that their livelihood was not threatened.[69] Edmund Grindal commented that the refugees should be granted a reduced rate of custom on goods which they had introduced into the country, noting that 'the Quenes Majestie should have a custome where she had none before'. Cecil's annotations show that he conceded that the Queen should suspend the excess customs normally paid by strangers, on goods which were newly introduced and produced in Southampton. This concession applied only to goods which were exported from Southampton and only for a seven year period.[70]

The third area of discussion centred on religious issues, a place for the refugees to worship and their form of worship. The strangers had emphasised their suffering for the Word of God in their petition to the Queen.[71] They asked the town corporation 'to have one church assigned whether wee may resort to learne to reverence both God and the magistrates, within which it may be lawfull to have sermons and other service and sacraments to be used apperteyning to the Christian Religion and administracion as it was used in the time of the Noble Prince of famous memorie King Edward the Sixth'.[72] Cecil however noted that the refugees should conform either to the Religious Settlement or to the order of the London stranger churches. A further note in another hand, at the base of this petition, stated that the refugees had offered to make a confession of faith to the Bishop of Winchester.[73] Robert Horne wrote to Sir William Cecil on the 30 June, appealing to his religious sympathies for the 'Banyshed netherlanders afflicted and forced oute of their natyve contrie for the self same faythe that we professe'. The Bishop went on to state that:

'they can not live without great disordres amonge themselves and sectes dangerous to the naturall subjectes, oneles by your good meanes also they may have lycence to gather to gether into some one churche and so to lyve undre some godly discipline . . . and there is for that purpose

[67] PRO, SP12/43/20.
[68] PRO, SP15/13/82.
[69] PRO, SP12/43/30.
[70] PRO, SP12/43/29.
[71] PRO, SP12/43/29.
[72] BL, Cott. MS Vesp. F.IX, f. 230.
[73] PRO, SP15/13/80.

a churche that may well be spared and fytt for them withoute the moles-
tation of any the parishes of Hampton'.[74]

The Bishop's approach seems to have tried to ensure a separate place for the
refugees to worship freely by warning of the dangers which would occur if
Cecil did not grant permission. However Horne's comments about 'sectes
dangerous to the naturall subjectes' may have awakened fears about Anabap-
tism and sectaries in the kingdom. The re-establishment of the stranger
churches had been seen as a means of controlling this and a proclamation had
been issued in September 1560 banning all Anabaptists from the kingdom.[75]

Before 22 July the refugees had informed Edmund Grindal that they would
conform to the doctrine and rites of the French Church in London as well as
providing a confession of faith for the Bishop of Winchester.[76] By September
the refugees suspected that questions about the religious orthodoxy of the community had hindered the establishment of the church. The refugees had provided the Bishop with written bonds assuring him that they would 'beware and
watchful that no corrupt sectes or opinions shal be suffered to growe among
them, for they them selves hate and deteste all soche'. The Bishop urged the
Privy Council to accept the refugees' suit and promised that 'as very prudently
and not without good cause they maye feare sectaries to crepe in under pretence of the Gospell, so shall I not fayle to be watchefull to prevent that evell
by Godes grace'.[77] This assurance seems to have allayed the fears relating to
the orthodoxy of the community.

The negotiations seem to have been completed by the end of September 1567.
The community's first service was held on the 28 October 1567 when the
sermon was delivered by Nicholas Baudouin, a minister from Guernsey. The
congregation included the town corporation led by the Mayor, Robert Ayre,
as well as the Bishop of Winchester.[78] The Bishop was given two gallons of
Gascon wine by the Corporation, presumably in recognition for his services.[79]
The attendance of the Bishop and the Corporation clearly attest to the official
support for the establishment of the stranger community.

[74] PRO, SP12/43/16.
[75] Pettegree, *Foreign Protestant Communities*, pp. 138–39.
[76] PRO, SP12/43/29.
[77] PRO, SP12/44/8.
[78] Hessels, *Ecclesiae Londino-Batavae Archivum*, III, pp. 2555–56.
[79] SRO, SC5/1/47.

THE FRENCH-SPEAKING COMMUNITY AND SOUTHAMPTON'S OVERSEAS TRADE, 1567–1616

Charles Phythian-Adams argued that 'by the *late* fifteenth and early sixteenth centuries even the more important towns and cities were under pressure; so much so indeed, that the period 1520–70, the culminating years of that period, might well be regarded as a time of acute urban crisis'.[1] At Southampton, the dramatic fall in customs receipts and the apparent insolvency of the Corporation were seen as being indicative of the town's economic stagnation. This was aggravated by the fall in cloth exports during the 1520s and 1540s. Urban poverty and the lack of growth in the town's population during the sixteenth century were seen as further symptoms of this urban crisis.[2] Dr. Alwyn Ruddock's research would also seem to support this view. In 1949 she wrote that 'the growth of London [in the early Tudor period] had sapped the trade and population of the southern port and the loss of her role as London's outport brought catastrophic commercial decline. Unable to furnish her required quota of ships and seamen to meet the Armada, the port sunk into a moribund condition until the coming of the railways in the nineteenth century once again opened up her former role as London's outport'.[3]

This belief in an overall urban crisis during the sixteenth century has not gone unchallenged.[4] Certainly the evidence for an urban crisis at Southampton is unconvincing. One of the symptoms of crisis was the lack of growth in the town's population. Southampton had a population of around 2,000 in the early 1520s after which it 'expanded only little, if at all, in the rest of the sixteenth century'. However the population did expand and rapidly because by 1596,

[1] C. Phythian-Adams, 'Urban Decay in Late Medieval England', in P. Abrams & E.A. Wrigley, (ed.), *Towns in Societies. Essays in Economic History and Historical Sociology,* (Cambridge, 1978), p. 183. See also P. Corfield, 'Urban Development in England and Wales in the sixteenth and seventeenth centuries', in J. Barry, (ed.), *The Tudor and Stuart Town. A Reader in English Urban History, 1530–1688,* (London, 1990), pp. 35–62; P. Clark & P. Slack, *English Towns in Transition, 1500–1700,* (Oxford, 1976).

[2] Phythian-Adams, 'Urban Decay in Late Medieval England', pp. 169, 180, 181–82; Corfield, 'Urban Development in England and Wales', pp. 43, 54–55.

[3] A.A. Ruddock, 'London Capitalists and the Decline of Southampton in the early Tudor Period', *Ec.H.R.,* Second Series, 2 (1949–50), 151. This image is perpetuated in the final chapter of Ruddock's book which is entitled 'The Decline of Southampton in the Sixteenth Century'. A.A. Ruddock, *Italian Merchants and Shipping in Southampton, 1270–1600,* (SRS, 1, 1951). Also see, Platt, *Medieval Southampton,* pp. 215–26.

[4] A. Dyer, 'Growth and Decay in English Towns 1500–1700', *Urban History Yearbook,* (1979), 60–72.

according to the Count of Heads, the town's population was 4,200.[5] The evidence for the town's economic stagnation is also unconvincing. Much of Ruddock's research relates to the first half of the sixteenth century and the evidence provided for the Elizabethan period has been questioned by Mrs J.L. Thomas in her unpublished thesis.[6] In particular Thomas challenged the evidence for a continuous economic decline, commenting that a distinction should be made between the Corporation's financial problems and the town's economic circumstances. Some of the sources which reveal financial difficulties should be treated with caution since they were the result of special pleading and were an attempt to avoid the exactions of central government. The evidence of decay presented by the Court Leet resulted from the work of a body which was charged with finding and drawing attention to problems in the town. While there were certainly some financial problems, there was not a continuous economic decline in Southampton. The town inevitably had to readjust as a result of the growth of London and other external forces but the town remained an important regional centre with excellent port facilities; the townspeople continued to depend upon trade for their livelihoods.[7]

Thomas identified two periods of prosperity in the town. The first was during the late 1560s and the 1570s and was 'characterized by the increasing proportion of trade being handled by the town merchants, by the development of the town's shipping and by the extension of the area of trade'. The second period was in the early 1590s and followed an economic depression which had begun in the early 1580s, thereby predating the outbreak of the Spanish War in 1585. This prosperity owed little to the town of Southampton itself and was shortlived, being followed by a period of economic stagnation.[8] In a study for the first half of the seventeenth century, D. Lamb identified a general increase in prosperity, after the Spanish War had ended in 1604, which lasted until 1610. This prosperity resumed again between 1613 and 1616 due to a growth in imports which more than offset the decline in Southampton's exports.[9]

Although Thomas' account remains the standard work for any consideration of Southampton's overseas trade in the Elizabethan period, she only fleetingly considered the involvement and significance of members of the exile community in the town's commerce. Although the negotiations for the establishment of the Walloon community had concentrated upon establishing the manufacture of the 'new draperies', some members of the Southampton community had wider commercial interests. There had been lengthy discussions concerning the payment of customs duties. It was agreed that the refugees

---

[5] Corfield, 'Urban Development in England and Wales', p. 43; SRO, SC3/1/1, f. 254v.

[6] J.L. Thomas, (née Wiggs), 'The Seaborne Trade of Southampton in the second half of the sixteenth century', (unpublished M.A. thesis, University of Southampton, 1955).

[7] Thomas, 'The Seaborne Trade of Southampton', p. 220; Dyer, 'Growth and Decay in English Towns', 69.

[8] Thomas, 'The Seaborne Trade of Southampton', pp. 220–22.

[9] D.F. Lamb, 'The Seaborne Trade of Southampton in the first half of the seventeenth century', (unpublished M.Phil. thesis, University of Southampton, 1972), pp. 23–24.

should not pay the usual higher rate of strangers customs on goods which were manufactured in the town by the new techniques for a seven year period.[10]

The involvement of the refugee merchants in the town's overseas trade can be divided into three main periods. The first period between 1567 and *c.* 1585 was dominated by several refugee merchants who took an active role in overseas trade but by 1585 had migrated from the town. The second period, *c.* 1585–95, coincided with the Spanish War when the refugees' involvement in foreign trade was dominated by the activities of Jean le Mercier. During the final phase, between *c.* 1595 and 1616, the refugee community was represented by the second generation of immigrants and more recent migrants, who became actively involved in the town's trade.

The refugee merchants, 1567–*c.* 1585

During this period several refugee merchants played an active role in the town's overseas trade: Jean de Beaulieu, Arnoul le Clercq, Mathieu Sohier and Anthoine du Quesne. The first three merchants were all related and came from Valenciennes. They also belonged to an extensive commercial network, the experience of which undoubtedly contributed to their mercantile activities in Southampton.

Mathieu Sohier was the younger brother of Claude Sohier, an Antwerp merchant who with his companions had retained factors at Rouen, Dieppe and London. Sohier's factor at Rouen seems to have been Henri de Beaulieu and at Dieppe, Augustin de Beaulieu.[11] In April 1567 Claude Sohier claimed that he had to leave Antwerp to see to his business affairs in Dieppe, Rouen and other places in England and France, but that he did not intend to move abroad.[12] However Claude Sohier died in London in 1568 and his will refers to his business interests on the continent; he divided his interest and stock in companies, including the company at Valenciennes, between his wife and children. Claude's brothers Mathieu, Pierre and Cornille Sohier were amongst those who were appointed as the executors of the will.[13] Although Pierre, Jehan and Cornille Sohier were all involved in Claude Sohier's business affairs, the extent of Mathieu Sohier's involvement is unclear.[14]

The business affairs of Jean de Beaulieu before 1567 are much clearer. He was a member of an Antwerp company with Jan Damman and Adrien de la Barre which had goods and interests at Seville. Henri de Beaulieu, Jean's brother, was apparently resident in Seville in 1564.[15] He had business dealings with his distant relatives, the Malapert brothers who had also migrated from

[10] See above pp. 32–33.
[11] In the 1572 survey of strangers in Rye, Augustin de Beaulieu was recorded as coming from Dieppe. SA, Certificatieboek 26, ff. 436, 514v; Hardy, 'Foreign Refugees at Rye', 569.
[12] SA, Certificatieboek 28, f. 117v.
[13] PRO, PCC Prob. 11/50 Claude Sohier.
[14] SA, Certificatieboek 22, f. 172.
[15] SA, Certificatieboek 20, ff. 61–62; van der Essen, 'Episodes de l'histoire religieuse', 360.

Valenciennes to Antwerp.[16] He may have also had commercial links with his father-in-law, Jan van Hof, who was based in London.[17]

These two examples provide some indication of the mercantile background and experience which some of the refugee merchants possessed. Unfortunately little evidence has survived concerning the activities of Mathieu Sohier's cousin, Arnoul le Clercq, before 1567. Little is known about Anthoine du Quesne; he became a member of the French church in April 1573, but it is not clear from where he originated.[18]

Besides this experience, the merchants possessed the necessary funds to become actively involved in Southampton's commercial life. The refugee merchants seem to have evaded the confiscation of their goods by the *Conseil des Troubles*. Mathieu Sohier and his wife certainly seem to have managed to dispose of their property before they left Antwerp.[19] Other refugees were less fortunate; one merchant, Roland Petit, was described by Jean de Beaulieu as 'beinge a pooreman by reason of the stay of his goods beyond the seas'.[20] Mathieu Sohier's brother-in-law, Guillaume Coppin, was forced, in October 1572, to revise his will due to his losses in the Netherlands. His wife was left only Coppin's moveable goods and jewels after his debts had been settled instead of the 2,700 *livres* which she had first been promised. Coppin's son's legacy of 1,400 *livres tournois* was reduced to 300 with a further 400 *livres tournois* 'when liberty shall be in the Low Countries and that profit and the sale of my goods which are at Valenciennes may be made and that my testament may be effected'. In fact Coppin's dilapidated position was such that he seems to have been in receipt of poor relief from the Threadneedle Street Church.[21]

Some indication of the extent to which the merchants were able to retain their assets is revealed in the 1571 lay subsidy returns. Jean de Beaulieu was assessed as having moveable goods worth £20, Mathieu Sohier goods worth £15 and Arnoul le Clercq also £15. While this was considerably less than the £50 assessment for John Crooke and also that of Richard Goddard senior (£30), it did mean that the refugees had similar resources to Southampton merchants such as Nicholas Caplin (£20), Lawrence Williams (£15), William Staveley (£20) and greater resources than those of men such as Richard Etuer (£6), Richard Goddard Junior (£8), Andrew Studley (£7) and John Errington (£5). These men formed the small élite of wealthy Southampton merchants,

---

[16]   SA, Certificatieboek 20, ff. 61–62, 66v.

[17]   M.E. Bratchel, 'Alien merchant colonies in sixteenth-century England: community organis-
        ation and social mores', *Journal of Medieval and Renaissance Studies*, 14 (1984), 54; *Returns
        of Aliens*, I, pp. 115, 237, 261.

[18]   *Registre*, p. 8.

[19]   AGR, Chambre des Comptes 111, f. 11v.

[20]   PRO, HCA 13/18, f. 266v. In spite of this claim, Roland Petit possessed goods worth £5
        according to the 1571 lay subsidy assessment, PRO, E179/174/387.

[21]   PRO, PCC Prob. 11/55 Guillaume Coppin; French Protestant Church of London Archives,
        Soho Square, DL/MS 194, ff. 7, 7v, 8, 10v, 11, 14, 22v, 23, 26v, 29, 88.

identified by Thomas, who engaged in the Gascon and Spanish trades.[22] Mathieu Sohier also had the means to lease West Hall for two years from the Southampton Corporation at £12 per annum in 1570.[23] This substantial property, complete with cellars and warehouses, had in the past been occupied by Italian merchants.[24]

Le Clercq and Sohier tend to overshadow other refugees who traded on a smaller scale and less widely. Refugees such as Emery Durant, Pierre Thieudet, Gaspard Desert and Pierre Trenchant appear infrequently in the royal port books, importing goods from St. Malo, Rouen and Caen. More significant was the cross-Channel trade of men such as Guillaume Hersent and Robert Cousin who regularly traded with Northern France. The small scale of this trade was no doubt a reflection on the merchants' more limited means; in 1571 Durant and Cousin were assessed as having goods worth £3 and Hersent less than that, so he was subject to the poll tax.[25]

Imports, 1567-c. 1585

The first reference to the refugee merchants appears in the petty customs accounts in March 1568 when Mathieu Sohier paid 2d on a barrel of oil; Jean de Beaulieu imported barrels of butter, soap, 'pack threde', rape oil, one packet of Holland cloth, one of [earthern] ware and two bundles of teasels.[26] In 1568–69 Mathieu Sohier was recorded as importing 27½ tuns of wine.[27] The petty customs accounts also refer to goods being imported and exported by other refugee merchants such as Arnoul le Clercq and Augustin de Beaulieu.[28] A clearer picture of the strangers' involvement in overseas trade can be seen from the surviving port books. These are dominated by the activities of Arnoul le

---

[22] PRO, E179/174/387; Thomas, 'The Seaborne Trade of Southampton', pp. 86, 99.

[23] SRO, SC4/3/58.

[24] Ruddock, *Italian Merchants and Shipping*, pp. 122–23, 130–31, 157, 234, 236, 241, 243–45. On West Hall, see Platt, *Medieval Southampton*, pp. 97–98.

[25] PRO, E179/174/387.

[26] SRO, SC5/4/64, entry dated 20/3/1568. Any study of the foreign trade in this period is limited by the only partial survival of the royal port books recording goods entering and leaving Southampton. For this period only two books survive which record not only imports and exports but also wine imports (which were recorded separately from 1575–76 onwards); in the other years, the records are incomplete or unavailable for consultation due to their condition. For various reasons the information provided by the port books should be treated with some caution and in particular because the Southampton port books include not only shipping from Southampton itself but also from the Isle of Wight and Portsmouth. The petty customs accounts also provide some evidence about the strangers' involvement in overseas trade. On the reliability of these sources, see D.M. Woodward, 'Short Guides to records: Port Books', *History*, 55 (1970), 207–10; Thomas, 'The Seaborne Trade of Southampton', pp. 23–26. One of the problems of using the port books is the identification of the different ports but variant spellings may be found from the index of H.J. Smit, (ed.), *Bronnen tot de geschiedenis van den handel met Engeland, Schotland en Ierland*, 2 vols. (Rijks Geschiedkundige Publicatiën, 9, 1950).

[27] SRO, SC5/4/65, not foliated.

[28] SRO, SC5/4/65, not foliated and the entries are undated, SC5/4/66, entries dated 6/11/1569, 19/10/1569 [sic], 4/12/1569, 16/1/1570, 17/3/1570, 20/5/1570, 28/7/1570, 9/8/1570, 5/9/1570.

Clercq and Mathieu Sohier, Jean de Beaulieu apparently having left Southampton before the period covered by these records.

Trade with Spain, Portugal and the Atlantic islands was dominated by the small élite of Southampton merchants who possessed the resources to charter vessels for such long journeys and were involved in what was essentially a luxury trade.[29] This therefore excluded many refugee merchants, although Mathieu Sohier and Arnoul le Clercq did play a small role in this trade. In 1577, Mathieu Sohier chartered the *Dove of Hampton* for a voyage to Lisbon.[30] In 1575–76 le Clercq imported to Southampton one tun of 'secke cask' compared with the 120 tuns and 16 butts of 'seck cask' imported from Andalucia by Southampton merchants. Besides wine, they imported cargoes of figs, raisins, ginger, brimstone, oil and Spanish salt and iron from Andalucia, Ayamonte, Bilbao and St. Sebastian.[31] The exiles also traded occasionally with the Atlantic islands of the Azores and the Canaries. In June 1574 the *John of Hampton* returned to Southampton with eighteen tuns of Canary wine for Mathieu Sohier and Anthoine du Quesne.[32] The principal commodity imported from the Azores was green woad; in 1574 the *Angel of Poole* returned with 3 score and 15 quintals of green woad for Arnoul le Clercq. However the élite Southampton merchants also dominated this trade and only insignificant quantities were imported by the refugee merchants.[33]

The refugee merchants were more actively involved in the town's trade with South Western France. This trade attracted only a few of the wealthiest Southampton merchants because of the necessary investment of capital in large ships for the long voyage and because it was a trade in semi-luxury goods.[34] In 1575–76 for example the *Dove of Hampton* sailed from Southampton on 28 November 1575 for Bordeaux, carrying cloth for le Clercq, Sohier and Richard Etuer and returned to Southampton from La Rochelle on 28 February 1576 carrying 30 weighs of bay salt and 3 tuns of Rochelle wine for the merchants. The *Dove of Hampton*, sailed with another cargo for the merchants to La Rochelle on 9 April 1576 and returned to Southampton on 24 July 1576.[35] The refugee merchants generally seem to have traded as individuals but on one

---

[29] Thomas, 'The Seaborne Trade of Southampton', pp. 96–97.

[30] SRO, SC2/6/5, f. 43.

[31] PRO, E190/814/10, ff. 19v, 20v, 21v, 22v, 25v, 27v, 32, 32v. On the Spanish trade with Southampton, see Thomas, 'The Seaborne Trade of Southampton', pp. 96–103; T.B. James, 'Southampton and Spain in the Sixteenth Century: A survey of sources for links with the Iberian peninsula to 1588', in C.M. Gerrard & A. Gutiérrez, (ed.), *Spanish Medieval Ceramics in Spain and the British Isles*, (British Archaeological Reports, (International Series), 610, 1995), pp. 41–49.

[32] PRO, E190/814/9, ff. 28, 29.

[33] Thomas, 'The Seaborne Trade of Southampton', pp. 103–4. In 1575–76, 406,300 lb of green woad was imported; Southampton merchants accounted for 197,500 lb of woad and other English merchants, 208,000 lb. Arnoul le Clercq imported to Southampton a mere 800 lb of woad. PRO, E190/814/10, ff. 21, 32, 32v, 33v, 36.

[34] Thomas, 'The Seaborne Trade of Southampton', pp. 86–87.

[35] PRO, E190/814/10, ff. 25, 37, 40v, 44–44v.

occasion there was a combined venture between refugee and native merchants. In a contract for the *Flying Dove of Hampton* in February 1583, the tonnage of the ship was divided between Richard Goddard (25 tons), Peter Janverain (12 tons), John Exton (5 tons), Alexander Pendry (5 tons), Mathieu Sohier (5 tons) and Arnoul le Clercq (15 tons).[36]

The refugee merchants only imported a limited quantity of wine into Southampton during 1575–76, a mere 9½ tuns of Gascon wine compared with the 96 tuns of Gascon wine imported by the Southampton merchants.[37] Wine was not the only cargo which came to Southampton from South West France; bay salt was the principal import for the refugee merchants. In 1575–76, 320 weighs of bay salt were imported to Southampton and its satellites, from La Rochelle, including one cargo of 70 weighs imported by one William Lounde of Yarmouth. The refugee merchants therefore accounted for 12.6 percent of the imported bay salt compared with the 54.3 percent imported by South-ampton merchants.[38] The town's importation of Toulouse woad had gradually been replaced by green woad from the Azores but small quantities of woad were still imported by refugee and Southampton merchants.[39]

The refugees' imports from South Western France seem to be of only lim-ited significance. However, the ships chartered by le Clercq and Sohier did not always return directly to Southampton. In September 1576, Arnoul le Clercq and Mathieu Sohier with Richard Etuer chartered the *Dove of Hampton* 'for one viage from hence [Southampton] to Rochell and ther to tarrie six dayes and from thence to Burdeux ther to tarrie xviij dayes to unlade & also to relade &c and from thence to tarrie at Guarnzie two tides to have awnswere of the merchants whether he shall goe to St. Mallowes or Suthampton'.[40] In September 1578 the merchants chartered the *Dove of Hampton* again to La Rochelle and then to Charente, the ship was then 'to reterne within th'isle of Wighte for annswere wher they shall passe to Midlebroughe, Duncarke or ostende in Flanders'.[41] The ship returned to Southampton from Middelburg

---

[36]   SRO, SC2/6/5, f. 117.

[37]   The 9½ tuns of Gascon wine were imported jointly by Arnoul le Clercq and Mathieu Sohier. The following Southampton merchants imported Gascon wine in 1575–76, the number of tuns each imported is given in brackets. They were: Nicholas Caplin (18), Richard Goddard (14½), John Crooke (15), Richard Etuer (7), John Errington (6 & 1 hogshead), Robert Moore (6), John Favor (6), Thomas Turner (5), John Calway (4), John Howper (4), James Betts (3), William Staveley (2½), Peter Stoner (2), Robert Knaplocke (2). One further tun of wine was imported by James de Marin.

[38]   Mathieu Sohier imported 10 weighs of bay salt, Arnoul le Clercq 31 weighs. Southampton merchants imported salt, the number of weighs of bay salt appears after each name in the list. They were: John Crooke (50), John Favor (30), Richard Biston (24), John Carew (16), Richard Goddard (11), Richard Etuer (10), Alexander Paynton (8), John Elsye (7), Martin Bewes (4), Thomas Demaricke (4), Thomas Turner (4), Mathew Mahalt (3), Peter Stoner (3), William Nutshawe (3).

[39]   Thomas, 'The Seaborne Trade of Southampton', p. 85.

[40]   SRO, SC2/6/5, f. 19v.

[41]   SRO, SC2/6/5, f. 62v.

on the 29 December 1578.[42] The merchants chartered the same ship for similar voyages in October 1579 and November 1580.[43]

The involvement of le Clercq and Sohier in trade between La Rochelle and Middelburg may in fact have been a continuation of their business interests from before the Troubles. Middelburg was the main entrepôt for foreign wines into the Netherlands, in particular those from Western France.[44] This trade had originally been handled by the Rochelais, but after 1555 the wine trade between La Rochelle and the Netherlands came to be dominated by merchants from the Netherlands and England as well as by German merchants. These merchants from the Netherlands had similarly taken over the importation of wine from Bordeaux.[45] The activities of the refugee merchants perhaps should be seen in this context rather than assuming that their interests were confined to trading directly between Southampton and the Western French ports. It is difficult to assess the significance of this trade network, but perhaps some insight can be gained from one cargo which went to Middelburg via Southampton. In a contract dated January 1577, le Clercq hired the *Grey Falcon of London* to transfer 171 'butts of wines of sheres commonlie called Seckes' from Southampton to Middelburg which was to be delivered to one Jasper Craiet.[46]

The refugee merchants imported goods from the Netherlands, presumably after their cargoes from La Rochelle or Bordeaux had been unloaded. The *Dove of Hampton* had sailed to Bordeaux but returned from Middelburg in 1578 with 1,200 lb of madder for Mathieu Sohier, 1,200 lb for Richard Etuer and 2,400 lb of madder and 4,000 lb of hops for Arnoul le Clercq. The ship sailed to La Rochelle on 27 January 1579 and returned in April from Middelburg, with a cargo of 3,000 lb of hops, 1,400 lb of madder, 3 lasts of pitch and tar and 2 lasts of Flemish soap for Arnoul le Clercq.[47]

Goods were not solely imported from the Netherlands by le Clercq and Sohier as a result of this triangular trade network. They also traded directly with the Netherlands. As has been seen le Clercq had hired the *Grey Falcon of London* in 1577 to sail to Middelburg; in the same year he chartered the *Prosperity of Rye* to Sluis in Flanders and then on to Bruges.[48] The refugee merchants also imported goods from the Netherlands through Dunkirk, Flushing and Ostend.[49] The use of a range of Netherlands ports may have been due to the political difficulties which made Antwerp inaccessible.[50] Generally bags of

[42] PRO, E190/815/5, f. 4v.
[43] SRO, SC2/6/5, ff. 74v, 84.
[44] Coornaert, *Les Français et le commerce international à Anvers*, I, pp. 118–20; J. Craeybeckx, *Un grand commerce d'importation. Les vins de France aux anciens Pays-Bas (XIIIᵉ – XVIᵉ siècle)*, (Paris, 1958), pp. 28–35.
[45] Craeybeckx, *Un grand commerce d'importation*, pp. 239–45.
[46] SRO, SC2/6/5, f. 35v.
[47] PRO, E190/815/5, ff. 4v, 9, E190/815/7, f. 7.
[48] SRO, SC2/6/5, f. 37.
[49] PRO, E190/814/9, f. 23, E190/814/10, f. 22, E190/815/5, f. 13.
[50] On these political difficulties, see G.D. Ramsay, *The Queen's Merchants and the Revolt of the Netherlands*, (Manchester, 1986), pp. 175–76, 180–81.

hops and madder were imported but small quantities of cloth also appear. In 1575–76, for example, Arnoul le Clercq imported 38 pieces of Ghentish cloth into Southampton and in addition English merchants imported small quantities of says, Holland cloth and mockadoes.[51] Southampton's trade with the Netherlands was generally limited and declined after 1580. It was not a trade which generally attracted the more important merchants and even the refugees' direct trade with their homeland seems to have been limited.[52]

The town's trade with the Baltic was also limited but reached its peak during the late 1570s.[53] The partnership of Etuer, Sohier and le Clercq also played a role in this trade. The *Peter of Hampton* returned from Danzig in August 1575 with a cargo of 9 lasts of pitch and tar, 50 bales of flax, 1,500 lb of hemp and 20 kegs of eels.[54] Similar cargoes were imported in the *Dove of Hampton* in September 1579 and the *Lyon of Hampton* in August 1581.[55]

Like many of the lesser merchants Arnoul le Clercq and Mathieu Sohier were also involved in the cross-Channel trade with Northern France. Occasionally cargoes were imported from Calais but their cargoes were generally similar to those which were imported from the Netherlands.[56] According to the port books, Arnoul le Clercq and Mathieu Sohier seem to have been less actively involved in trade with Rouen than the lesser merchants, Robert Cousin and Guillaume Hersent. Cousin imported a variety of goods from Rouen which were often related to the production of the 'new draperies' such as teasels, woolcards and woad. He also imported small quantities of Normandy canvas, vinegar, paper, prunes, rape oil and, on one occasion, a tun and one 'ponchion' of French wine, from Rouen and other Norman ports. Cousin seems to have traded regularly until his death in 1584. Hersent also imported small quantities of vinegar, Normandy canvas, teasels etc. from Norman ports but in particular he regularly imported woad from Caen. In 1580–81, for example, he imported 56,000 lb of woad.[57]

Le Clercq and Sohier were more actively involved in trade with St. Malo. The importation of canvas from Brittany represented a significant element of Southampton's import trade until the mid-1580s.[58] The quantity of canvas imported by the refugee merchants seems to have varied. In 1575–76 the refugee merchants do not seem to have imported any goods from St. Malo. In 1580–81 however Arnoul le Clercq imported 69½ 'fardels' of vitry canvas, 3

---

[51] PRO, E190/814/10, ff. 22, 23, 33v.

[52] Thomas, 'The Seaborne Trade of Southampton', pp. 104–5.

[53] Thomas, 'The Seaborne Trade of Southampton', pp. 111–12.

[54] PRO, E190/814/10, f. 34v.

[55] PRO, E190/815/5, f. 14v, E190/815/11, f. 23.

[56] For example, on 16 January, 1581 the *Dolphin of Hampton* returned with a cargo for Arnoul le Clercq of 1,200 lb of hops, ten ½ pieces of frizadoes and two ½ pieces of frizadoes for his own use. Further quantities of hops were imported later that year for le Clercq and Sohier. PRO, E190/815/11, ff. 6, 12v, 13. See also, Thomas, 'The Seaborne Trade of Southampton', p. 83.

[57] PRO, E190/815/11, ff. 3, 10, 24.

[58] Thomas, 'The Seaborne Trade of Southampton', pp. 69–71.

Table II – Export of says and bays, 1567–*c*. 1585

	1573–74	*1575–76*	*1578–79*	*1579–80*	*1580–81*	*1583–84*
Refugee Merchants	253 says	185 says	421½ says	575 says	382 says	34 says
			11 bays	14 bays	6 bays	
Other Merchants	81½ says	219 says	93½ says[1]	207 says	259 says[2]	81 says
	140½ bays	107½ bays	109 bays	132 bays	344 bays	131 bays
TOTAL	334½ says	404 says	515 says	782 says	641 says	115 says
	140½ bays	107½ bays	120 bays	146 bays	350 bays	131 bays

[1] This figure excludes 25 pieces of Hondschoote say.
[2] This figure excludes 7 yards of say.

'fardels' of Rumbelo canvas and a further 90 bolts of unspecified canvas from St. Malo, as well as 3,100 lb of prunes.[59] The Breton trade, however, generally attracted the lesser merchants due to the lower costs involved; in particular small-scale Southampton merchants and merchants from Salisbury and the Channel Islands dominated the importation of canvas.[60]

Exports, 1567–*c*. 1585

While the refugee merchants imported a range of different goods to South-ampton, they had only one major export, the cloths of the 'new draperies'. Although the export of the 'old draperies', in particular the Winton or Hampshire kerseys reached its height in the 1570s, the refugee merchants rarely exported these cloths.[61] An analysis of the surviving Exchequer Port Books reveals the extent of the trade in the 'new draperies' as well as the distribution of these exports.

The export of says and bays increased rapidly until 1579–80; the total number of says exported in that year was twice the quantity exported in 1573–74. The export of says declined in 1580–81 (which may be linked with the beginnings of the town's economic decline in the early 1580s) and collapsed in 1583–84 to less than half the total in 1573–74. This collapse in exports was probably precipitated by the outbreak of plague, which lasted from April 1583 through to April 1584 and caused seventy-one deaths in the French com-munity.[62] The collapse also coincided with the departure of Mathieu Sohier

59 PRO, E190/815/11, ff. 1v, 4, 5v, 8, 10v, 15, 16v, 18v, 20v, 21v, 25.
60 Thomas, 'The Seaborne Trade of Southampton', p. 86.
61 On the export of the 'old draperies', see Thomas, 'The Seaborne Trade of Southampton', pp. 74–76. Two examples of refugee merchants exporting 'old draperies' can be found in the 1573–74 port book. PRO, E190/814/9, ff. 32, 38v.
62 *Registre*, pp. 102–4.

Table III – Percentage of total number of says exported by the refugees

	1573–74	1575–76	1578–79	1579–80	1580–81	1583–84
le Clercq	35.3%	17.6%	34.75%	24.8%	31.1%	22.6%
Sohier	13.5%	21.0%	18.1%	10.5%	7.0%	1.7%
Others	26.9%	7.2%	29.0%	38.2%	21.5%	5.2%
TOTAL	75.7%	45.8%	81.85%	73.5%	59.6%	29.5%

and Arnoul le Clercq from Southampton.[63] In 1583–84, the refugee merchants exported a mere thirty-four says, less than a third of the cloths of the 'new draperies' which were exported.[64]

The export of bays from Southampton was dominated by non-refugee merchants. In some years there was a single large consignment of bays exported by one merchant, and this does distort the figures. For example in 1575–76, William Merryvall of Salisbury exported 55 bays to Bayonne. In 1580–81, 50 bays were sent to the Azores by the Southampton merchants Richard Biston, Edmund Caplin and John Crooke.[65] It is surprising that the refugee merchants did not become involved in the exportation of bays, but before 1579 the principal markets for bays seem to have been in areas such as Andalucia, Bayonne and the Azores, which were dominated by the élite of Southampton merchants.[66]

As can be seen from Table III, the refugee merchants dominated the export of says. The table analyses the refugee merchants' share of the export of says. In 1573–74 the refugees exported 75.7 percent of the says which left Southampton and 81.85 percent in 1578–79. The refugees' share of the exports declined after 1578–79, even though the total number of says exported peaked in 1579–80. The sharp fall in the refugees' share of say exports in 1575–76 to a mere 45.8 percent of the total is intriguing. Arnoul le Clercq's share of say exports fell to a mere 17.6 percent and may in part account for the decline. However the fall may have been due to the increase in the customs duties for refugees. Permission for the refugees to be exempt from the higher strangers customs rate for goods produced by the new techniques was for a period of seven years.[67] Presumably this exemption ended in 1574 and they would have had to pay a higher rate for the export of says. Consequently Southampton merchants were then able to export the cloths of the 'new draperies' more cheaply than the

[63] See below p. 52.
[64] See Tables II and III.
[65] PRO, E190/814/10, f. 43, E190/815/9, f.13.
[66] See above p. 40.
[67] See above p. 33.

refugees. However any such fall in the refugees' share of say exports was temporary and they had clearly recovered their dominance by 1578–79.

An analysis of the surviving royal port books for 1567–85 reveals the distribution of 'new drapery' exports from Southampton.[68] Initially Spain and Portugal, in 1573–74, accounted for 15.8 percent of these exports but this had declined rapidly. By 1580–81 it accounted for only 5.9 percent of say exports and at its lowest point, a mere 2.2 percent. Although in 1573–74 le Clercq sent 37 says and Sohier 8 says to Spain and Portugal, no other refugee merchants were attracted to this trade. From this date the refugees' exports to Iberia declined, possibly as a result of the restoration of the strangers' rate of customs which made it more difficult for the refugee merchants to compete in that market.[69] The English merchants generally maintained a steady trade in the 'new drapery' cloths with Iberia but this was on a very small scale. In particular they exported significant quantities of bays; in 1573–74, 114 bays were exported which accounted for 81.1 percent of total bay exports. The significance of these bay exports also declined over this period. The exports to Iberia slumped in 1578–79, possibly due to the establishment of the Spanish Company, although the data for 1579–80 shows a recovery.

The export trade with the Atlantic islands underwent similar changes. Initially the refugee merchants actively exported the 'new draperies' to the Azores and other Atlantic islands; in 1573–74, le Clercq exported more says to the Atlantic islands than any other merchant. However after that date, the refugee merchants ceased to be involved in this trade which seems to have fallen to the English merchants who exported says and in particular significant quantities of bays.[70] Again the reason for this may have been the restoration of the strangers' rate of customs.

The principal destination for the 'new draperies' was France. The more lucrative trade was with the ports of Western France, in particular Bordeaux and La Rochelle. In this period this area accounted for between 15.6 percent and 32.6 percent of the total number of says which were exported.[71] Small quantities of bays were exported to South Western France, principally to Bayonne. La Rochelle and Bordeaux were both important for the import of wine to Southampton and the export of the 'new drapery' cloths represented the other half of this trade for the refugee merchants. Arnoul le Clercq and Mathieu Sohier were the major exporters of says to these ports. By 1579–80 other refugee merchants had also begun to export cloth. Le Clercq's son-in-law, Jean le Mercier, exported says to Bordeaux and La Rochelle; two other Southampton refugees, Gaspard Desert and Peter Poché, also exported small quantities to Bordeaux.[72] Previously English

[68] Spicer, 'The French-speaking Reformed community', pp. 97–101.
[69] See above, p. 33.
[70] Spicer, 'The French-speaking Reformed community', pp. 97–101.
[71] Spicer, 'The French-speaking Reformed community', pp. 97–101.
[72] PRO, E190/815/6, ff. 17, 20v, E190/815/9, ff. 6v, 7, 19.

merchants had exported the 'old draperies' as well as quantities of tin, wax and lead to these ports but they gradually began to encroach upon the refugees' domination of say exports.[73] In 1580–81, English merchants exported more says than the refugee merchants to La Rochelle and Bordeaux.[74]

The ports of Northern France generally attracted the lesser merchants presumably because this trade required less capital.[75] However the level of trade was significant and in some years was the principal destination for say exports. The cloths were exported to several Norman ports: Dieppe, Caen, Rouen, Honfleur, Quillebeuf-sur-le-Seine and Le Havre. The volume of these exports fluctuated during this period. In 1573–74, 19.1 percent (64 says) of the total number of says exported from Southampton sent to Northern France. This increased to 62 percent (319½ says) in 1578–79 only to fall to 22.8 percent (146 says) in 1580–81.[76] This trade was dominated by the refugees and generally only negligible quantities were exported by non-refugee merchants. Although le Clercq and Sohier were actively involved in this trade, significant quantities of the 'new draperies' were also exported by other refugees. In 1579–80, Sohier and le Clercq accounted for 33.9 percent of the says exported to Northern France but other refugee merchants exported 65.3 percent of the says.[77] In this cross-Channel trade, two principal merchants stand out: Guillaume Hersent and Robert Cousin. Generally, however, the quantities of says exported by these other refugee merchants were quite modest.

Rouen was one of the destinations for cloth exported to Northern France. Goods sent to this city had to be sold immediately after unloading unless a congé was obtained from the municipal authorities permitting the merchants to store their goods. Since many Spanish, Italian and Flemish merchants tended to avoid the need to apply for congés by retaining legally resident factors in Rouen, the majority of the congés refer to English merchants.[78] Although merchants from Southampton were amongst those who applied for congés from the Rouen authorities,[79] only three congés refer to the refugee merchants. This suggests that the refugees either sold their goods immediately on arrival in Rouen or that they exploited their contacts in Rouen's 'Flemish' community. Jehan le Mesureur may have acted as a

[73]   Thomas, 'The Seaborne Trade of Southampton', p. 85.
[74]   PRO, E190/815/9; Spicer, 'The French-speaking Reformed community', p. 101.
[75]   Thomas, 'The Seaborne Trade of Southampton', p. 86.
[76]   Spicer, 'The French-speaking Reformed community', pp. 97–101.
[77]   PRO, E190/815/6; Spicer, 'The French-speaking Reformed community', p. 100.
[78]   Benedict, 'Rouen's Foreign Trade', 38–39. On the English in Rouen, see C. Douyère, 'Les marchands étrangers à Rouen au XVIe siècle', *Revue des Sociétés Savantes de Haute-Normandie, Lettres et Sciences Humaines*, 69 (1973), 24–43.
[79]   *Congés* granted to Southampton merchants in the period 1563–75. Archives Communales de Rouen, B2, ff. 167, 179, 184v, 187, 218, 223, 229, 253, 338, B3, ff. 59v, 90v, 116, 116v, 117v, 166v, 174v, 177, 211v, 212, 245, 252, 271, 273, 273v, 280, 280v.

factor; certainly he arranged a *congé* on behalf of Arnoul le Clercq and Mathieu Sohier, in which he was described as a *'stippulant'*.[80] (A *'stippulant'* was probably a broker.) In a *congé* authorised in June 1572, the merchants stored their goods at the home of Richard le Nud's widow who may have passed through Southampton in 1569.[81] The final *congé* was issued to Robert Cousin in November 1575.[82] The value of the *congés* as a source for studying Rouen trade declines from the mid-1570s onwards, as the information they contain becomes less detailed.[83]

Significant quantities of the 'new draperies' were also exported to Brittany and the Channel Islands during this period. Initially the refugee merchants were not attracted to this trade, but by 1580–81 they exported 59.3 per cent of the says sent to Brittany and the Channel Islands.[84] The cloths were principally exported to St. Malo with smaller quantities of cloths being sent to Morlaix and Nantes.

Only negligible quantities of the 'new draperies' were exported to the Netherlands. Le Clercq and Sohier were the only merchants who exported cloths there but even so it remained a very small part of their export trade.[85] This should not perhaps be surprising in view of the political situation in the Netherlands but also because the 'new drapery' cloths were produced there anyway. In fact, Orange had reluctantly granted the Merchant Adventurers in 1573 safe passage for four ships to sail along the Scheldt estuary, which was controlled by the rebels, to Antwerp so long as they only contained English produce and not the 'new draperies' which would compete with the Dutch textile industry.[86]

Migration and decline

The 'Flemish' community in Rouen seems to have attracted several of the early refugee settlers in Southampton.[87] Indeed some of these merchants may have had earlier links with Rouen for there were trading links between that city and both Antwerp and Valenciennes. Henri de Beaulieu, who stood as the godfather for his nephew Jean de Beaulieu in 1570, apparently migrated to Rouen. Similarities in the heraldry of the de Beaulieus and the fact that the Rouen Henri de Beaulieu originated from Valenciennes, suggest that the sponsor in Southampton and his namesake in Rouen were in fact one and the same

[80] Archives Communales de Rouen, B3, f. 211v; Douyère, 'Les marchands étrangers à Rouen', 28.

[81] Archives Communales de Rouen, B3, f. 243v; *Registre*, p. 5; see above, pp. 18–19.

[82] Archives Communales de Rouen, B3, f. 353.

[83] On the reliabilty of the *congés*, see Benedict, 'Rouen's Foreign Trade', 38–39.

[84] Spicer, 'The French-speaking Reformed community', pp. 97–101.

[85] Spicer, 'The French-speaking Reformed community', pp. 97–101.

[86] Ramsay, *The Queen's Merchants*, p. 179.

[87] 'Flemish' was the generic term for anyone from the Low Countries. See Douyère, 'Les marchands étrangers à Rouen', 45–60.

person.[88] He had been the factor of Claude Sohier and settled in Rouen from about 1568 onwards where he may have remained during the disorders in the Netherlands. In June 1571 Henri de Beaulieu became a naturalised Frenchman. He took an active part in Rouen's commercial life and by 1576 was described as a citizen of Rouen.[89] Pierre de Beaulieu, the brother of Jean and Henri de Beaulieu, also appears to have settled in Rouen. He had been admitted to the first Lord's Supper in Southampton, but was active in Rouen between 1570 and 1572.[90]

Nicholas Dorville was another exile who settled in Rouen after being admitted to the Lord's Supper in Southampton in 1567. He traded with Rouen and was described in March 1571 as being resident in England but by November, Dorville had settled in Rouen.[91] He was also involved in commerce with Henri de Beaulieu.[92] Dorville's uncle, Jehan le Mesureur also migrated to Rouen where in February 1572 he arranged a *congé* on behalf of Arnoul le Clercq and Mathieu Sohier.[93] Dorville was not recorded again in Southampton after December 1567 and the final entry relating to le Mesureur is dated 18 July 1568.[94]

The migration to Rouen began very soon after the establishment of the exile community in Southampton. Other refugee merchants traded for slightly longer before leaving the town. In May 1571 Jean de Beaulieu claimed that he had 'occupied and used the makinge of bayes & sayes and nothinge ells' but 'for theise iiij or v monthes space he hathe litle or nothinge tradid the makinge of bayes and sayes as before'.[95] Yet according to the town's petty customs

---

[88] The de Beaulieu family which settled in Normandy bore arms which were described as: '*d'azur à un chevron d'or accompagné de trois grelots de même*'. The de Beaulieu family in Valenciennes, members of which migrated to Southampton, bore the following arms: '*quintier au chevron d'argent, accompagnié de trois grelots de même*'. The similarities in these arms would suggest that 'differencing for cadency' had taken place whereby slight changes or modifications were made to arms but retaining their distinctive and principal features. This is because 'armorial bearings should be distinctive not only of the family as a whole, but also of its several branches and individual members'. Bibliothèque Municipale de Valenciennes, Manuscrits 809–818 Casimir des Sars, livres généalogiques, I, pp. 713–15; *Dictionaire des Familles Françaises anciennes ou notable à la fin du XIXe siècle*, (Evreux, 1904), III, pp. 169–70; C.W. Scott-Giles, *Boutell's Heraldry*, (London, 1958), pp. 108–9.

[89] Archives Communales de Rouen, B3, f. 414v; *Armorial Général de la France. Registre premier (-sixième)*, ed. L.P. d'Hozier, 6 vols. (Paris, 1738–68), Registre Premier, Première Partie, p. 56; *Dictionaire des Familles Françaises*, III, pp. 169–70; Douyère, 'Les marchands étrangers à Rouen', 46.

[90] *Registre*, p. 3; Douyère, 'Les marchands étrangers à Rouen', 46.

[91] Archives Communales de Rouen, B3, ff. 86, 97v, 104, 117v, 193v, 194v.

[92] ADS-M, Meubles 1 (1 oct. 1571 / 31 mars 1572) -29 mars, 1572. I am grateful to Mme. C. Demeulenaere-Douyère for providing me with details from Rouen's notarial archives concerning the 'Flemings'.

[93] Archives Communales de Rouen, B3, f. 211v.

[94] *Registre*, pp. 3, 39.

[95] PRO, HCA 13/18, f. 264v.

books, he had been actively involved in the town's trade before 1570.[96] De Beaulieu seems to have migrated soon after 1571, for in that year he was assessed for the lay subsidy and paid his 'stall & art' dues and was described in October as being resident in 'Hampton'.[97] Although he apparently had lodgings in London by May 1571, he does not appear in any of the surveys of aliens made in the capital.[98] A similar move to London was made by de Beaulieu's brother Augustin although his name does periodically reappear in the Southampton archives.[99]

The impact of such merchants on the economy of Southampton was limited when set beside the contribution of merchants like Arnoul le Clercq and Mathieu Sohier who traded from Southampton throughout the 1570s. By the early 1580s Southampton had begun to experience economic difficulties. In 1582 an account of the decayed state of Southampton was written by an anonymous author. After recounting the town's prosperity earlier in the sixteenth century, the author went on to identify the reasons for Southampton's decline.[100] He stated that:

> The most part of our Merchants were nowe become rych and so taryed at home taking their rest, and in their places sett yong men to the seas for their factors, trusting them with great stockes: so that these factors in short time by their factorshippes and provision allowed them, gott good sommes of money, and fell to occupying for them selves lustely: but in shorter tyme then they had to gett this wealth, by lusteness, banquetting and gamming, they spent away all their owne, and yet were so bolde with their Masters as to consume their substance, and so brought them home such accomptes as manie of them feele the smarte therof unto this daye. In this article you must understande that after a man hath borne anie good office in the towne, it is some discredit unto him to goe any more to the seas, but must still tarie at home & keepe some state and countenance. This case and state ys manie times dearly bought.

The author clearly had some particular merchants in mind when he wrote this moralistic attack though the reference to holding municipal office would suggest that the refugee merchants were not amongst the accused.

The memorialist went on to identify piracy as a more pressing problem, as well as the trade in prize goods. He wrote:

> For these eight or tenne yeares last past pyrates have styll haunted about these costes, who have not only taken manie ships bounden into this port

---

[96] SRO, SC5/4/64, ff. 25v, 27, SC5/4/65, ff. 20v, 22, 22v, 23, 26v, 33v, 34, SC5/4/66, ff. 5v, 8v, 11, 40v. The royal port books have not survived for this period.

[97] PRO, E179/174/387; SRO, SC6/1/8.

[98] PRO, HCA 13/18, f. 317v.

[99] PRO, E190/816/4, f. 10v, E190/816/10 entry dated 17/3/1586, E190/816/11, entry dated 11/8/1587; SRO, SC2/6/5, f. 41v; *Registre*, pp. 45, 47; *Returns of Aliens*, II, p. 240.

[100] PRO, SP12/156/43–44; Thomas, 'The Seaborne Trade of Southampton', pp. 7–9. For his comments on the state of Southampton's religious life, see below pp. 98–99.

and sold away their commodities ... to the great hindrance of our Merchants ... [they] have also robbed and spoyled many of our Merchants even at their owne dores, & so sold away their good as it were before their owne faces, to the undoing of many which shall never be able to recover themselves againe.

Piracy was certainly something which affected the refugee merchants directly. Some refugees such as Jean de Beaulieu were actively involved in financing the operations of the Sea Beggars and benefited from the trade in prize goods. Other Southampton merchants, possibly including the refugees, merely traded in the prize goods auctioned at Meadhole.[101] While dealing in prize goods could be lucrative, piracy damaged trade. A petition came before the Privy Council in 1575 concerning the *Black Raven* which had been carrying £1,000 worth of goods for Arnoul le Clercq, Richard Etuer and one Roger Perrye of Poole when it was attacked by Portuguese pirates. Unfortunately the appropriate port book has not survived so it is impossible to identify the cargo or the ship's destination. The merchants obtained letters of reprisal 'for the staie of certein Portingalls' goodes in recompense of the losse of a ship called the *Black Raven* ... spoiled by the subjectes of the Kinge of Portingall'. A ship called the *Flying Ghost* was seized together with its cargo of salt. However Andrew Ruiz, based at Nantes and a member of the prominent Spanish merchant family, claimed that the cargo of salt belonged to him. The dispute was still unresolved in February 1577.[102] This is the only recorded case of refugee merchants having experienced financial losses and difficulties as a result of piracy but given the prevalence of freebooters in this period, it would be surprising if this experience was unprecedented.

The Spanish trade was of particular importance for the town's economy but with the establishment of the Spanish Company in 1577 the memorialist suggests that trade became increasingly restricted. While this may have been the case, the Southampton merchants were not entirely excluded from the trade with Spain as has been sometimes implied. In fact when the Company was established in 1577 twenty-six Southampton merchants were listed as founder members, including Richard Etuer who had close links with the refugee community.[103] Furthermore it was possible for ports such as Yarmouth to continue to trade with the Iberian peninsula ignoring the monopoly of the Spanish Com-

---

[101]   PRO, HCA 13/18, ff. 281v–85; O.G.S. Crawford, 'Mead Hole and Shoesflete', *PHFC*, 17 (1949–52), 114; see below, pp. 132, 135–36.

[102]   *Acts of the Privy Council*, 1575–77, pp. 62–63, 279–80. Thomas has also identified an entry in the Southampton archives which may also relate to the same ship and its cargo of salt, which according to depositions taken in December 1575 belonged to one Adrian Cornellis and Lawrence Hendrickson. This reference may in fact have been part of the merchants' attempts to disprove Ruiz's claim to the cargo of salt. SRO, SC9/3/2; Thomas, 'The Seaborne Trade of Southampton', pp. 139–40. On Andrew Ruiz, see H. Lapeyre, *Une Famille de Marchands, les Ruiz. Contribution à l'étude du commerce entre la France et l'Espagne au temps de Philippe II*, (Paris, 1955), pp. 47–59.

[103]   *The Spanish Company*, ed. P. Croft, (London Record Society, 9, 1973), p. xvii; *CPR, Elizabeth*, VII, p. 318.

pany.[104] In view of the limited trade that the refugee merchants had with Spain and Portugal before 1577, the establishment of the Company probably did not seriously affect their business interests.

The refugees with their burden of a higher rate of customs duties after 1574 may have experienced financial difficulties as a result of the farming of customs duties. The farming of customs was certainly another complaint made by the anonymous memorialist in 1582 who implied that this resulted in the stricter collection of the customs. Whether this had any great impact is unclear because apart from several specific instances of fraud, the port books seem generally to have been reliable.[105]

These problems may have contributed to the economic decline of Southampton but in any event Arnoul le Clercq and Mathieu Sohier left Southampton in 1583. Le Clercq made a 'stall & art' payment of 20s in 1582 and in the following year exported three consignments of cloth from Southampton.[106] In July 1582, however, le Clercq had appointed Jean le Mercier as his attorney for collecting and paying debts.[107] Le Clercq migrated to Middelburg although he does not seem to have become a member of the Walloon church in the town.[108] He exported cargoes of herrings to Southampton from Middelburg in 1585 and 1586 and a further cargo of raisins in April 1587.[109] Two of these cargoes were transported in the *Flying Dove of Hampton*, a ship which le Clercq had used while he was living in Southampton and which he again hired when he was in Middelburg in December 1585.[110]

In 1583 Mathieu Sohier made a payment of 6s 8d for his 'stall & art' dues; this is the last reference to him living in Southampton.[111] A 'Duch' merchant called Mathieu Sohier was recorded in a survey of strangers in London in 1583 as living in Walbrooke ward in the company of a distant relative and prosperous merchant, Guido Malapert.[112] Although Sohier continued occasionally to import and export goods through Southampton, he remained in London until his death in 1605.[113]

[104]   *The Spanish Company*, p. xvii.
[105]   PRO, SP12/156/43; Thomas, 'The Seaborne Trade of Southampton', pp. 24–26.
[106]   PRO, E190/816/1, ff. 2v, 4v, 10; SRO, SC6/1/17.
[107]   SRO, SC2/6/5, f. 95.
[108]   The archives of the Walloon Church at Middelburg were destroyed by enemy action in May 1940 but a card index of the archives was compiled before their destruction. An Arnoul le Clercq was admitted, with his wife, as a member of the church in 1601 but it is unclear whether this could be the same person. Bibliothèque Wallonne, Amsterdam.
[109]   PRO, E190/816/8, f. 4, E190/816/11, entries dated 30/12/1586, 19/4/1587.
[110]   PRO, E190/816/8, f. 4, E190/816/11, entry dated 30/12/1586; SRO, SC2/6/5, f. 117; Smit, *Bronnen tot de geschiedenis*, II, p. 1299.
[111]   SRO, SC6/1/18.
[112]   Another Mathieu Sohier was recorded in this survey as living in Langbourne ward. This may have been Mathieu Sohier, son of Simon, who was admitted to the Lord's Supper in Southampton in 1571, and the nephew of his namesake. *Returns of Aliens*, II, pp. 323, 336, 340; *Registre*, p. 6.
[113]   PRO, E190/816/6, f. 2, E190/816/10, entry dated 17/3/1586, E190/817/3, f. 3v; PCC Prob. 11/106 Mathieu Sohier.

The Refugees and Overseas Trade, c. 1585–c. 1595

The economic decline of Southampton in the early 1580s was exacerbated by the political situation in the Netherlands and the renewal of war against Spain. In the Netherlands, the Company of Merchant Adventurers had left Antwerp for the relative safety of Middelburg in October 1582. Antwerp surrendered to Parma's forces in August 1585 and further anxiety was caused amongst the Merchant Adventurers by the Spanish capture of Sluis, which threatened the island of Walcheren. These events combined with the difficulties being experienced at Emden, the Company's German mart, resulted in a fall in the export of English cloth.[114] The consequent unemployment amongst the clothworkers was exacerbated by the poor harvest of 1586. The combination of social crisis and heightened anxiety about possible Spanish attack may have played some part in the Hampshire Beacon Plot of 1586 when a group of plotters, who included several weavers and tailors, intended to loot barns and storehouses for grain.[115] The crisis of 1586–87 ended with the Merchant Adventurers' establishment of a suitable outlet for English cloths at Stade.[116] The significance of such a dislocation for Southampton's commerce is debatable as the trade with the Netherlands was of only minor importance during Elizabeth's reign.[117]

As a result of Parma's reconquest of Brabant and Flanders, which culminated with the fall of Antwerp in August 1585, Elizabeth concluded the Treaty of Nonsuch by which she agreed to provide assistance openly to the Dutch cause. This disrupted not only trade with the Netherlands but also with Spain. The situation worsened when Philip II seized English ships in December 1585, in reprisal for Drake's actions in the Caribbean. With the renewal of civil war in France trade became more difficult as the west coast of France and the Channel became the haunt of pirates.[118]

The disruption of trade with Iberia and the Atlantic islands bore much more heavily on Southampton than the difficulties in the Netherlands. The trade with Spain had been an important element of the town's prosperity until the outbreak of hostilities when it generally ceased. A limited degree of trade was maintained by alien merchants using alien ships, in some cases with the protection of the English authorities. Commerce with the Azores was also technically affected following the annexation of the Portuguese kingdom and empire by Philip II in 1580 but a regular trade does seem to have continued, in spite of losses through privateering.[119]

---

[114] Ramsay, *The Queen's Merchants*, pp. 188–90; J.D. Gould, 'The Crisis in the Export Trade, 1586–1587', *English Historical Review*, 71 (1956), 212–15.
[115] J.D. Jones, 'The Hampshire Beacon Plot of 1586', *PHFC*, 25 (1968), 105–18.
[116] Gould, 'The Crisis in the Export Trade', 220.
[117] Thomas, 'The Seaborne Trade of Southampton', p. 105.
[118] G. Parker, *The Dutch Revolt*, (London, 1977), pp. 214–15, 217–18; Benedict, 'Rouen's Foreign Trade', 60.
[119] Thomas, 'The Seaborne Trade of Southampton', pp. 102–4.

Privateering became an important element of the town's trade during the Spanish war. Merchants, such as John Crooke, John Errington and Richard Goddard, had all been actively involved in trade with Spain and the Atlantic Islands but finding this trade disrupted by war, resorted to privateering in order to obtain their imports.[120] One of the largest shipowners in Southampton, Henry Ughtred, received letters of reprisal from the Duke of Anjou in 1582 authorising him to equip three ships to sail against the Spaniards at Peru and 'other islands'. One of his ships, the *Susan Fortune* attacked the Portuguese fishing fleet off Newfoundland that summer.[121] One ship which was taken as a prize during this period, was the *Jacques of Dieppe* with its cargo which belonged to one Nicholas Sohier of Rye, presumably a relative of Mathieu Sohier's brother Cornille.[122] Privateering became an important element in Southampton's economy and was probably partly responsible for the revival in trade between 1592 and 1596.[123] It seems that there was also a brief recovery in the town's trade with France and the Channel Islands in the early 1590s but this faded by the end of the century.

Jean le Mercier

Between 1585 and 1595, only one refugee merchant, Jean le Mercier, matched the activity of le Clercq and Mathieu Sohier in the town's overseas trade. Le Mercier originated from Tournai and was the son of François Cocquiel dit le Merchier, a prominent Calvinist merchant who had migrated to Antwerp and was associated with the Sohiers. He first appeared in Southampton in 1579 when he married the daughter of Arnoul le Clercq.[124] Le Mercier first became involved in Southampton's overseas trade in the early 1580s. He exported 18 says to Bordeaux in September 1580 and the following month a further 14 says were sent to La Rochelle; in August 1584 he exported 6 says to St. Malo with Arnoul le Clercq.[125] But it was not until 1585 that le Mercier played a prominent part in the town's trade. However le Mercier's commercial connections were not as extensive as those of his father-in-law, Arnoul le Clercq, or those of Mathieu Sohier, but this may in part have been due to the foreign situation.

---

[120] Thomas, 'The Seaborne Trade of Southampton', pp. 99, 103, 147–52; K.R. Andrews, *Elizabethan Privateering. English Privateering during the Spanish War, 1585–1603*, (Cambridge, 1964), p. 15.

[121] SRO, SC2/6/5, f. 104; Andrews, *Elizabethan Privateering*, p. 202.

[122] The *Jacques of Dieppe* had been loaded in Spain for Nicholas Sohier of Rye, Peter de Caulx and Peter de Bourdevill who were described as being burgesses of Dieppe. The ship was taken by the *Godspeed of Southampton*. The cargo included 'sack wine', figs, olives, cork and sweet oils. Nicholas Sohier sold the cargo of the ship, on behalf of the company, to John Errington and John Sedgewick for £400. SRO, SC2/6/5, ff. 178–79; Thomas, 'The Seaborne Trade of Southampton', p. 163; *The Third Book of Remembrance*, III, pp. 92–93.

[123] Thomas, 'The Seaborne Trade of Southampton', pp. 54, 136–65.

[124] *Registre*, p. 86; *The Book of Examinations and Depositions, 1622–1644*, ed. R.C. Anderson, 4 vols. (PSRS, 29, 31, 34, 36; 1929, 1931, 1934, 1936), I, p. 59.

[125] PRO, E190/815/6, f. 20v, E190/815/9, ff. 6v, 7, E190/816/4, f. 10.

Although le Mercier does not seem to have traded with Spain, he apparently imported one cargo of green woad from the Azores in 1588.[126] He imported wine from Bordeaux, as well as raisins and prunes on occasion, and salt from La Rochelle. Trade with these ports even attracted one of the town's smaller merchants whose trade was normally confined to Northern France. Guillaume Hersent imported bay salt, dates and oats from La Rochelle in 1588–89.[127] Le Mercier's trade with South Western France does seem to have been less frequent than that of le Clercq and Sohier but again this may have been due to the political situation. In fact it became necessary to protect the wine fleet to Bordeaux with a convoy against pirates, which was financed by a levy imposed on the imported goods.[128]

Le Mercier traded regularly with Middelburg with several cargoes being imported each year.[129] It is unclear what, if any, links there were between le Mercier and le Clercq who had migrated to Middelburg in 1583. Le Mercier imported goods which had been produced or manufactured in the Netherlands such as hops, madder, rape oil and 'Holland linings' but he also imported goods which were redistributed through Middelburg in particular sack wine but also pitch and tar, cables and tarred ropes from the Baltic.[130] Trade with the Low Countries was however always liable to disruption on account of the war there.

He frequently traded with Brittany and the Channel Islands. In 1585–86 twelve ships returned from St. Malo with cargoes for Jean le Mercier and in 1587–88 another 14 ships returned from the port. These ships generally carried cargoes of canvas. This trade was an important element of Southampton's imports and reached its peak between 1578–79 and the mid-1580s.[131] Canvas was also imported from the Channel Islands, for example in 1586–87 only four ships sailed from St Malo to Southampton but 15 ships sailed from the Channel Islands.[132] The neutrality of the Channel Islands meant that trade with Brittany could be sustained even during trade embargoes and periods of political disruption.[133] Wine was imported from St. Malo and also from Guernsey to Southampton; for example in 1587–88 le Mercier imported 46

[126] PRO, E190/817/2, f. 8.

[127] PRO, E190/817/4, entries dated 23/6/1589, 19/8/1589, 13/9/1589.

[128] Thomas, 'The Seaborne Trade of Southampton', p. 89, which cites *Acts of the Privy Council*, 1591–92, pp. 86, 320.

[129] PRO, E190/816/8, ff. 7, 9, E190/816/11, entries dated 18/11/1586, 13/2/1587, 6/4/1587, 5/5/ 1587, E190/817/2, ff. 4, 10v, 13, E190/817/4, entries dated 23/12/1588, 11/8/1589, E190/ 817/6, entries dated 1/10/1589, 20/11/1589, 6/3/1590, 23/4/1590.

[130] For example in April 1586, the *Peter of Hampton* had a cargo of 6 hogsheads and 8 barrels of rape oil, 800 lb of madder and the *Hare of London* had a cargo of 2,400 lb of hops. In March 1586 the *Hare of London* had a cargo of 6½ barrels of sack wine cask and the *Peter of Hampton* imported a further 3 barrels. PRO, E190/816/8, E190/816/10.

[131] Thomas, 'The Seaborne Trade of Southampton', pp. 69–71.

[132] PRO, E190/816/11.

[133] On the neutrality of the Channel Islands, see J.C. Appleby, 'Neutrality, Trade and Privateering, 1500–1689', in A.G. Jamieson, (ed.), *A People of the Sea. The Maritime History of the Channel Islands*, (London, 1986), pp. 59–71.

butts of 'seck' wine in casks.[134] The Channel Islands played an important role in this cross-Channel trade by redistributing goods.[135] The trade with Brittany and the Channel Islands also attracted some of the smaller refugee traders such as Guillaume Hersent. In 1587–88, for example, he imported cochineal, prunes, vitry canvas and oleron canvas from St. Malo.[136]

Trade with Northern France also continued although le Mercier only traded infrequently with these parts. In particular he imported quantities of Normandy canvas and along with these consignments also came other goods such as prunes, vinegar and millstones. In June 1587, he imported in one shipment four packets of Normandy canvas and one packet of buckrams as well as 80 dozen woolcards and ten tuns of wine.[137] Guillaume Hersent and other lesser merchants also continued to trade with Northern France as they had before 1585. Charles Heslin seems to have become involved in the cross-Channel trade after 1585 and imported a range of goods from the Northern French ports, such as vinegar, rape oil, millstones as well as Rouen canvas, buckrams and quilts.[138]

The cross-Channel trade was however vulnerable to privateering. In July 1587 a ship was brought into Southampton which had sailed from St. Malo to Guernsey with a cargo of canvas belonging to Jean le Mercier and several other merchants. The ship was brought to Southampton by 'menn of warr' after it had been taken near Guernsey by one Thomas Shrive and his company.[139]

Although privateering became an important element in the town's prosperity during this period, le Mercier does not seem to have been directly involved but he did trade in prize goods. Sir Thomas Leighton, the Governor of Guernsey, had seized a cargo of oil and other goods which were suspected as being Spanish. When however the cargo was shown to have belonged to a Monsieur de Bordeaux, a Paris merchant, the Privy Council wrote to the Mayor and Corporation of Southampton requiring them to ensure that the raisins were returned to de Bordeaux's agent, John Melhorne, and that appropriate restitution was made for any raisins which had been sold. Jean le Mercier had apparently bought a cargo of raisins from this ship.[140] Possibly the cargo of Malaga raisins which had been imported by le Mercier from Guernsey in the *Pearl of Hampton* in April 1587, may have been those to which the Council referred.[141] Le Mercier and other refugees also imported other goods to

---

[134] PRO, E190/816/11, entries dated 2/6/1587, 11/7/1587, 10/8/1587, E190/817/2, ff. 18, 19, E190/817/5, entries dated 3/1/1589, 8/2/1589, 24/2/1589.

[135] Appleby, 'Neutrality, Trade and Privateering', pp. 75, 81.

[136] PRO, E190/817/2, ff. 4v, 7v, 9, 9v, 10.

[137] PRO, E190/817/2, f. 8, E190/816/11, entry dated 15/6/1587.

[138] PRO, E190/816/8, ff. 1, 6v, E190/816/11, entries dated 11/11/1586, 29/8/1587, 15/6/1587, E190/817/2, f. 6v, E190/817/6, entry dated 30/3/1590. After 1590, Heslin became increasingly involved in trade with the Western French ports, see below pp. 62–63.

[139] PRO, E190/816/11, entry dated 11/7/1587.

[140] *Letters of the Fifteenth and Sixteenth Centuries from the Archives of Southampton*, ed. R.C. Anderson, (PSRS, 22, 1921–22), pp. 111–12; *Acts of the Privy Council*, 1587–88, pp. 146–47.

[141] PRO, E190/816/11, entry dated 19/4/1587. A further quantity of raisins was imported from Guernsey by le Mercier in May 1587 in the *Barbara of Alderney*, entry dated 27/5/1587.

Southampton which may have been legally redistributed through Guernsey or may have been prize goods. For example, in April 1588 le Mercier imported eight bags of Carthaginian alum from Guernsey, and in February 1589 the *Barbara of Guernsey* brought to Southampton a cargo of currants for le Mercier, figs for Pierre le Gay and Claude Moutonnier; canvas, prunes and figs for Esay Bernay; canvas and a barrel of cochineal for Guillaume Hersent.[142]

A more significant example of le Mercier purchasing prize goods occurred after the Portuguese expedition of 1589.[143] The venture, led by Sir John Norris and Sir Francis Drake, was largely a failure but a number of ships was taken as prizes and brought back to England. On 30 June 1589 permission was given for the cargoes of perishable goods and corn to be sold from these ships and commissioners were appointed to oversee these sales.[144] At Portsmouth these commissioners included Thomas Heaton, the Customer of Southampton, Andrew Studley and Richard Goddard of Southampton and Thomas Thorney of Portsmouth.[145] The Privy Council also decreed that the grain from one of these prize ships could be used to repay the money owed to the Mayor and Corporation of Southampton for the supplies they provided for the soldiers who had embarked from the port for the expedition. A prize ship, the *Young Froe* [sic], was therefore despatched to Southampton with its cargo of grain.[146]

The sale of grain from these prize ships did not proceed smoothly and several Portsmouth commissioners were summoned before the Privy Council accused of exploiting their position to purchase grain at the lowest possible price of 6s 6d per quarter for wheat and 4s per quarter for rye.[147] It is unclear whether or not Jean le Mercier was a commissioner but he seems to have taken advantage of the this low rate to purchase a quantity of poor quality grain. Since le Mercier agreed to buy further quantities of grain, paying 10s per quarter for wheat and 5s 4d per quarter of rye, regardless of the quality, the Privy Council decided that le Mercier should also be allowed to purchase some of the better quality grain from the *Young Froe* which had been earlier earmarked for the Mayor and Corporation of Southampton. The profits from this sale were to be used to repay the debt owing to Southampton.[148]

The Privy Council permitted le Mercier to export the grain from Portsmouth to Holland, Zealand or any part of France not subject to the Catholic

---

[142] PRO, E190/817/2, f. 9v, E190/817/4, entry dated 24/2/1589.

[143] For an account of this expedition, see W.T. MacCaffrey, *Elizabeth I. War and Politics, 1588–1603*, (Princeton, 1992), pp. 73–96; J. Sugden, *Sir Francis Drake*, (London, 1990), pp. 263–84; R.B. Wernham, (ed.), *The Expedition of Sir John Norris and Sir Francis Drake to Spain and Portugal, 1589*, (Navy Records Society, 127, 1988).

[144] Wernham, *Expedition of Sir John Norris and Sir Francis Drake*, pp. lvii, 199.

[145] Wernham, *Expedition of Sir John Norris and Sir Francis Drake*, pp. 310–11.

[146] 1,950 men embarked from Southampton for Portugal together with a regiment of 200 men under Captain Huntley. Wernham, *Expedition of Sir John Norris and Sir Francis Drake*, pp. 305, 344–45.

[147] *Acts of the Privy Council, 1589–90*, p. 68; Wernham, *Expedition of Sir John Norris and Sir Francis Drake*, pp. 310–11.

[148] *Acts of the Privy Council, 1589–90*, p. 75.

League, free of customs duties. Previously, Andrew Studley had exported 58 sacks of wheat and 130 sacks of rye to Middelburg. The Council was also prepared to sell le Mercier further quantities of grain from the captured ships if he so wished.[149] The sale of this grain to le Mercier provides a clearer impression of his stature as a merchant than can be gleaned from the royal customs books.

Besides purchasing prize goods, le Mercier was involved in the illegal trade with the League towns of Northern France. On 11 July 1588 English ships were prohibited from trading directly with the ports of Normandy, Brittany and Picardy and were required to trade through the Channel Islands. By October 1588 however direct trade with these ports had resumed.[150] In April 1591 the Queen issued a proclamation forbidding her subjects from 'repairing to any port or creek of Picardy, Normandy or Brittany where the rulers of the same ports or creeks do not manifestly obey the French king'. Furthermore all trade either directly or indirectly with the League towns was prohibited but the Crown was aware of smuggling of goods to these ports and also the use of the Channel Islands as a staging post for exports.[151] The proclamation failed to halt supplies and munitions being exported to the League and complaints were made by the merchants of Zealand about the Catholic League being supplied by English merchants through Jersey and Guernsey.[152]

In March 1593 the Privy Council began an enquiry into merchants who continued to trade with St. Malo and the League towns. Le Mercier was identified as one of these merchants and in January 1592 had 3,000 crowns worth of goods which belonged to two St. Malo merchants. The embargo had had little impact upon le Mercier's commercial activities; he frequently imported canvas from Guernsey thereby exploiting the island's neutrality. The Council directed the Mayor of Southampton to examine le Mercier as to his trading interests and to search his premises for any goods which originated from St. Malo or League towns, which were then to be inventoried and stored.[153] Le Mercier's examination provides some valuable details about his trading operations and shows how the neutrality of the Channel Islands was exploited by merchants. Two fardels of vitry canvas were found in le Mercier's possession.

[149] *Acts of the Privy Council*, 1589–90, pp. 74–77; Wernham, *Expedition of Sir John Norris and Sir Francis Drake*, p. 311.

[150] HMC, *Calendar of the Manuscripts of the Most Hon. Marquis of Salisbury K.G. preserved at Hatfield House, Hertfordshire*, 24 vols. (London, 1883–1976), III, p. 338; Thomas, 'The Seaborne Trade of Southampton', p. 87. Goods were imported to Southampton from St. Malo by Jean le Mercier on 9/9/1588, 24/9/1588 (two cargoes), 16/7?/1588. PRO, E190/817/2, ff. 14, 14v, 15, 19.

[151] *Tudor Royal Proclamations*, ed. P.L. Hughes & J.F. Larkin, 3 vols. (New Haven-London, 1964–69), III, pp. 77–79.

[152] *List and Analysis of State Papers, Foreign Series, Elizabeth I*, ed. R.B. Wernham, (London, 1964–), III June 1591–April 1592, p. 175 No. 209. Appleby wrote that the complaint from these merchants prompted the 1591 proclamation. However the complaint was dated July 10/20 1591 and also from its contents it is clear that the complaint postdates the proclamation. Appleby, 'Neutrality, Trade and Privateering', p. 70.

[153] *Acts of the Privy Council*, 1592–93, p. 119.

These had been purchased by a Vitré merchant, John le Moine, and then sent to Pontorson in Brittany from where they were despatched to one Phillipp Journois, le Mercier's factor on Jersey. The factor then arranged for the canvas to be shipped to le Mercier in Southampton. It is possible that le Mercier may have also retained a factor on Guernsey. Le Mercier denied trading with any of the League either directly or indirectly. He did however admit, on further questioning, that the previous January he had in his possession some goods which belonged to one of the St. Malo merchants identified by the Privy Council.[154] Le Mercier was summoned before the Privy Council and duly appeared on 25 March 1593. He was required to attend daily and not depart without a special licence from the Council. The enquiry was deferred in April 1593 because of complaints from some West Country merchants that le Mercier was being detained from his business and there were two ships loaded and waiting to sail. Le Mercier was licensed to leave for a month but there is no further record of his appearing before the Privy Council on this matter.[155]

The difficult international situation also had an impact upon the export of goods from Southampton. The refugee merchants continued to be principally involved in exporting the cloths of the 'new draperies' from the town and le Mercier played a prominent role in this trade. The refugee community had however been seriously weakened by the impact of the plague in 1583–84 which had adversely affected the production of the 'new draperies' in the town.

The export of the 'new draperies' from the town slowly recovered from the nadir of 1583–84 when a mere 115 says and 131 bays had been exported.[156] This meant that any increase in the export of these cloths during this period started from a very low base. The exports by non-refugee merchants in 1586–87 were inflated by the substantial quantities of cloth exported by Guido Malapert and two other merchants.[157] By 1588–89 the total number of says exported was almost equal to the number exported in 1579–80, when 782 says had been exported. However more than five times the number of bays (735½ bays) were exported in 1588–89 than almost a decade earlier when 146 bays had been exported. The gradual increase in exports continued until 1593–94 and a similar increase can be seen in the export of these cloths by non-refugee merchants. This growth clearly reflects the revival in Southampton's economic fortunes in the early 1590s which Mrs Thomas identified.[158] Some impression of the scale of the Southampton export of the 'new draperies' can be obtained by comparing the Southampton exports with exports from London. Unfortunately the evidence does not survive for the same years to allow a direct comparision between the exports of the two ports. The figures survive for

[154]   *Books of Examinations and Depositions, 1570–1594*, ed. G.H. Hamilton, (PSRS, 16, 1914), p. 108.
[155]   *Acts of the Privy Council*, 1592–93, pp. 136, 170.
[156]   See above p. 44.
[157]   PRO, E190/816/11, ff. 1, 1v, 2, 3, 5.
[158]   Thomas, 'The Seaborne Trade of Southampton', pp. 54–55.

Table IV – Export of says and bays, 1585–94

	1585–86	1586–87	1587–88	1588–89	1590–91	1593–94
Refugee Merchants	138 says 120 bays	201½ says[2] 136 bays	88 says 176 H. says 90 n. bays	262½ says 41 bays 35 H. says	548½ says 2 bays 21½ H. says[5]	1516 says 12 s. bays 26¼ H. says
Other Merchants	241 says 247½ bays[1]	577½ says 823 bays[2]	446½ says 238 bays 291 H. says 65 s. bays	520 says 694½ bays 85 H. says[4]	414½ says 246½ bays 80 H. says[6]	826 says 6 bays 646 s. bays 19 d. bays 182 H. says
TOTAL	390 says★ 367½ bays	779 says 959 bays	534½ says 238 bays 467 H. says 90 n. bays 65 s. bays	782½ says 735½ bays 120 H. says	963 says 248½ bays 101½ H. says	2,342 says 6 bays 658 s. bays 19 d. bays 208½ H. says

(Abbreviations: H. says – Hondschoote says; s. bays – single bays; d. bays – double bays; n. bays – narrow bays).

[1] This figure excludes 24 yards of bays
[2] This figure excludes 2 remnants of says
[3] This figure excludes 40 yards of bays
[4] This figure excludes 20 yards of serge
[5] This figure excludes 20 yards of stammell bays
[6] This figure excludes one remnant of say.
★ The total includes 11 says whose destination cannot be identified.

Table V – Percentage of total number of says exported by the refugees

	1585–86	1586–87	1587–88	1588–89	1590–91	1593–94
le Mercier	21.0%	19.0%	13.9%	12.8%	2.5%	13.5%
Others	14.4%	6.9%	4.5%	20.8%	54.5%	51.2%
TOTAL	35.4%	25.9%	18.4%	33.6%	57.0%	64.7%

1594–95 when in total 10,976 bays, 4,256 says, 33,455 pairs of worsted stockings and 168,065 cottons were exported from London.[159] In 1593–94, 2,342 says, 208½ Hondschoote says, 6 bays, 658 single bays and 19 double bays were exported from Southampton. Solely in terms of say exports those sent from Southampton were significant but in comparison with the London exports for the 'new draperies', Southampton's contribution was limited.

The refugee merchants began to export other 'new drapery' cloths besides says during this period. In 1585–86 120 bays were exported, 136 the following year and in 1587–88 176 Hondschoote says were exported. However says remained the principal cloth exported by the refugee merchants and, with the exception of 1588–89, more says were exported by the refugees than other types of cloth. As can be seen from Table V, the refugees' share of the total number of says exported initially declined together with those of the French community's principal merchant, Jean le Mercier. After 1587–88 when le Mercier's share of say exports continued to decline, other refugee merchants increased their share of exported says, to over fifty percent of the total number exported in 1590–91. Certainly in 1590–91 the 24 says and 20 Hondschoote says exported by le Mercier seem insignificant compared with the 242 says exported by Pierre le Gay. By 1593–94 le Mercier's share of say exports had recovered and he was again the principal refugee merchant, exporting 316 says and 8 Hondschoote says compared with the 283 says exported by Claude Moutonnier and 271 by Pierre le Gay.[160]

From an analysis of the surviving port books, it is clear that the trade in the 'new draperies' with Spain continued after 1585; the total number of cloths sent to the Iberian peninsula in 1585–86 and 1586–87 exceeded the number exported in previous years.[161] However these exports were the result of the activities of a few London merchants. In 1586–87, Guido Malapert and two other alien merchants based in London were responsible for all of the cloth exported to Iberia.[162] Traditionally Southampton's Iberian trade had been

---

[159]   Stone, 'Elizabethan Overseas Trade', 45.

[160]   PRO, E190/817/7, E190/818/1; Spicer, 'The French-speaking Reformed community', pp. 122–27.

[161]   Spicer, 'The French-speaking Reformed community', pp. 122–27.

[162]   Of the 54 says and 631 bays, only 6 says were not exported by these three merchants. PRO, E190/816/11, ff. 1, 1v, 2, 3, 5.

focussed upon Andalucia but during this period cargoes were directed to Lisbon.[163] Guido Malapert was responsible for the only consignment exported to the Atlantic islands before 1593.[164] From 1588 onwards even these exports by London merchants ceased and this area of trade had not revived by 1593–94 unlike other areas of trade.

Trade with the ports of Western France only gradually recovered from their low point in 1583–84. In 1580–81, 209 says had been exported there but this total was not exceeded until 1588–89 when $471\frac{1}{2}$ says were exported from Southampton to these ports. To an extent this disruption may have been due to the dangers caused to shipping by the renewal of piracy in this area after 1585.[165] Arnoul le Clercq and Mathieu Sohier had played an important role in this trade before they left Southampton in 1583 but generally the consignments sent to La Rochelle and Bordeaux before 1588–89 were exported by substantial Southampton merchants such as John Crooke and George Heaton. Sohier did, however, still continue to export some cloths, as did Richard Etuer, through Southampton although he was now resident in London.[166] The refugees' share of the 'new drapery' cloths which were exported to these ports gradually increased so that by 1590–91 they were responsible for 66.8 percent of the says exported to the Western French ports and by 1593–94 this had increased to 81.4 percent of says. Le Mercier began again to export cloths to these ports from 1587–88 and the totals increased to 165 says by 1593–94. However by this date other refugee merchants such as Claude Moutonnier and Pierre le Gay had also begun to export significant quantities of the 'new draperies' to these ports. Other members of the French community also exported smaller quantities. For example Jean Hersent exported 145 says to La Rochelle in 1593–94, Balthasar des Maistres exported 86 says, Charles Heslin 60 says, Daniel Seulin 27 says and Peter Poché exported 16 says. The latter four merchants sent all of the cloths which they exported during that year to La Rochelle.[167]

La Rochelle was certainly the principal destination for 'new drapery' exports in Western France, with 1,120 of the 1,185 says exported to these ports being sent to that city.[168] A variety of cloths was exported to La Rochelle by English merchants but those exports from Southampton seem to have been particularly prized. The trade however remained in the hands of English merchants with the cloths being sold to the La Rochelle merchants by *commissionaires* who were resident in the town.[169] By the end of the sixteenth century one of these *commissionaires* was Charles Heslin. Heslin had become increasingly involved

163 The only exception was a cargo of 90 Hondschoote says exported by Richard Staper of London to San Lucar de Barremada. Thomas, 'The Seaborne Trade of Southampton', pp. 97–98; PRO, E190/817/1, f. 1v.

164 PRO, E190/816/11, f. 5.

165 Benedict, *Rouen during the Wars of Religion*, pp. 172–73.

166 PRO, E190/816/6, ff. 2, 4, 4v.

167 PRO, E190/818/1.

168 PRO, E190/818/1; Spicer, 'The French-speaking Reformed community', p. 127.

169 E. Trocmé & M. Delafosse, *Le Commerce Rochelais de la fin du XVe siècle au début du XVIIe*, (Paris, 1952), pp. 132–33, 149.

in exporting cloths to Western France and by January 1599 had migrated to La Rochelle.[170] In 1624 Daniel Hersent had two resident factors in La Rochelle.[171] The settlement of an agent in the town perhaps reflects the importance of this cloth trade with La Rochelle for the refugee community by the end of the century.

While the trade in the 'new draperies' with La Rochelle prospered, the cross-Channel trade with the Northern French ports of Normandy declined. Only in 1593–94 did the total number of says exceed the totals reached in 1580–81 and even this was below the peak of 319½ says in 1578–79. In that year 62 percent of the total number of say exported were sent to Northern French ports but in 1593–94 they accounted for a mere 8.2 percent of say exports.[172] In 1588–89 no cloths at all were recorded as exported to these ports perhaps as a result of the royal proclamation forbidding exports not only to Norman ports but also to those of Picardy and Brittany.[173]

The decline in the exports of cloths undoubtedly owed a great deal to the economic and political situation in France. By the early 1580s the heavy taxation imposed by Henry III began to damage Rouen's economy; in addition there was also a serious shortage of money in circulation in Normandy. These economic problems were exacerbated by the renewal of the French religious wars after the 'Day of the Barricades' in May 1588. Normandy was ravaged by war between the royalists and the League forces for five years. Rouen was secured by the League in February 1589; there was an abortive siege in 1589 by Navarre and a more intense but unsuccessful siege in 1591–92. Trade suffered from this conflict with ships having to travel in armed convoys down the Seine to Rouen while merchants migrated, especially the English merchants who became the focus of attention for the city's Leaguer authorities. This disruption in trade continued until Rouen finally submitted to Henry IV in 1594.[174]

The political disturbances in Normandy also affected the export trade with Brittany and the Channel Islands. After the assassination of Henry III in August 1589, the Guise assumed control seizing royalist strongholds and leaving only small isolated pockets loyal to Henry of Navarre. The Spanish also attempted to establish a base for themselves in Brittany. England intervened in Breton affairs after a request for assistance from the royalist governor and English troops arrived in May 1591.[175] Trade was inevitably the victim of such

---

[170]   Heslin was mainly involved in the cross-Channel trade until about 1588. After that date he seems only to have traded with La Rochelle and Bordeaux. In January 1599, he was described as 'of' La Rochelle rather than Southampton. PRO, E190/817/3, f. 3, E190/817/7, f. 6, E190/818/1, ff. 1, 2v, E190/818/6, ff. 6, 7v, 12v, 13, E190/818/10, f. 4v.

[171]   *Examinations and Depositions, 1622–1644*, I, p. 44.

[172]   Spicer, 'The French-speaking Reformed community', pp. 99, 101, 124.

[173]   Spicer, 'The French-speaking Reformed community', p. 125; see above p. 58.

[174]   Benedict, *Rouen during the Wars of Religion*, pp. 161, 211–12, 217; Benedict, 'Rouen's Foreign Trade', 60–65.

[175]   MacCaffrey, *Elizabeth I. War and Politics*, pp. 148–49, 152–53.

instability, and as has been seen there were proclamations against trade with Northern France in July 1588 and 1591.[176]

Neverthless the trade with Brittany and the Channel Islands continued despite the political upheavals. In 1587–88, when the trade was at its peak, 51.7 percent of says and 97.9 percent of bays were exported there and even in 1590–91 when trade diminished, it accounted for 23.1 percent of say exports and 23.3 percent bay exports.[177] There were significant changes in the destination for the cloths exported during this period. In 1587–88, 229½ says were exported to St. Malo, 99 says in 1588–89 but in 1590–91 no 'new drapery' cloths were exported there.[178] This decline was only partially offset by an increase in the quantity of cloths exported to Guernsey and Jersey. The cloths exported to the Channel Islands were probably re-exported to Brittany exploiting the Islands' neutrality but in spite of this, the war did apparently diminish the total volume of exports in this period.

Small quantities of the 'new draperies' were exported elsewhere. Le Mercier maintained a very limited trade with the Netherlands sending cloths to Middelburg and in 1593–94 exporting ten says to Flushing.[179] Other 'new drapery' cloths were exported to Danzig and in 1587–88 to Wexford in Ireland.[180]

While says were certainly the principal commodity exported by le Mercier, he did periodically export cloths of the old draperies. For example in 1585–86 he exported twelve Hampshire kerseys and two Winton kerseys to Middelburg and ten northern dozens were sent to St. Malo. Occasionally he exported cottons, 'friezes' and 'buffins'.[181] Limited quantities of tin were also exported from Southampton by le Mercier, for example in 1588 he sent 3 barrels containing 1,000 lb of tin to Morlaix. A further 200 lb of tin was exported from Southampton by Pierre le Gay.[182] Sometimes le Mercier exported goods from Southampton which had originated elsewhere. For example, pitch and tar which presumably came from the Baltic was exported to St. Malo while Portuguese salt was exported to Danzig. In 1592 he exported a cargo of dried pilchards and hake from Plymouth to Bordeaux.[183] These different exports were however exceptional; the principal export for le Mercier and other refugee merchants remained the 'new draperies'.

[176] See above p. 58.
[177] Spicer, 'The French-speaking Reformed community', pp. 124, 126.
[178] PRO, E190/817/1, E190/817/3, E190/817/7.
[179] PRO, E190/816/6, ff. 5, 6, E190/817/3, ff. 4, 7v, E190/817/7, f. 3v, E190/818/1, entry dated 9/9/1594.
[180] PRO, E190/816/6, f. 5v, E190/817/1, f. 5v, E190/817/3, f. 1v, E190/818/1, entry dated 8/7/1594.
[181] PRO, E190/816/6, ff. 5, 5v, 6v, E190/816/11, f. 5, E190/817/3, f. 9v, E190/817/7, f. 8v, E190/818/1, f. 6.
[182] PRO, E190/817/3, ff. 2v, 9.
[183] PRO, E190/816/11, entries dated 7/2/1587, 9/2/1587, 10/5/1587; *Examinations and Depositions, 1570–1594*, p. 134.

The refugees and overseas trade, *c*. 1595–*c*. 1620

The prosperity of the early 1590s was shortlived and the town's overseas trade began to decline.[184] There was also a change in the refugee merchant community at this time. Particularly significant was the sudden change in the fortunes of Jean le Mercier after 1594. His name does not appear in the 1596–97 port book and his lay subsidy payment fell from 53*s* 4*d* based on goods valued at £10 in 1594 to a poll contribution in 1599.[185] This financial trouble was the result of 'great losses on the seas and by the evill dealinge of his factours and copartners, and by suites of lawe in forraine partes for the recovery of his goodes whereof he was spoiled at the seas'.[186] It is possible that some of these losses were the result of his illegal trade with the League towns.[187] A petition was made to the Privy Council on le Mercier's behalf which requested that he should be allowed time to settle his debts which would be possible if he continued to trade and recovered the money owed to him. It seems that the two most rigorous creditors were James Parkinson and John Jeffries, a Southampton merchant, who were eager to recover these debts through the courts. There were further creditors in London, in particular one Richard French.[188] Jean Rochefort, a member of the stranger community, had apparently lent le Mercier £135.[189] The Privy Council responded to the petitioners by requesting that they should see le Mercier's creditors and urge them to pursue a more tolerant approach in the settlement of his debts. The results of this intervention are unclear, but le Mercier does not seem to have been able to recover his former prominent role in the town's trade. There are only occasional references to le Mercier importing small quantities of goods after 1600.[190] However le Mercier does not seem to have been impoverished as he received the maximum lay subsidy assessment of 8*s* 4*d* in 1602. He remained in Southampton until his death in 1626.[191]

There were other noticeable changes amongst the refugee merchants. Guillaume Hersent, who had been actively involved in the cross-Channel trade and had later exported small quantities of says further afield, died in 1590. His son, who had become involved in trade before Guillaume's death, and then

---

[184]   Thomas, 'The Seaborne Trade of Southampton', pp. 54–56.
[185]   PRO, E179/174/415, E179/174/446.
[186]   *Acts of the Privy Council*, 1598–99, pp. 211–13.
[187]   Another Southampton merchant, Thomas Heaton, had been actively involved in privateering and seems to have experienced severe financial difficulties by 1595 and was later imprisoned for debt. Thomas, 'The Seaborne Trade of Southampton', pp. 154–56.
[188]   *Acts of the Privy Council*, 1598–99, pp. 211–13.
[189]   HRO, Wills 1606/B/46.
[190]   Le Mercier's name does not appear in the port books between 1596 and 1599. He reappears in January 1601 when he imported 14 packets of Holland cloth and 6 barrels of rape oil from Dieppe. In 1605 he imported Gascon wine from Bordeaux and French wine from Flushing. PRO, E190/818/13, f. 11, E190/819/4, entries dated 19/11/1605, 21/11/1605.
[191]   *Registre*, p. 113; *Assembly Books*, I, p. 5; Southampton City Record Office, *Southampton in 1620 and the Mayflower. An Exhibition of Documents*, (Southampton, 1970), p. 50 (No. 136).

his grandsons became leading refugee merchants during the early seventeenth century.[192] Claude Moutonnier who had become a significant exporter of says in the late 1580s and early 1590s had migrated to Caen, Normandy, by 1598.[193] Another merchant, Estienne Michellet, also seems to have left Southampton by the mid-1590s.[194] Several other merchants who had emerged in the early 1590s continued to trade into the seventeenth century but died shortly afterwards, such as Pierre le Gay who died in 1604 and Balthasar des Maistres who died in 1605.[195]

Southampton's mercantile community in the early seventeenth century has been analysed by D. Lamb. His analysis was based upon a list of proposed contributions to be made by Southampton merchants towards the cost of sending a fleet to suppress the North African pirates. While the list is not exhaustive (three merchants appear to have been omitted) it does give an indication of the state of the merchant community in 1619. The following 'French' merchants were identified: Peter Seale, Peter Priaulx, John Clungeon, William Marinell, Peter Clungeon, Paul Desert, Jean Hersent, John Guillam, Judith de la Motte, Daniel Hersent, Isaac Herevill, Matthew Vibert, Jan de la Bye, James Roberts and John Piton.[196]

The 'French' merchant community identified by Lamb can be divided into two groups. The first group consists of merchants from refugee families, such as the Hersents, Paul Desert, James Roberts, Judith de la Motte and Jan de la Bye. With the exception of the last two merchants, these were second or third generation immigrants who had been born in Southampton. The other two merchants, Judith de la Motte and Jan de la Bye, were both natives of Armentières.[197] However Judith de la Motte was the daughter of Balthasar des Maistres and the widow of the minister Philippe de la Motte, who had both been involved in the town's overseas trade.[198]

The second group which can be identified is that of the Channel Island merchants and includes the Clungeons, Isaac Herevill, William Marinell, John Piton, Peter Seale and Peter Priaulx.[199] These merchants seem to have been first generation settlers in Southampton and worshipped at the French church. Matthew Vibert may have also belonged to this group or may have been a

[192] *Registre*, p. 105.
[193] *Les Actes des Colloques des Eglises Françaises et des Synodes des Eglises Etrangères réfugiées en Angleterre 1581–1654*, ed. A.C. Chamier, (HSQS, 2, 1890), pp. 36, 37, 38, 41.
[194] Spicer, 'The French-speaking Reformed community', p. 133.
[195] *Registre*, pp. 108, 110.
[196] Lamb, 'The Seaborne Trade of Southampton', pp. 500–3.
[197] *Registre*, p. 89.
[198] PRO, E190/818/1, entries dated 8/1/1594, 3/6/1594, E190/818/1, ff. 2, 3, 4v, 7, 9, 12, 13, 15, 18, E190/818/6, ff. 2v, 6, 6v, 7v, 8, 10, 10v, 11, 12v, E190/818/6, f. 25, E190/818/7, entries dated 14/2/1598, 28/3/1598, 1/10/1597, 4/10/1597, 4/1/1598, 17/2/1598, 17/4/1598, 6/7/1598, 14/8/1598, 27/9/1598, E190/818/9, entry dated 12/2/1598, E190/818/10, ff. 2, 2v, 4, 5, 6, 10v, 11v, 18v, 20v, 31, E190/818/12, entry dated 23/1/1600, E190/818/13, ff. 2, 12v, 17v, 18, 19v, 20v, 24, 28, E190/819/2, ff. 22v, 25v; HRO, Wills 1615/A/24; *Registre*, p. 89.
[199] *Registre*, pp. 87, 89, 92.

member of a Channel Island family well-established in Southampton.[200] Priaulx had close links with the refugee community. He traded on a small scale from 1585 and may have been a factor or apprentice of Jean le Mercier, subsequently marrying his daughter.[201]

A glimpse of the commercial interests of one of the refugee merchants, Jean Rochefort, can be gained from examining his will and the probate inventory of his goods. He originated from Rouen and was admitted to the Lord's Supper in Southampton in December 1594.[202] Rochefort was a substantial merchant; his goods were valued at £528 4s 7d at the time of his death in 1606. He was actively involved in the production of the 'new draperies', owning four serge looms, and was still trading at the time of his death. According to the probate inventory one balette of five pieces of serge and a further two small pieces of black dyed serge had been sent to John Piton and Peter Seale of Jersey. The balette was then to be delivered to one Pierre Paumier in St. Malo. Rochefort also traded with Western France. Six hogsheads of Rochelle wine and a balette of canvas, valued at £24, arrived at Southampton in *The Mayflower* after his death. Rochefort may also have imported salt from this area because he was owed £19 by Edward Barlow for 142 quarters of salt. This situation was not unique. Robert le Page was another merchant who died while actively involved in the town's trade and after his death consignments worth £60 came from La Rochelle and another consignment from Dieppe which was worth £34.[203]

There is a degree of continuity in Southampton's overseas trade from Elizabeth's reign into the early seventeenth century. However any study of the town's overseas trade between the mid-1590s and c. 1620 is limited by a hiatus in the surviving royal port books. These record foreign trade between 1596 and 1602 but there is then a break of a decade in the records until 1612. Furthermore during this gap in the records, the port books ceased to be calculated from Michaelmas to Michaelmas but from Christmas to Christmas, rendering direct comparision between the earlier and later port books difficult.

Although the conclusion of the war with Spain undoubtedly had an impact upon overseas trade, the general direction of this trade in the early seventeenth century remained largely unchanged. The import trade was principally centred upon the Channel Islands, St. Malo and Morlaix; trade with the ports of Western France and Normandy was of only secondary importance. The trade with the Netherlands and the Iberian peninsula was of limited significance.[204]

Linen and canvas from Brittany and Normandy were the most important commodities imported to Southampton during this period, accounting for 73.6

---

[200]   James, 'Geographical Origins and Mobility', pp. 511, 512, 619; *Assembly Books*, I, p. 8.

[201]   PRO, E190/816/11, ff. 1, 3v, E190/817/5, entry dated 24/2/1589, E190/817/7, f. 8v, E190/818/1, ff. 2v, 9; *Registre*, pp. 45, 55, 56, 57, 114; *Southampton in 1620 and the Mayflower*, pp. 41 (No. 87), 50 (No. 136).

[202]   HRO, Wills 1606/B/46; *Registre*, p. 25.

[203]   HRO, Wills 1612/A/58.

[204]   Lamb, 'The Seaborne Trade of Southampton', pp. 42–44.

percent of total imports in 1613 and this increased to 84.7 percent of imports in 1619.[205] The refugee merchants such as Pierre le Gay, Jean Hersent, Balthasar des Maistres and Robert le Page were all engaged in this trade.[206] Besides canvas these merchants imported other goods from St. Malo such as aniseed, almonds, raisins and Seville oil.[207] Members of the French community also continued to trade with the Northern French ports; the principal merchant who exported goods from Caen to Southampton was David Moutonnier, probably the son of Claude.[208] Some of the refugees also traded with the Netherlands, for example Philippe de la Motte imported twelve barrels of rape oil and four bags of madder from Flushing in 1601-2.[209] The import of wine doubled between 1606 and 1609, the most marked growth being in the import of Spanish wine which quadrupled. By 1617 the level of imports seems to have fallen back to the lower levels of 1606.[210] This would not have affected many strangers directly for few of them had imported wines.

The 'new draperies' were Southampton's most important export in the first half of the seventeenth century, although the actual volume of 'new drapery' exports seems to have peaked in the second decade of the century. It is difficult to calculate the actual quantities of 'new drapery' exports due to the inconsistencies in the surviving port books and because of the emergence of even more varieties of the 'new draperies'.[211] New cloths such as perpetuanas first appear in 1612-13. There were also several changes in terminology; the cloth which had been exported as says had by 1596-97 come to be called serge. This name seems to have changed again by 1613 to 'cloth rash'.[212] These changes in terminology and in the types of cloth makes any direct comparisions with earlier 'new drapery' exports difficult.

By the seventeenth century, the term 'new draperies' had also come to embrace other types of cloth which were not produced by the refugee community. The export of the 'old draperies' declined markedly in the first half of the seventeenth century. In Southampton the export of the 'old draperies', of which the Hampshire and Winton kerseys were the most important, had declined after reaching their peak in the early 1570s. The 'new draperies' offered a lighter and cheaper alternative to the English broadcloths. Gradually new cloths had emerged outside the refugee communities in response to the

---

[205] Lamb, 'The Seaborne Trade of Southampton', p. 49.

[206] PRO, E190/818/10, ff. 14v, 15v, 16v, 17v, 18, 18v, 20v, 21, 22, 22v, 23, 23v, 24, 24v, 26v, 27, 28, 31.

[207] PRO, E190/818/10, ff. 22, 26v.

[208] Lamb, 'The Seaborne Trade of Southampton', p. 69.

[209] PRO, E190/819/2, ff. 22v, 25v.

[210] Lamb, 'The Seaborne Trade of Southampton', p. 128.

[211] Some figures for the volume of different types of 'new drapery' exports have been calculated. Lamb, 'The Seaborne Trade of Southampton', p. 57.

[212] In 1593-94 the phrase 'sayes al. sarges' was used and by 1596-97, 'sarge' seems to have become the common term. There are still references to says but these were presumably what had earlier been called Hondschoote says. PRO, E190/818/1, E190/818/6. On the adoption of the term cloth rash, see Lamb, 'The Seaborne Trade of Southampton', p. 54 which cites *Examinations and Depositions, 1622-1644*, I, p. 48.

changing patterns of demand. The rapid growth of serge-production in Devon was typical of this development. In Southampton, cottons were an important export in the first two decades of the seventeenth century. These 'new draperies' were probably produced in the counties of Southern England. As a result of this 'expansion' of the 'new draperies', the cloths produced by the refugee community only represented a share, albeit the most important, of the total volume of the 'new draperies' exported in the early seventeenth century.[213]

The involvement of the 'French' merchants in the town's overseas trade in 1619 was also examined by Lamb. In terms of imports, the most active 'French' merchants were John Clungeon, Peter Clungeon, John Guillam and Peter Seale who imported 73 of the 224 consignments imported by the principal Southampton merchants. In general these merchants seem to have imported cloth from St. Malo. These merchants together with the Hersents, Peter Priaulx and James Roberts were all actively involved in exporting cloth from Southampton which was principally sent to St. Malo, La Rochelle and Bordeaux.[214]

The presence of the 'French' merchants continued to be felt in Southampton's overseas trade later into the seventeenth century, through the activities of merchants such as the de la Mottes, Paul Mercer and the Clungeons. However as the members of the community gradually began to penetrate municipal government and became increasingly integrated into Southampton society, it becomes less valid to identify these merchants as a separate group in the town's economic life.[215]

Conclusion

The refugee merchants clearly made a substantial contribution to Southampton's overseas trade in the second half of the sixteenth century. While there were a number of small traders who regularly engaged in the cross-Channel trade, the principal benefit to Southampton's economy came from a very small group of prominent merchants: Arnoul le Clercq, Mathieu Sohier and Jean le Mercier. In importing goods to Southampton, these merchants were generally engaged in a similar trade to the indigenous Southampton merchants. However their most important contribution was in the development of a new export trade, the 'new draperies'. These merchants rarely encroached upon the types of goods exported by Southampton merchants. Refugee merchants were responsible for on average about 70 percent of the says exported from Southampton between 1573 and 1580. The merchants' contribution to Southampton's overseas trade was however tempered by war and plague as

---

[213] Thomas, 'The Seaborne Trade of Southampton', pp. 74–76; Lamb, 'The Seaborne Trade of Southampton', pp. 54–58; D.C. Coleman, 'An Innovation and its Diffusion: the "New Draperies"', *Ec.H.R.*, Second Series, 22 (1969), 428; R. Brenner, *Merchants and Revolution. Commercial Change, Political Conflict, and London's Overseas Traders, 1550–1653*, (Cambridge, 1993), pp. 36–39.

[214] Lamb, 'The Seaborne Trade of Southampton', pp. 504–5, 514.

[215] See below, p. 147.

well as local economic crises during the 1580s. As a result some merchants left Southampton while others such as Jean le Mercier adapted to the changed circumstances. By the early seventeenth century, the 'new draperies' had become the most important export from Southampton and of these the most significant were the serges which had been introduced by the refugee community.

CHAPTER FOUR

THE REFUGEES AND THE PRODUCTION OF THE 'NEW DRAPERIES'

During the 1560s, Cecil and the Privy Council became alarmed that the value of luxuries being imported to England could not be met by the value of the country's exports. Cecil therefore attempted to encourage the domestic production of goods in order to offset this damaging adverse balance of trade.[1] Part of this encouragement of domestic production meant supporting proposals made for the introduction of new skills and products to England.[2] The establishment of the 'new draperies' by the exile communities should be seen against this background.

In 1561 the Privy Council granted permission for a community of Dutch refugees to be established in Sandwich. It was hoped to revitalise Sandwich's flagging economy through the introduction of the skills of the 'new draperies'.[3] Other towns also cherished the hope that their economies would benefit from these new techniques introduced by exiles; communities were soon established in Norwich (1565), Maidstone (1567) and Stamford (1567).[4] The introduction of the 'new draperies' also played an important part in the negotiations for the establishment of the refugee community in Southampton.[5]

The economy of Southampton depended largely upon overseas trade. Despite several attempts to establish textile production in Southampton during the late fifteenth and early sixteenth centuries, the town still lacked any substantial manufacturing industry.[6]

---

[1] See above p. 23.

[2] Pettegree, *Foreign Protestant Communities*, pp. 139–42.

[3] Pettegree, *Foreign Protestant Communities*, p. 141; Backhouse, 'The Strangers at Work in Sandwich', 74.

[4] Pettegree, *Foreign Protestant Communities*, pp. 263–64.

[5] See pp. 31–33, 72.

[6] Thomas, 'The Seaborne Trade of Southampton', p. 44. This is to an extent confirmed by an examination of the probate inventories produced for residents of Southampton before 1567, which reveals the dominance of mercantile and maritime trades. In 1483 attempts were made to settle foreign clothworkers in the town and to educate the English in the new techniques for the dyeing and finishing of cloth. Anthony Spinola revived this scheme in Henry VII's reign but it came to nothing. The plans of Antonio Guidotti, to introduce twenty four silkweavers from Messina to the town in 1537, were also unsuccessful. *Southampton Probate Inventories 1447–1575*, ed. E. Roberts & K. Parker, (SRS, 34–35, 1992), I; *Calendar of the Patent Rolls, preserved in the Public Record Office: Edward IV, Edward V, Richard III*, (London, 1901–), p. 342; Ruddock, *Italian Merchants and Shipping*, p. 217; A.A. Ruddock, 'Antonio Guidotti', *PHFC*, 15 (1941–43), 37–38.

By 1569 the refugees had 'set vp in ye towne a dyenge house, wevinge & fullinge' for the production of the 'new draperies'.[7] These cloths had been developed in Flanders 'partly in a commercialization of peasant techniques drawing into the market economy; and partly in a copying and adaptation of Italian textile models'.[8] They offered an alternative to the 'old draperies', the Hampton and Winton kerseys, for which the county had been an important centre of production.[9] The refugees proposed *'composer sayes de Honscooten, draps d'Armentiere et couvertures d'Espagne, desqueles sortes de marchandises jusques à présent la manifacture ne s'est faicte, ny cognue'*.[10] In fact they seem never to have introduced the *'draps d'Armentiere'* or the *'couvertures d'Espagne'* to Southampton. The production of *'draps d'Armentiere'* at Coventry from 1568 onwards may have prevented the manufacture of this type of cloth in Southampton, and the Flemish community at Norwich briefly produced *'couvertures d'Espagne'*.[11]

The Southampton community concentrated on the production of says. These cloths had been produced in Flanders since the twelfth century using local wool and a variety of says had emerged with different types of spun warps and wefts.[12] By the sixteenth century the term 'say' had come to be applied not just to 'says' but also to 'serges'. Technically there was very little difference between the two types of cloth which both had jersey warps and carded wefts; a say had a warp which was made to appear prominent through doubling and twisting of the yarn, whereas the warp in a serge was inconspicuous.[13] In the royal port books for Southampton for 1593–94, these cloths were described as 'sayes al. sarges' and by 1596–97 'sarge' seems to have become the common term for the cloths exported.[14]

The refugees produced several varieties of this cloth. They produced narrow cloths, suitable for making doublets, and broad cloths for cloaks.[15] The broad serge seems to have been produced more widely than the narrow serges. As the broad loom required two people to operate it, it was less easily adapted for serge production in rural areas. By the early seventeenth century the 'Hampton broad serges' came to be called 'cloth rashes'.[16]

A coarser cloth, pinnion serge, had been developed in the West Country and came to challenge the Hampton serges. According to Kerridge, the refugees also manufactured pinnion serge.[17] However his evidence comes from the mid-seventeenth century, but this cloth was made in the town in the late six-

---

[7] *Court Leet Records*, p. 60.
[8] Coleman, 'An Innovation and its Diffusion', 421.
[9] Brenner, *Merchants and Revolution*, pp. 37–38.
[10] PRO, SP12/43/30.
[11] E. Kerridge, *Textile Manufactures in Early Modern England*, (Manchester, 1985), pp. 34–35.
[12] Kerridge, *Textile Manufactures*, pp. 6–7.
[13] Kerridge, *Textile Manufactures*, pp. 7, 60, 111, 113.
[14] PRO, E190/818/1, E190/818/6.
[15] Kerridge, *Textile Manufactures*, p. 111.
[16] Kerridge, *Textile Manufactures*, p. 113; *Examinations and Depositions, 1622–1644*, I, p. 48.
[17] Kerridge, *Textile Manufactures*, pp. 113–14, 116–17.

teenth century.[18] In 1590 Gilles Seulin left 40 lb of 'pynyon earne' while in 1606 Jean Rochefort left 5 tods 7 lb of 'middell pinion' as well as some pieces of coarse serge.[19] Another type of say made by the community were the Hondschoote says. These traditionally had a rockspun weft and a slackly twisted wheelspun warp.[20] These cloths were distinct from the main production of says/serges produced by the community and were recorded separately in the royal port books.[21]

The refugees did not however confine themselves to producing says or serges; in 1574 the Court Leet referred to those 'that mak serge & estammel'.[22] 'Estammel' was a cloth known as 'stammet' (and later as tammy), in which the yarn had been scoured in order to make it smoother or finer. The immigrants from the Netherlands introduced the production of stammet kerseys to England, though only limited quantities of this cloth were manufactured by the refugee communities and little was exported from Southampton.[23]

Silk weaving was also introduced to Southampton by the refugees. In 1574 Anthoine Jurion was described as being a silk weaver and was accused by the Court Leet of the retail selling of silk and ribbon lace.[24] When he died in 1578, he left amongst his goods 28 lb 3 oz of different coloured silks which together with a range of other silks, threads and laces were assessed as being worth £76 4s.[25] References to silkweaving in Southampton are sparse. Another refugee who was described as a silkweaver was Vincent Nérin, who in 1582 married Jurion's widowed daughter-in-law.[26] In 1584 a certain John Cordon, the son of a woollen draper, was apprenticed to Nérin who was 'to teach him to weaue silke'.[27]

The variety of 'new drapery' cloths exported from Southampton can be seen from the royal port books. Between Michaelmas 1573 and Michaelmas 1574, 334½ pieces of say and 140½ bays were exported from Southampton; refugee merchants exported 253 of these says (75.8%) and no bays.[28] In addition the refugee merchants exported small quantities of other cloths: forty pieces of blankets, twenty-nine pieces of mockadoes, four pieces of Holland cloth and three score 'goads' of cottons.[29] The more varied cloths exported may not have been produced in Southampton and may have already been imported to the town. Members of the refugee community occasionally imported small quan-

[18] Kerridge, *Textile Manufactures*, p. 299 n.289.
[19] HRO, Wills 1590/Ad/42, 1606/B/46.
[20] Kerridge, *Textile Manufactures*, p. 7.
[21] PRO, E190/818/1, E190/818/6.
[22] *Court Leet Records*, p. 106.
[23] SRO, SC5/4/65; Kerridge, *Textile Manufactures*, pp. 110–11.
[24] *Court Leet Records*, p. 106.
[25] HRO, Wills 1578/B/53.
[26] Catherine des Plus had initially married Abraham Jurion in 1575, but he died in May 1579, three months after his father. HRO, Wills 1578/B/53; *Registre*, pp. 85, 88, 102.
[27] SRO, SC2/6/5, f. 168v.
[28] PRO, E190/814/9; see above p. 44.
[29] PRO, E190/814/9, ff. 32, 35v, 36.

tities of 'mockadoes' (which were described as being 'of Flanders making'), Holland cloth and Ghentish cloth.[30]

Initially some members of the stranger communities in London and Sandwich returned to the Netherlands to purchase yarn. One Cool Boye often returned to Tournai while a refugee from Sandwich went to purchase yarn at Tourcoing. A certain François Ente, who had been banished from the Netherlands, had been seen buying yarn in Armentières.[31] There is no evidence to suggest that the refugees in Southampton made similar journeys to the Netherlands to purchase yarn, perhaps because of the distances involved. Arnoul le Clercq, Mathieu Sohier, Augustin de Beaulieu, Jean de Beaulieu and Robert Cousin occasionally imported sacks of wool, but there is no evidence about where these sacks originated.[32] At Norwich small quantities of finer grades of wool were imported but generally these seem to have been brought to the city by sea from London.[33]

By the 1570s the community at Sandwich had begun to manufacture yarn themselves and were generally supplied with wool by Flemish dealers who mainly bought their wool within Kent, in particular from the Romney Marsh area.[34] The refugees in Southampton seem also to have begun to manufacture their own yarn, as spinning wheels or 'tournes' were mentioned in some probate inventories.[35] It seems that the Southampton clothiers used long Buckinghamshire and Oxfordshire combing wool to produce their warps and, for the weft, initially Hampshire and Berkshire wool, though by the early seventeenth century Devon and Cornwall wool, was considered better for some fabrics.[36] Probably the clearest insight into the wool used in the manufacture of the 'new draperies' in Southampton comes from the probate inventory of the goods of Jean Rochefort compiled in 1606.[37] He possessed the following quantities of wool:

13 stone 4 lb of Leominster wool	£16	1s	4d
45 tods 14 lb of fleece wool	£72	16s	
17 tods of Spanish wool, valued at 42s per tod	£35	14s	
5 tods 8 lb of Spanish wool, valued at 40s per tod	£10	11s	[sic]
7 tods 24 lb of Spanish wool, valued at 12d per lb	£11		

---

[30] PRO, E190/814/9, f. 34, E190/814/10, f. 22.

[31] E. de Coussemaker, *Troubles religieux de XVIe siècle dans la Flandre Maritime, 1560–1570*, 4 vols. (Bruges, 1876), I, pp. 346–54.

[32] Unfortunately these entries can not be confirmed by comparision with the royal port books because the entries do not coincide. SRO, SC5/4/64, SC5/4/65, entry dated 19/7/1569, SC5/4/66, entries dated 15/2/1570, 13/4/1570, 18/7/1570, 18/8/1570, SC5/4/67, entry dated 10/7/1571, SC5/4/73, entries dated ?/11/1577, 16/7/1578.

[33] N.J. Williams, *The Maritime Trade of the East Anglian Ports, 1550–1590*, (Oxford, 1988), p. 177.

[34] Backhouse, 'The Strangers at Work in Sandwich', 81.

[35] HRO, Wills 1603/Ad/52, 1606/B/46.

[36] P.J. Bowden, *The Wool Trade in Tudor and Stuart England*, (London, 1962), pp. 63–64.

[37] HRO, Wills 1606/B/46.

5 tods 7 lb of 'middell pinion', valued at 6*d* per lb	£3 13*s* 6*d*	
One small barrel full of wool valued at	10*s*	
Four small baskets with certain wool valued at	£1	

Leominster wool was considered to be the best type of wool for carding; March wool, which came from the Welsh Marches around Wenlock and the Clun Forest, was the second best wool.[38] In the same inventory a clear distinction was made between serges made with Leominster wool and those made from March wool.

The dues paid on the wool brought into the town by the sergemakers became the centre of a dispute in the early seventeenth century. The brokage dues were farmed by Michael Nutley but the sergemakers refused to pay the duties imposed upon wool brought into the town. In 1609, Estienne Latelais, Isaac le Gay, Pierre Thieudet and Richard Robert were all ordered to pay their arrears to Nutley, while John Clungeon and Isaac Herevill were ordered to pay the arrears owing up to the time when they became burgesses.[39] The sergemakers were ordered by the Corporation to reach an agreement with Nutley in July 1612, concerning the brokage dues on wool entering the town.[40] The matter had still not been resolved by January 1614 when Nutley complained to the Corporation about Jean Hersent and other Frenchmen who refused to pay the customary rate of a penny on each tod of wool.[41] In January 1616 the clothiers reached an agreement with the Corporation about the brokage dues. The clothiers agreed to pay 4*d* on every sack which contained thirteen tods of wool and 2*d* for every half sack of wool brought into the town.[42]

Although some probate inventories mention spinning wheels, by the early seventeenth century the spinning of yarn seems to have been largely put out by the sergemakers.[43] This was inevitably due to the large number of spinners who were needed to supply one weaver. Whereas the ratio of spinners to weavers in the production of the broadcloths had been 3 : 1, in the production of fine serge it was 10 : 1.[44] The wool was prepared for spinning by being carded or combed, it was then 'seamed', i.e. dressed with grease before spinning. When Pierre Thieudet died in 1612, he left fifty pounds of combed wool and two dozen pounds of wool at the spinners. His goods also included five tods of wool 'seamed' ready for the spinners.[45]

---

[38] Kerridge, *Textile Manufactures*, pp. 2, 20.
[39] SRO, SC5/15/1–3; *The Third Book of Remembrance*, III, pp. 117–18; *Assembly Books*, II, pp. 14, 64.
[40] *Assembly Books*, III, pp. 40–41. On the same occasion the sergemakers were ordered to pay their employees in English money, see below p. 81.
[41] *Assembly Books*, III, p. 81.
[42] *Assembly Books*, IV, p. 37.
[43] HRO, Wills 1603/Ad/52, 1606/B/46. See below p. 80.
[44] D. Seward, 'The Devonshire cloth industry in the early seventeenth century', in R. Burt, (ed.), *Industry and Society in the South West*, (Exeter, 1970), p. 49.
[45] HRO, Wills 1611/B/65.

Again the probate inventory of Jean Rochefort's goods provides further information about the type of yarn which was used:[46]

363 lb of Leominster yarn, valued at 2s per lb	£36 6s
54 lb of 'Devyse yarne', valued at 20d per lb	£4 10s
112 lb of March wool yarn, valued at 12d per lb.	£5 12s
216 lb of coarse yarn, valued at 9d per lb	£8 2s
164 lb of very coarse yarn, valued at 6d per lb	£4 18s
216 lb of the same yarn, valued at 22d	£3 3s
60 lb of small 'torne' yarn, valued at 2s 8d per lb.	£8
One pack of 'list yarne' valued	4s
One 'chaine warpt of litle-torne yarne' valued	£2 10s

By 1601 Hampshire yarn was considered inferior to yarn produced in Devon and Cornwall which 'serveth best for the abb of some sort of sarges and stuffs' and 'that without the same they cannot make the said stuffes vendable and for use'. The Mayor and Corporation of Southampton appointed an agent to purchase yarn in the South West, but after being arrested he was prohibited by the Justices in Devon from buying more yarn. The Southampton authorities protested to the Privy Council arguing that the production of serges was important for the local economy. The Privy Council acquiesced and wrote to the Justices of the Peace in Devon and Cornwall authorising agents to purchase West Country yarn as this would not cause a shortage but the agents were not however to purchase more than between sixty or eighty pounds of yarn per week.[47]

By the early seventeenth century the cloth was woven on either broad or narrow looms. A certain James Flower was apprenticed in 1618 and was to be 'instructed in weaving serge both upon the broad and narrow looms'.[48] The broad loom seems to have been operated by two men because when the Corporation drew up regulations for the Company of sergemakers, they forbade two apprentices to operate the loom.[49] While some sergemakers such as Clement Graunt possessed a single loom other manufacturers had several looms; Jean Rochefort had 'three loomes for great sardges furnished and one loome for small sardges furnished 4 tornes and polles to dryv chaines upon'.[50]

The woven serges were dyed 'in the piece', in a range of colours: black, tawny, minom [grey], 'grisburn' or 'French russet', silver and white.[51] When the refugees first arrived in Southampton, they had requested permission to be able to export cloths undyed because they were uncertain that sufficient num-

46   HRO, Wills 1606/B/46.
47   *Acts of the Privy Council*, 1601–4, pp. 347–48.
48   *A Calendar of Southampton Apprenticeship Registers, 1609–1740*, compiled by A.J. Willis & ed. A.L. Merson, (SRS, 12, 1968), p. 8.
49   *Assembly Books*, II, p. 50, IV, p. 77.
50   HRO, Wills 1584/Ad/25, 1590/Ad/42, 1603/Ad/52, 1606/B/46, 1611/B/65.
51   *Examinations and Depositions, 1622–1644*, I, p. 48.

bers of says would be produced to allow them to employ a dyer. It was also considered that the quality of the local water would not ensure that the colour of cloths would be fresh. They were given permission to export undyed cloths for a limited period but it seems that they soon found somewhere suitable to dye the cloths.[52] In this respect Southampton was not ideally suited for the cloth industry because it frequently experienced problems over its water supply, which since the thirteenth century had been piped from the Hill area of Southampton.[53]

Dyeing clearly required a significant quantity of water and it may have been for this reason that at least one dye-house was set up in the Hill district. In 1584 Robert Cousin bequeathed to his late wife's son-in-law, Claude Moutonnier, 'that dyeng shope which I have at the hill with the tubbes, chaudrons and all the Instruments belonginge or servinge to the said dyenge'.[54] By the early seventeenth century this dyehouse was in the possession of the le Gay family.[55] Isaac le Gay also had a second dyehouse attached to his home, West Hall, in the parish of SS. Michael & John.[56]

The Court Leet periodically attacked dyeing in the town. In 1602 they complained that Jean Hersent had taken a water pipe to his house from the town cistern and had drawn off water for dyeing. He was accused of taking sufficient water to supply a quarter of the town and of causing a water shortage.[57] The Court Leet complained in 1616 about 'the servants of mr. philipp delamote for castinge their oade [woad] and dyenge water out of the dye house in the backe parte of Bull Street, which is most vnseemelye & Causeth vnsavorie smells to the people passing bye'.[58] De la Motte's widow was similarly accused in 1619 and 1624.[59]

After dyeing, the cloths were finished by the clothworkers who were skilled in 'rowinge', 'burling', 'fulling', 'dressing and pressing of kerseys, serges and other draperies'.[60] Some cloths were fulled; Robert Cousin owned a fulling shop and 'all that which belongeth to the occupacion of a ffuller' when he died in 1584.[61] Other cloths were felted; after dyeing the nap on cloth was raised using teasels and then the cloth was sheared.[62] Cousin also bequeathed

---

[52] PRO, SP12/43/29, SP15/13/78. The different sources of water were also important for dyeing. Apparently 'well water . . . was only suitable for reds or for dyeing cloths made wholly or largely of cotton wool. River water was essential for clear blue, yellow or green wools or woollens'. Kerridge, *Textile Manufactures*, p. 164.

[53] Platt, *Medieval Southampton*, pp. 65, 144, 181, 207.

[54] PRO, PCC Prob. 11/67 Robert Cousin.

[55] PRO, PCC Prob. 11/106 Pierre le Gay, Prob. 11/122 Isaac le Gay.

[56] PRO, PCC Prob. 11/122 Isaac le Gay; SRO, SC4/3/121.

[57] *Court Leet Records*, p. 367.

[58] *Court Leet Records*, p. 503.

[59] *Court Leet Records*, pp. 557, 599.

[60] *Assembly Books*, IV, p. 80.

[61] PRO, PCC Prob. 11/67 Robert Cousin.

[62] This was the case with the *saies drappées* which had been produced at Bruges, Armentières, Lille, Arras, St. Omer, Mechlin and Liège. Kerridge, *Textile Manufactures*, p. 7. See below, pp. 81–82.

to Moutonnier 'all the greate sheeres which I have servinge for to sheare withall and alsoe the shearing tables handells telses [*sic*] and all other thinges servinge to the dressing of clothes'.[63] In 1613 the shearmen and clothiers of the town were admonished by the Court Leet because on a Sunday they 'hange there Clothes to be stretched and dryed uppon severall Racks as well in Godeshowse Greene as in other places'.[64] These racks presumably needed a sizeable area: the Court Leet presented Lionel Awsten, in 1587, for weakening the town walls by cutting into a defensive bank in order to stand his racks.[65] The Corporation leased part of God's House Green, for twenty-one years, to another shearman, John Wyatt, so that he could to set up his racks.[66]

A final stage in the finishing process was the pressing of the serges, which gave the cloths a sheen. William Terrie petitioned the Privy Council in 1597 and claimed that he had lived in Southampton for sixteen years and had made his living through pressing serges.[67] Recently according to Terrie, strangers, who had previously been employed in dying cloth, now also pressed serges. Terrie requested that the Privy Council should order the dyers to cease pressing cloths. The Privy Council wrote to the Mayor and several aldermen in Southampton for their advice on this issue.[68]

The Mayor's response to this letter is unknown. It is however clear that Terrie had not had a monopoly in the pressing of serges in the town since at least *c.* 1584 when Robert Cousin bequeathed to Claude Moutonnier 'my presse serge or washe clothes after the fashion of fflorence, with all the thinges belonginge and servinge to the saide presse'.[69] Moutonnier was certainly dyeing and pressing serges by 1593.[70]

Apparently Terrie's wife pursued her husband's claims for a monopoly. On 20 September 1598 the minister and elders of the French church wrote to Sir Robert Cecil and explained their reasons for opposing the grant of such a

[63] PRO, PCC Prob. 11/67 Robert Cousin; HRO, Wills 1603/Ad/52.

[64] *Court Leet Records*, p. 456.

[65] *Court Leet Records*, pp. 259–60.

[66] *Assembly Books*, III, p. 24. Several racks can be seen in Speed's map of Southampton.

[67] William Terrie [Guillaume Thiery] originated from the Pays de Caux, Normandy and mar- ried Rachel le Roy dit Bouillon at the French church in August 1580. He was occasionally involved in the cross-Channel trade. He initially lived in the ward of Holy Rood where he was assessed for the 'stall & art' dues in 1581 and 1587. By 1594 he was living in the ward of SS. Michael & John where he was assessed for the lay subsidy on goods worth £3. Terrie seems to have been sufficently respected to act as a *parrain* on a number of occasions. Four of the couple's children were baptised in the church, the last being in April 1598. In Sep- tember 1598, Terrie was described as being in debt and had been living in La Rochelle for the previous one and a half years. His wife remained in Southampton. PRO, E179/174/415; SRO, SC6/1/16, SC6/1/19; Hatfield House, Salisbury MSS, CP64/37–38; *Registre*, pp. 43, 44, 45, 46, 48, 50, 51, 52, 87.

[68] *Acts of the Privy Council*, 1597, pp. 9–10.

[69] PRO, PCC Prob. 11/67 Robert Cousin.

[70] See below p. 83.

monopoly to Rachel Terrie. They complained that many strangers would be damaged financially by such a grant because some refugees had imported and set up presses from the continent costing a hundred crowns or more. Furthermore without competition, the cost of pressing says would probably increase such that it would not be viable for them still to be produced. Besides the consequences of such a monopoly, Terrie was accused of being an unsuitable character to operate such a monopoly; furthermore in the past when serges were taken to her and her husband for pressing, they were sometimes lost or secretly sold.[71]

The request for this privilege was referred for consideration to a tribunal which consisted of Sir Julius Caesar and two others. The Mayor and Corporation of Southampton petitioned these men in July 1599. Their letter argued against the granting of this privilege to Rachel Terrie (whom they described as being 'verie idle, a prattlinge Gossipp, unfitt to undertake a matter of so great a charge') and reiterated the points made by the refugees the previous year.[72] It would seem that Terrie's petition was unsuccessful as several sergemakers, including Judith de la Motte, seem to have owned their own serge presses in the early seventeenth century.[73]

During the negotiations for the establishment of the community, the strangers had requested that they might employ 'men and maid servants of their own country' for the manufacture of the 'new draperies' because the employment of unskilled Englishmen could be damaging. The Council permitted twenty families of strangers to settle in the town on condition that they trained two English apprentices for seven years and then took two Englishmen for every two strangers.[74] However while the strangers agreed to train English men they appealed to be allowed sufficient servants to produce the 'new draperies'. While Cecil noted that there should be a 'competent nomber' of Englishmen after three years, he permitted twelve strangers per household but there were to be no more than forty households.[75]

Interestingly the term 'household' used in these negotiations referred to a working unit, i.e. the master craftsman and his employees or apprentices, rather than to the man's family.[76] Bishop Grindal wrote in 1567: 'I suppose it were good no limitation were made, for limitinge of the membre[s] of familyes ... restrayne excessive numbre of servauntes'.[77] In the letters patent drawn up for the establishment of the community in Norwich, the phrase '... being all householders or master workmen' is used and at Maidstone in 1567 the total

[71]   Hatfield House, Salisbury MSS, CP64/37–38.
[72]   BL, Lansdowne MS 161, f. 127.
[73]   *Examinations and Depositions, 1622–1644*, I, pp. 48, 50.
[74]   PRO, SP15/13/82.
[75]   PRO, SP12/43/29–30.
[76]   For a discussion of household structure, see N. Goose, 'Household size and structure in early Stuart Cambridge', *Social History*, 5 (1980), 347–85.
[77]   PRO, SP12/43/29.

was to include '200 persons being householders, children or servants, men and not women'.[78]

The lists of the Sandwich strangers drawn up in the early 1560s demonstrate that a similar form of organisation had also been established there. The first list compiled in 1561 reveals that there were 173 bay workers divided into seventeen groups and 74 say workers divided into eight groups. A master headed each of these groups. A similar pattern appears in the list compiled in 1563, in which 285 names were divided into groups of bay workers with their masters and groups of say workers with their masters.[79] In 1573 a survey of the Sandwich community listed the twenty-five masters separately.[80] This structure reflects the guild-controlled organisation of the urban-based cloth industry in the Southern Netherlands, which can also be seen to an extent in some English towns.[81] Probably the production of the 'new draperies' in Southampton was initially organised in a similar way.

This household form of organisation was however modified because of the large quantities of yarn that were required for the production of the 'new draperies'.[82] By the early seventeenth century, some producers of the 'new draperies' began to act as entrepreneurs and to develop the putting-out system for spinning wool. Jean Rochefort's probate inventory included 47 lb of combed wool with the spinners, a further 23 lb of combed wool and 283 lb of wool 'for the great torne'.[83] Nor was this an isolated example, Pierre Thieudet left £11 worth of wool 'abrod a spyning' and when Robert le Page died in 1612 he owed 14s to diverse spinners.[84]

The use of the putting-out system for spinning resulted in complaints being made to the Corporation in 1609. Isaac le Gay and other sergemakers were accused of employing people in the countryside rather than townsmen in spinning yarn. The sergemakers denied the charge and Isaac le Gay claimed to have one hundred and forty people within the town on his books. However the sergemakers complained that some of the poor people they employed stole the wool or yarn but they agreed to employ any person who approached them for work so long as they had been given a testimonial by the Mayor.[85] The sergemakers seem to have employed workers as far afield as Lymington

[78] *CPR, Elizabeth*, III, pp. 39–40, IV, pp. 209–10.

[79] Backhouse, 'The Strangers at Work in Sandwich', 81; M.F. Backhouse, 'De Vlaamse vluchtelingenkerk in Sandwich in 1563. Twee manuscripten uit het British Museum', *Bulletin de la Commission Royale d'Histoire*, 147 (1981), 84–113.

[80] M.F. Backhouse, 'De Vlaamse vluchtelingenkerk in Sandwich in 1573. Een derde manuscript uit het British Museum', *Bulletin de la Commission Royale d'Histoire*, 148 (1982), 229–67.

[81] E. Coornaert, 'Draperies rurales, draperies urbaines. L'évolution de l'industrie flamande au moyen age et au XVIᵉ siècle', *Revue Belge de philologie et d'histoire*, 28 (1950), 86–90; R.S. DuPlessis, *Lille and the Dutch Revolt. Urban Stability in an Era of Revolution, 1500–1582*, (Cambridge, 1991), pp. 96–99; Clark, 'An Urban Study', pp. 29–45; Kerridge, *Textile Manufactures*, pp. 179–86.

[82] See above p. 75.

[83] HRO, Wills 1606/B/46.

[84] HRO, Wills 1611/B/65, 1612/A/58.

[85] *Assembly Books*, II, p. 69.

because in 1608 they were warned not to deliver or receive 'anie yearne works' from workers there, due to an outbreak of plague in that town.[86]

Although the sergemakers clearly employed a large number of spinners there were complaints made about the way they paid them. In 1604 a complaint was made in the Court Leet against Philippe de la Motte, Pierre le Gay, Estienne Latelais, Jean Hersant, Balthasar des Maistres and Robert le Page who were accused of paying their spinners 'in wares at a verie hard rate, which the poore people are Constrayned to sell againe to whomsoever they cann gett to buye it and that at least by two pence in a shillinge losse, they the said aliens refusinge to pay them in monie'. The Court Leet demanded that the offenders be called before the Town Assembly and be ordered to desist from making such payments in kind.[87] The matter does not appear to have been resolved because in 1612 the following sergemakers were called to the Town Assembly: Isaac Herevill, Jean Hersent, Isaac le Gay, Andrew Harris, Richard Allen, Roger Morse, Mr. Palmer, Richard Goare, Clement Audley, Hugh Newe, Robert Rochefort.[88] They were ordered 'to paie good English money to their worcke folkes in respect they are not otherwise able to live'. The sergemakers promised to conform to this request.[89]

The 'putting-out' system was also used in other areas of cloth production. Although Jean Rochefort seems to have owned a sizeable and well-equipped establishment, the probate inventory of his goods refers to 'a peece of sarge to be woven at lindost [Lyndhurst] in the forest' and to a piece of serge 'at the sherman'.[90] When Robert le Page died, he had significant quantities of wool and yarn but he does not seem to have owned any equipment for the making or finishing of cloths. His probate inventory reveals that le Page owed money to various spinners as well as to a certain Joseph who was a weaver.[91] It is difficult to establish from this fragmentary evidence the extent to which the weaving of cloth may have been 'put out'.

By the early seventeenth century, the production of the 'new draperies' in Southampton was divided between cloth production and cloth finishing. Jean Rochefort also owned a large workshop which would have employed a number of workmen. He had 'an old torne' in the gallery, three looms for weaving broad serges and a loom for small serges in his shop, while above the shop there was a combing chamber, a rack for drying serges on in the garden and in the courtyard there was 'a pearche to rowe sarges'.[92] It is however clear that Rochefort lacked the means to dye or finish the cloths which were produced in his workshop. The probate inventory of the goods of Peter Poché reveals that he possessed the necessary equipment for spinning yarn (one old 'tourne',

[86]   *Assembly Books*, I, p. 72.
[87]   *Court Leet Records*, p. 414.
[88]   Robert Rochefort was the son of Jean Rochefort and seems to have taken over his father's business interests. HRO, Wills 1606/B/46.
[89]   *Assembly Books*, III, pp. 40–41.
[90]   HRO, Wills 1606/B/46.
[91]   HRO, Wills 1612/A/58.
[92]   HRO, Wills 1606/B/46.

a 'warpenbare', and a dozen bobbins), for weaving cloth (two old looms, one large and one small), dyeing the cloth (Poché owned a dye house), for shearing (in the shearing chamber he had six pairs of old shears with a shearing table and all the furniture that went with it) and for pressing of the serges (he had two presses with their furniture 'for 12s of serges' [sic]).[93] Poché would seem to have been primarily engaged in finishing cloth, as he possessed more equipment for finishing cloth than manufacturing it. There is also evidence of cloth manufacturers sending their cloths to be finished outside their workshops. Clement Graunt left two pieces of serge at the dyers before he became ill in 1584; Rochefort left a piece of serge, worth £6, at the dyers.[94]

This division between cloth manufacture and the finishing of cloth can be clearly seen in the early seventeenth century. In October 1624 a deposition made by Judith de la Motte describes how cloth, which had been produced elsewhere, was finished on her premises:

> [The cloths] which were woven in or neare Southampton aforesaid, and were dyed dressed and packed upp in this deponents dwelling house at Southampton aforesaid . . . And the said John de la Motte and John Sledge doe depose and say that they dyed all the before mencioned serges within the said dwelling house of the said Judith de la Motte And the said Tobie Roberts and John Rawlings doe depose and say that they did sheare and dresse all the before mencioned serges within the said dwelling house of the said Judith de la Motte And the said Anthonie Roberts doth depose and say that hee with other his fellowes did measure ffold make upp in buckroms and presse all the foresaid serges within the said dwelling house of the said Judith de la Motte and did afterwards packe them upp in seven ballets or trusses which were marked and numbred as is abovesaid.[95]

Another deposition was made by the merchant Daniel Hersent at the same time:

> . . . the sayd Daniell Hersent doth depose and say that the Nineteene peeces of Hampton great serge and xxij peeces of hampton small serge numbred marked Coloured . . . were woven dyed dressed and packed upp in or neare Southampton aforesaid And the said John Mingin doth depose and say that hee dyed all the said serges in the dwelling house of the said Daniell Hersent And the said James Paule doth depose and say that hee and other did sheare all the said Serges at the place abovesaid And the said Thomas wayte doth depose and say that hee pressed and packed upp all the sayd Serges at the place aforesaid into six balletts'.[96]

The separation between cloth manufacture and cloth finishing was confirmed by the regulation of the trades into two separate companies in 1616.[97]

[93] HRO, Wills 1603/Ad/52.
[94] HRO, Wills 1584/Ad/25, 1606/B/46.
[95] *Examinations and Depositions, 1622–1644*, I, p. 48.
[96] *Examinations and Depositions, 1622–1644*, I, pp. 49–50.
[97] See below p. 86.

The finishing of cloth was a capital-intensive and specialised business. The sizeable establishments operated by Judith de la Motte and Daniel Hersent required them to purchase significant quantities of cloth for finishing. These entrepreneurs were able to combine cloth-finishing with their mercantile activities, exporting the cloths which they produced.[98] Other merchants also purchased cloth from the local markets which was then finished by specialist craftsmen. In the following deposition made in 1593, cloth belonging to a merchant, Edward Barlow, was sent to be finished and each stage of the process was overseen by a master.

> John Lovell, shereman having received in his possession into his howse of the goods of Edward Barlowe, merchant, the number of xij pieces of sarges white to be trymed and dressed. They these deponents with the aide and helpe of the said master [Lovell] did dresse them and having so done did at severall tymes cary those xij peeces unto the house of Gland Mountayne [Claude Moutonnier] to be dyed and having so done they being died, the same xij peeces were brought by Gland's servaunte backe againe unto the said masters howse to be trimed, shorne and dryed as they ought to be. And they saye that after they had so trymed, shorne, dressed and dryed these pieces of Sarge they these deponents together with there said master at severall tymes as they were readie and drye did carry Tenn of these peeces of Sarge backe againe unto the howse of the said gland mountayne to be by him pressed and ordered as they ought to be. And this they do know of a verie certaine to be true for that these deponents at severall tymes did themselves carry them the said Tenn peeces backe unto the said glands his howse and delivered them to the servaunte by the name of the goods of Mr. Barlowe.[99]

Evidence of this entrepreneur/merchant form of industrial organisation can also be seen in the Southern Netherlands as well as in the manufacture of the 'new draperies' in England.[100]

Two forms of organisation can be discerned in the production of the 'new draperies' in Southampton. Initially the 'new draperies' were manufactured by households, a group of workmen organised under their master. By the early seventeenth century, merchants as well as those involved in the finishing processes, bought cloth which was dyed and finished before being exported. This form of organisation of the cloth industry may indeed have existed from the establishment of the community. Refugees such as le Clercq, Sohier and de Beaulieu were not only actively involved in the town's overseas trade, exporting the 'new draperies', but also manufactured these cloths.[101] In Valenciennes, from where these men had originated, the wealth-

---

[98] See above pp. 66, 68.

[99] *Examinations and Depositions, 1570–1594*, p. 117.

[100] Coornaert, 'Draperies rurales, draperies urbaines', 88–89; Clark, 'An Urban Study', p. 35; Seward, 'The Devonshire cloth industry', pp. 41–45.

[101] PRO, HCA 13/18, f. 264v; *Court Leet Records*, p. 106; see pp. 44–48, 144.

ier *marchands de saye* seem to have operated their own workshops as well as trading in the finished cloths.[102] The entrepreneur/merchant system was well established by the early seventeenth century. Entrepreneurs such as Jean Rochefort and Robert le Page, were involved in the manufacture of the 'new draperies', as well playing a prominent role in the town's overseas trade.[103]

At Norwich, the Corporation attempted in 1571 to regulate the town's cloth industry through the Book of Orders which was drawn up six years after the establishment of the refugee community. The book contained detailed regulations about the sale of cloth in several halls but also regulated the quality of the cloths that were produced in the city. Searchers were to examine every package of cloths to ensure that it did not include anything unlawful. Englishmen had been producing cloths akin to the 'new draperies' before the exiles' arrival, but the Corporation stated that their cloths, in particular bays, 'hath not had ther full perfeccion, by reason they have nott passed vnder searche, nor the defawlters corrected orderlye'. As a result the Corporation required not only the strangers but also Englishmen to submit 'enye manner of baye or bayes, stammett kersies, hownscott saies, carrelles, mockados, fustian of Naples, or suche lyke clothes' to be examined 'for the trewe makynge and trewe cowlleringe'. After examination the cloths were then to be sealed.[104] The Norwich authorities also drew up other regulations from time to time, which detailed the production of particular types of cloth (e.g. for the production of mockadoes in 1577) or the size of the cloth that was to be produced.[105] The community at Sandwich also had detailed regulations concerning the production of the 'new draperies'.[106] The Southampton community was not regulated in the same way although there were some trading restrictions imposed on the refugees through the town ordinances.[107]

By the early seventeenth century, however, the Corporation became increasingly alarmed about the numbers of newcomers in Southampton. The beadles were ordered to make a list of all the clothiers and shearmen in the town and they were ordered to appear before the Town Assembly at the beginning of March 1609.[108] The clothiers were required to provide the Corporation with a list of all their workmen and journeymen. The Corporation complained 'that there comon entertaynment of all sorts of people aswell married as unmarried to worcke at there works hath allreddie greatly pestered [crowded] the Towne with inmates, and undertennaunts and licklye to be the occasion of the utter

---

102 In 1559, Mathieu Sohier was described in the Antwerp notarial archives as a saye merchant. SA, Certificatieboek 14, f. 3; Clark, 'An Urban Study', p. 44.
103 See above pp. 67, 81.
104 'Book of Orders for the Strangers at Norwich', in Moens, *The Walloons and their Church at Norwich*, pp. 257–58. On the production of the 'new draperies' before the establishment of the exile community, see below p. 91.
105 Moens, *The Walloons and their Church at Norwich*, pp. 77–78.
106 Kerridge, *Textile Manufactures*, p. 97.
107 See below pp. 141–42.
108 *Assembly Books*, II, p. 19.

impoverishment of the state of this Towne'. The clothmakers and sergemakers were ordered not to employ any newcomers as journeymen without the consent of the Mayor. A fine of £5 was imposed for breaches of these regulations. A similar order was made by the Assembly to the shearmen.[109] After 1609 a clear distinction was made by the Corporation in its attempts to regulate the serge industry between those who produced the cloth (clothiers, sergemakers, woolcombers) and those employed in the finishing process (clothworkers).

The Corporation's ordinances were breached by a shearman, one Lionel Awsten, who had employed two journeymen without the Mayor's consent. Awsten was pardoned because he agreed to send away the one journeyman and act as bond to the other.[110] In July 1609, Awsten and other shearmen complained about the clothworkers who employed newcomers and provided the Town Assembly with the names of these men.[111] As a result the clothworkers were ordered to draw up regulations for admittance to their trade which were approved by the Assembly although no record of them or the modified version of 1612 has survived.[112]

In May 1609 the Corporation attempted to regulate the employment of apprentices by the weavers, shearmen and woolcombers. All those who were taken on as apprentices had to have their names enrolled by the Town Clerk at the cost of 12d. Furthermore those who had not been apprenticed were not permitted to work as journeymen for any clothier. The Corporation appointed six sergemakers (Henry Ayres, Andrew Harris, William Martin, John le Plus, Isaac Lamoureux and William Harding) as overseers to the trade to ensure that there was no abuse of these regulations.[113]

The regulations which the Corporation approved in July 1609 for the sergemakers, sergeweavers and woolcombers established a trade company and provided regulations for the employment of apprentices and newcomers. Sergemakers were not permitted to take apprentices unless they themselves had completed a seven-year apprenticeship. No-one was permitted to become a sergemaker unless he had completed this apprenticeship or had 'otherwise exercised therin for so long time' and had been enrolled by the Corporation. Two apprentices were not permitted to use a broad loom, unless one of them was in the final year of training, because there were many journeymen in the town who were seeking employment. Newcomers would not be employed unless they could produce a certificate proving that they had completed a seven year apprenticeship.[114]

There continued to be breaches of the regulations about the employment of newcomers. In 1612 a Richard White had come to Southampton and was employed by M. le Gay (presumably Isaac le Gay) as a journeyman but he

[109] *Assembly Books*, II, p. 20.
[110] *Assembly Books*, II, p. 33.
[111] *Assembly Books*, II, p. 48.
[112] *Assembly Books*, II, pp. 48, 54, III, p. 42.
[113] *Assembly Books*, II, pp. 36–37.
[114] *Assembly Books*, II, pp. 50–51.

and his wife and family were ordered to leave the town.[115] In 1615 a wool-comber, Robert Webber, who had been employed by Judith de la Motte, was ordered to leave Southampton, within three weeks.[116]

In March 1616 the sergemakers, sergeweavers and woolcombers met at the Audit House where it was agreed that the orders of the trade should be revised.[117] The Mayor and Corporation approved these new regulations for the sergemakers, sergeweavers and woolcombers in December 1616 and at the same time approved new regulations for the clothworkers.

The Company of sergeweavers, sergemakers and woolcombers was reorganised in 1616, and provision made for the election by the Company of two officers 'for the better orderinge of the said Company and receiving disbursinge & disposinge of such money and duties as shall happen or growe due or paieable unto or by the said Company'. The Company's funds came from fines imposed for the failure to observe certain regulations, and these fines were divided between the Company and the Corporation. The regulations reiterated earlier orders about the enrollment of new apprentices and the employment of newcomers in the town.[118] These ordinances were part of an attempt by the Corporation to reorganise the trade companies in Southampton and to overcome the irregularities of people setting themselves up in business. The Corporation was attempting to assert control over the craft guilds through the imposition of these regulations, a process which can be seen in other towns in the late sixteenth and early seventeenth centuries.[119] As a result there was considerable similarity in the wording of the regulations for the different companies.

The Company of clothworkers was established for those who practised the 'Art or mistery within the said towne viz rowinge burlinge fullinge dressinge and pressinge of Kerseys serges and other draperies'. The dyers would seem to have been excluded from this company. The regulations concerning the organisation of the Company, the conditions of apprenticeship and the employment of journeymen were similar to those for the Company of sergemakers, sergeweavers and woolcombers.[120] The Company's regulations included several specific clauses such as prohibition from working on the sabbath; 'noe person of the said Companie shall sett or cause to be sett uppon Racke or Tenters any Serges Kerseys or other drapery uppon the saboth daie Nor shall at any tyme worcke any Cloth Kersey Serge or other like draperie with cardes'. This clause may have been inserted due to the complaint made before the Court Leet in 1613 about the breaches of the sabbath by cloth-

[115] *Assembly Books*, III, p. 46.
[116] *Assembly Books*, IV, p. 1.
[117] *Assembly Books*, IV, p. 41.
[118] *Assembly Books*, IV, pp. 74–79.
[119] *Assembly Books*, IV, pp. xxii–xxx; V. Pearl, 'Change and stability in seventeenth-century London', in J. Barry, (ed.), *The Tudor and Stuart Town. A Reader in English Urban History, 1530–1688*, (London, 1990), p. 148.
[120] *Assembly Books*, IV, pp. 79–84.

workers.[121] One further clause only appears in the regulations for the Clothworkers, concerned the position of widows of freeman should they marry again. This clause may have been inserted as a concession towards Judith de la Motte who pursued the trade of a clothworker after her husband's death.[122]

The regulation of the cloth industry clearly forms a part of a more wide-ranging strategy to overcome the problems of overcrowding in the town of Southampton and to clarify the town's regulations; it was not an attempt to keep the cloth industry in check or to regulate the cloth that was produced although the regulations concerning apprenticeship were reinforced.

The success of the 'new draperies'

An important condition made during the negotiations for the establishment of the French community was that after the community had been established for a year, that they should 'teach and instruct in their sciences without frawde' two English-born apprentices and after seven years they should employ one Englishman for every two strangers.[123] Such training by the refugees in the skills of the 'new draperies' has left few traces in the records. The town does not seem to have kept a register of apprenticeship enrollments in the later sixteenth century and a register only seems to have been kept after 1609 due to the regulation of the serge industry because of the intrusion of untrained men.[124]

Some evidence of the earlier apprentices may be gained from the register of the French community. Sometimes those admitted to the Lord's Supper were described as living at '*Chez Bourdel*', for example. This may be purely a domestic arrangement but in most cases those admitted seem likely to have been apprentices, for they were usually young men. Between 1578 and 1584 nine young men at the home of the sergemaker, Adrien Bourdel, were admitted to the Lord's Supper. Twelve men were described as living at Guillaume Hersent's home between 1577 and 1583.[125] There is only one example of anyone being described in the register as an '*apprentis*': one Thomas, apprenticed to Jan le Maire.[126]

A partial record of apprenticeships does survive for the later sixteenth century in the town's books of instruments. These enrollments do provide some insight into the diffusion of the 'new draperies'. Peter Poché seems to have been particularly active in the training of apprentices; he instructed seven apprentices in sergemaking between 1577 and 1600.[127] Poché's apprentices came from a wide area; from around Southampton, Millbrook, Fordingbridge and the Isle of Purbeck, while two apprentices came from Jersey and another

[121] *Assembly Books*, IV, p. 83; *Court Leet Records*, p. 456. See below p. 100.
[122] *Assembly Books*, IV, pp. 83–84.
[123] PRO, SP15/13/82.
[124] *Calendar of Southampton Apprenticeship Registers*, pp. xi–xiv.
[125] *Registre*, pp. 13, 14, 15, 16, 17, 18.
[126] *Registre*, p. 109.
[127] SRO, SC2/6/5, ff. 39, 40, 41, 42v, 112v, 136v, SC2/6/6, f. 45.

from Silo in Normandy. It is interesting to note that only one of these apprentices seems to have been admitted to the Lord's Supper, although we would
not expect English apprentices to have become members of the French
church.[128] The following refugees all undertook to train apprentices in the cloth
industry: Jan de Bavais, Denis du Gard, Pierre le Gay, Estienne Latelais,
Nicolas Ponthieu, the widow of Gilles Seulin and Ambrose le Vasseur.[129]

An analysis of the surviving apprenticeship enrollments and registers reveal
the growing importance of the clothmaking industry in Southampton. The
serge industry rapidly came to employ large numbers of apprentices. In most
years the number of apprentices in cloth-making appears to have been virtually
equal to the number who entered the mercantile trades. While it should be
remembered that the material for the period 1575–1604 is fragmentary, it does
point to the rapid growth and significance of the industry which the refugees
introduced.[130]

Yet by the early seventeenth century the refugee community had ceased to
be as prominent in Southampton's serge industry. The petition for the setting
up of the Company of sergemakers, sergeweavers and woolcombers in 1616
was signed by thirty-eight sergeweavers and woolcombers on behalf of themselves and their colleagues in the town.[131] Although the list of names is not
exhaustive, it does give a clear impression of who in Southampton were the
main producers of serges in 1616. Men such as Isaac le Gay and John le Plus
who had been appointed as overseers for the trade had died by 1616, but
others such as Andrew Harris and Henry Ayres appear amongst the petitioners.[132] When we examine these thirty-eight signatories, we find that only
six were linked with the French church. Four of these men – John Clungeon,
Isaac Herevill, Daniel Hersent, Robert Prevost – were admitted to the Lord's
Supper.[133] Isaac Lamoureux does not seem to have been admitted to the
Lord's Supper but he frequently acted as a *parrain* and his death was recorded
in the church's register in 1626.[134] Only Matthew Vibert's death was recorded

---

[128] John Havie, who was apprenticed to the sergeweaver Ambrose le Vasseur in 1577, may have
been the Jan Haruier who was admitted to the Lord's Supper in April 1586. SRO, SC2/6/5,
f. 40v; *Registre*, p. 20.

[129] SRO, SC2/6/5, ff. 39, 40, 40v, 41, 42v, 43, 65v, 112v, 136v, 137, 141v, 142v, 160, 161,
167v, SC2/6/6, ff. 45, 48.

[130] Spicer, 'The French-speaking Reformed community', pp. 161–63.

[131] Assembly Books, IV, pp. 74–75. The Sergemakers who signed were: John Clungeon, Isaac
Herevill, Andrew Harris, Richard Goare, Roger Morse, Henry Ayres, Daniel Hersent, Richard
Allen, Robert Toldervey, William Peare, Hugh Newe, Matthew Vibert, Clement Audley,
Edward March, Edmond Hayes, Richard Readinge, Edward Tackney, Bartholomew Tolder-
vey, Robert Provoe and John Osman.
Sergeweavers and woolcombers: Thomas Nutley, John England, Isaac Lamoureux, Robert
Waterman, Thomas White, George Levett, Joseph Prowse, Leonard Morris, John Dawes,
Francis Hampton, Samuel Allen, Robert Edmondes, John West, Walter Barlinge, John Snowe,
William Chaplin, Thomas Brown and William Brading.

[132] *Registre*, p. 111; *Assembly Books*, II, pp. 36–37.

[133] *Registre*, pp. 16, 17, 21, 29.

[134] Isaac may have been the son of Bastien Lamoureux, one of the founding members of the
community. *Registre*, pp. 53, 54, 55, 56, 60, 113.

by the French Church but he married Marie le Page, the widow of Robert le Page, in 1612.[135] One of the other signatories, Richard Allen, had been apprenticed to a member of the French community, Pierre le Gay.[136] The remaining signatories do not seem to have been associated with the French church, in fact some of these sergeweavers had only recently arrived in Southampton. Clement Audley had not completed all of his apprenticeship in Southampton and in 1610 Francis Hampton had been required to provide sureties upon his arrival in the town.[137] The absence of French names is even more marked amongst the petitioners for the Company of clothworkers which does not include any members of the French community.[138]

The absence of refugees amongst the petitioners for these two companies may testify to the success of the diffusion of the technology of the 'new draperies' through apprenticeship. However as refugees migrated from the town or became increasingly integrated, it was inevitable that their domination of the industry would decline.

Whereas earlier attempts to establish industries in Southampton seem to have been unsuccessful, the manufacture of the 'new draperies' did make a significant contribution to the town's economic life and overseas trade. Contemporaries recognised that the industry has provided significant employment. The Mayor and Corporation recognised the value of the 'new draperies' and wrote in 1601 'that divers straingers inhabiting in that towne doe use the trade of makeing of sarges and other stuffs, whose contynuance there by takeing of Englishe apprentices have sett up a trade in that towne not onely beneficyall to the common wealth but by setting the poorer sort on worke they doe relieve and maintaine a great number of people and their whole famelyes'.[139] These do not seem to have been idle claims. In 1615 Judith de la Motte and other clothiers offered to employ 'dyvrs poore children of this Towne which use to begge for waunt of worcke'.[140] Isaac le Gay claimed in 1609 to employ 140 spinners within the town of Southampton and in 1618 it was claimed that the decay of the cloth industry would cause distress for at least 3,000 poor people employed within the towns of Southampton and Winchester besides the large numbers employed in the immediate locality.[141]

The production of the 'new draperies' made an important contribution to the town's overseas trade. The refugee merchants were actively involved in

[135]   HRO, Wills 1612/A/58; *Registre*, p. 113.
[136]   SRO, SC3/5/1, f. 3v.
[137]   SRO, SC3/5/1, f. 2; *Assembly Books*, II, pp. 99, 100, 101.
[138]   *Assembly Books*, IV, p. 79. The signatories were: Lionel Awsten, William Suffield, John Appleton, Nicholas Wheate, George Fuckett, John Sares, William Wheat, Andrew Awsten, Averye Toft, Edward Lake, Roger Searle, William Esraell and Stephen Mason. It should however be noted that by 1624 Nicholas Wheat was employed by Judith de la Motte, *Examinations and Depositions, 1622–1644*, I, pp. 47–49.
[139]   *Acts of the Privy Council*, 1601, p. 347.
[140]   *Assembly Books*, IV, p. 3.
[141]   PRO, SP14/98/54; *Assembly Books*, II, p. 69.

exporting these cloths and by the early seventeenth century a particularly important market for these cloths had developed at La Rochelle.[142]

While the cloth industry established by the refugees in Southampton was particularly important for the town's economy, in comparison with other refugee communities the cloth production in Southampton was limited. Unfortunately there are no accurate records of the volume of cloths produced in Southampton, such as survive for Norwich where the collection of a petty custom duty called 'alnage' has meant that there are detailed records of the number of cloths sealed in the city's cloth halls.[143] A list, compiled in June 1578, of the main centres where the strangers produced the 'new draperies' ranked towns according to the volume of production: Norwich (with the greatest production), London, Sandwich, Canterbury, Rochester. Southampton was not included in this list although it did appear, with Hampshire, on a more general list of the places where the 'new draperies' were produced.[144] This list is very general and fails to recognise that the cloth produced differed between communities. At Norwich the production of bays, mockadoes, carrels and velvets was important whereas the Southampton community concentrated on say production. During the 1580s there was a noticeable collapse in the production of bays and in 1581 Norwich seems to have begun to produce says.[145] In the absence of any accurate figures for the numbers of 'new draperies' produced, it is not possible to assess the significance of the production in Southampton.

Serge-making seems to have developed at Romsey, Dibden, Lymington, Newport and Winchester.[146] The extent to which the refugee community at Southampton, or the manufacture of serge in Southampton generally contributed to this development remains unclear. People were however attracted to Southampton from Hampshire and beyond to be apprenticed to sergemakers and in other related trades. Yet the diffusion of the new techniques may have been more to do with the problems facing the Hampshire textile industry than the arrival of refugees in Southampton. The Hampshire kersey and Winton kersey ceased to be able to compete in overseas markets with the cheaper and lighter fabrics. The consequent decline in exports is evident in the Southampton port books.[147] As a result the 'new draperies' did develop tentatively in the county before 1620.[148] The manufacture at Christchurch, of 'frizadoes'

[142] See above pp. 62–63.
[143] N.J. Williams, 'Two documents concerning the New Draperies', *Ec.H.R.*, Second Series, 4 (1951–52), 356–58.
[144] PRO, E101/347/19.
[145] The manufacture of bays seems to have collapsed at Sandwich during the 1580s. At Norwich, the numbers of bays sealed fell from a peak of 13,652 in 1581–82, to a mere 2,813 in 1587–88. Backhouse, 'The Strangers at Work in Sandwich', 81; Williams, 'Two documents', 356, 357.
[146] Kerridge, *Textile Manufactures*, p. 113; A. Rosen, 'Winchester in transition, 1580–1700', in P. Clark, (ed.), *Country towns in pre-industrial England*, (Leicester, 1981), p. 149.
[147] Brenner, *Merchants and Revolution*, pp. 37–38; Thomas, 'The Seaborne Trade of Southampton', pp. 75–76.
[148] Rosen, 'Winchester in transition', p. 149.

after the manner of Haarlem, by an Englishman underlines the fact that the 'new draperies' were not the sole preserve of the refugees.[149] D.C. Coleman concluded that 'the really rapid diffusion of the new techniques into an industry such as textiles organized on a putting-out basis was probably dependent upon non-economic forces, such as war and religious persecution, to ensure movement of skills on a large enough scale'.[150] This may well have been the case in Southampton which lacked a textile industry before the arrival of the refugees. Elsewhere it would seem that the role of the refugees is debatable. The new techniques seem to have been known about in Norwich before the arrival of the refugees and cloths akin to the 'new draperies' were produced there throughout the sixteenth century.[151] These new techniques were also able to spread to areas like Devon, which became important for serge production, without any immigrant community to act as a focus.

[149]   *The Victoria History of the Counties of England. Hampshire and the Isle of Wight*, ed. H.A. Doubleday *et al.*, 5 vols. (London, 1900–12), V, pp. 486–87.
[150]   Coleman, 'An Innovation and its Diffusion', 429.
[151]   U. Priestley, *The Fabric of Stuffs. The Norwich textile industry from 1565*, (Norwich, 1990), pp. 8–9.

CHAPTER FIVE

REFUGEE ARTISANS

Trade and the textile industry dominated the commercial life of Southampton in the second half of the sixteenth century. The refugees made a significant contribution in both of these areas but others found employment elsewhere.

While town corporations were willing to admit refugees who were going to introduce new techniques and skills, they were reluctant to allow them to compete with the town's native inhabitants. At Norwich, article 10 of the Book of Orders stated 'ye shall nott occupie the trades of merchauntdise, that is to saye, of Foreine comodities browght from beyonde the sea, here, to putt to sale, but by whole bolke, and in grosse'. Another article forbade any tailors, butchers, shoemakers and cobblers from displaying their wares and restricted them to selling their goods to members of the refugee community.[1] Similar restrictions were placed on the Sandwich community and there were frequent presentments for breaches of these decrees. Some refugees were licensed by the Corporation in Sandwich to pursue trades which were not permitted under the initial terms of the settlement. In 1582, 95 refugees were recorded as pursuing unauthorised trades in the town.[2] This caused considerable tension between the refugees and the town's inhabitants, so the Privy Council ruled that the exiles were 'not to be retailours or shopkepers, and especiallie not use the misteries of tailours, showmakers, cobblers, coopers, masons or bricklayers, bakers, blacksmiths, shipwrightes and cowkeepers'.[3] The controversy was not however settled, and continued for several years.[4]

At Southampton, the refugees initially petitioned that some members of the community should be allowed to pursue their trades as shoemakers, tailors etc. However, if this was not to be permitted, they asked that they might be able to compound in order to pursue these trades.[5] The Corporation however objected 'because there be many of that science alreadye'.[6] This request was however modified because, in the letter sent by Edmund Grindal to Sir William Cecil, it was suggested that the refugees occupied in these trades should only serve

---

[1] Moens, *The Walloons and their Church at Norwich*, pp. 257, 258.
[2] Backhouse, 'The Strangers at Work in Sandwich', 81–83.
[3] *Acts of the Privy Council*, 1581–82, p. 372.
[4] Backhouse, 'The Strangers at Work in Sandwich', 84–86.
[5] BL, Cott. MS Vesp. F.IX, f. 230v.
[6] PRO, SP15/13/80. The Corporation's concern finds confirmation in the analysis of the occupational structure of the town in 1585 when there were fifteen shoemakers and fourteen tailors. James, 'Geographical Origins and Mobility', p. 575.

their own community. The town seems to have been left to reach a decision on this matter.[7]

A few references do survive to the refugees involved in these 'unauthorised trades'. A probate inventory of the goods of John Enough, a shoemaker, was drawn up in March 1613, who may be the 'Jean Enouf' who was admitted to the Lord's Supper the same month. There is not however any other reference to this name in the French Church.[8] There were instances of people being described as brewers while another was a cooper.[9] In 1575, Jan Blondel at that time living in Winchester, was admitted to the French Church at Southampton on which occasion he was described as a cutler.[10]

Some of the refugees pursued several different trades. Pierre Thieudet was described as a goldsmith on several occasions and in August 1577 was indeed paid 5s 10d by the Corporation for mending the town plate and at a later date, 5s for mending a flagon.[11] Yet the probate inventory of his goods drawn up after his death in 1611 records a number of pieces of cloth and quantities of wool and yarn as well as two looms; there is no mention of the necessary tools for being a goldsmith.[12] Another refugee, Robert Cousin, was involved in the finishing of the 'new drapery' cloths but also bequeathed 'all the Instruments, Tooles and thinges servinge to the occupacion of beating of pewter as stones to beate uppon, hammers, mooles and also a myll which serveth for to make colors withall and a copper platt for to guilt uppon'.[13]

Refugees were also engaged in the professions such as ministers and school-masters.[14] Between 1509 and 1820, as many as 470 refugees in England were recorded as being involved in the medical professions.[15] Henricus Lems, one of the initial settlers in Southampton, was a doctor and several other settlers were also in the medical profession. Marc Clem, who was admitted to the Lord's Supper in 1571, was a doctor, and his son, Jan, was a surgeon.[16] It is unclear if Masse Blondel was a doctor or whether he had been appointed as a visitor of the sick by the consistory during the outbreak of plague in 1604. At the time of his death he was recorded as 'estant venu pour mediciner les malades'.[17] The occupation of Guillaume Chambrelen is not recorded in the

[7]   PRO, SP12/43/29.
[8]   HRO, Wills 1613/Ad/32; *Registre*, p. 32.
[9]   Two men were described as *brasseurs* in the *Registre*, Jan de Lotte and Michel le Grant. Jan le Clauier, who was admitted in July 1582, was described as '*demeurant chez Courtené, brass-eur*'. The daughter of Guillaume du Moulin, a cooper, was baptised in May 1587. *Registre*, pp. 10, 15, 17, 47.
[10] *Registre*, p. 11.
[11] SRO, SC5/3/1, ff. 166, 185v; SC6/1/9–12, SC6/1/19.
[12] HRO, Wills 1611/B/65.
[13] PRO, PCC Prob. 11/67 Robert Cousin.
[14] See below pp. 116, 117–25 *passim*.
[15] W.R. le Fanu, 'Huguenot Refugee Doctors in England', *HSP*, 19 (1952–58), 113.
[16] *Registre*, pp. 3, 6, 109.
[17] *Registre*, p. 109.

Southampton records but he is credited with the invention of forceps, and with his sons, he pursued a career in midwifery.[18]

Rather more is known about the eight glassworkers who were admitted to the Lord's Supper between October 1576 and January 1579.[19] The glassworks were sited at Buckholt, about fifteen miles from Southampton on the Wiltshire border; Buckholt Forest provided fuel and ashes for the glasshouses.[20] Although they became members of the French Church, the glassmakers were in fact 'country' members of the French community in Southampton – their names do not appear in any of the local tax returns. It is unclear how frequently they attended the French church and the extent to which they were subject to the church's discipline.[21]

Although the glassworkers lived at Buckholt they did visit Southampton. 'A Frenchman of Buckhole' was fined 12*d* by the town Corporation in 1576 'for throwing of his dagger at an Englishman in anger'.[22] There may have been some friction between the glassworkers and the pre-1567 aliens in the town. Edward Barker, Peter Breme and Peter Fox were all glaziers and the latter two paid the Corporation 10*s* in 1577 to be the sole glaziers in the the town.[23]

The development of the glass industry in England has been studied in some depth by industrial historians who have credited Jean Carré with the re-establishment of the industry in early modern England. He fled from Antwerp, where he had come to the attention of the *Conseil des Troubles*, and in 1567 he obtained permission from Cecil to establish glass production in England. He recruited skilled glassmakers from Normandy and Lorraine to work for him.[24] The names of the Buckholt glassworkers were similar to those of some of the established Norman and Lorraine *'gentilhommes verriers'*: le Vaillant, du Tisac, du Houx.[25] It is unclear whether the glassworkers migrated directly to Buckholt or whether they came there from the earlier Sussex glassworks.[26]

[18]   *Registre*, pp. 5, 40; J. Rushen, 'The Secret "Iron Tongs" of Midwifery', *The Historian*, 30 (1991), 12–14; T. Murdoch, (ed.), *The Quiet Conquest. The Huguenots 1685 to 1985. A Museum of London exhibition in association with the Huguenot Society, 15 May to 31 October, 1985*, (London, 1985), pp. 120, 121.

[19]   *Registre*, pp. 12, 14. They were: Jan du Tisac, Pierre Vaillant, Glaude Potier, Monsieur de Hennezé & his wife, Louis de Hennezé, Arnoul Bisson, Jan Perné, Monsieur du Houx.

[20]   E.S. Godfrey, *The Development of English Glassmaking, 1560–1640*, (Oxford, 1975), p. 141.

[21]   Special provisions for Reformed worship had been made for the workers at the Sussex glassworks. There was a minister and consistory at Fernfold Wood, while permission for a minister to serve the community at Wisborough Green was obtained in 1579. PRO, PCC Prob. 11/54 Jean Carré; Godfrey, *Development of English Glassmaking*, p. 34.

[22]   SRO, SC5/3/1, f. 159.

[23]   SRO, SC5/3/1, f. 160.

[24]   See Godfrey, *Development of English Glassmaking*, pp. 16–37; Marnef, 'Antwerpen in Reformatietijd', Appendix V No. 132, 137.

[25]   Godfrey, *Development of English Glassmaking*, p. 6; G.H. Kenyon, *The Glass Industry of the Weald*, (Leicester, 1967), pp. 124–31, 214, 215; E.G. Clark, 'Glass-making in Lorraine', *Journal of the Society of Glass Technology*, 15 (1931), 107–19.

[26]   Kenyon, *The Glass Industry of the Weald*, p. 215.

There seem to have been two glasshouses at Buckholt; one was probably used for making window glass and the other for vessel glass.[27] Further light can be shed upon the glassworks at Buckholt from a lease in the Southampton archives which has previously been overlooked. In 1578, the 'great glasse house with the store house and the dwelling house' at Buckholt, which had been recently in the tenure of one James Knollis, was leased to Pierre du Houx by Sir William West, Lord de la Warr, for five years at £20 per annum. The agreement was witnessed by two prominent members of the French Church, Gaspard Desert and Pierre Thieudet. There was a further agreement reached between the glassmaker and West on the same day. This agreement stated that de Houx was to 'receive and take of the saide Lorde de la Ware or his Assignes as much glasse as shall amounte unto the somme of x*li* lawfull monie of England and upon everye halfe yers daye ended to make payment unto the said Lord de la War or his Assignes the saide tenne poundes for the said glasse so by him receaved'.[28] This curious agreement suggests that de Houx was employed by de la Warr but this would seem to conflict with his lease of the glasshouse.

It has been assumed that the Buckholt glasshouses flourished between 1576 and 1579, an assumption apparently based on the dates of admission to the Lord's Supper in the French Church of Southampton.[29] But the *Registre* only refers to the date of admission to the Lord's Supper and does not refer to attendance at the Church. The glasshouse at Buckholt could therefore have functioned for longer than has been supposed especially since the evidence for the migration of some of these glassmakers from Buckholt appears to be inconclusive.[30] In fact Jean du Houx was still living at Buckholt in September 1580; the glassmakers had however probably departed by 1586 because they do not appear in the lay subsidy return for that year.[31]

The glassworkers at Buckholt form an exceptional group in the context of the Southampton French-speaking community, but like their counterparts in

---

[27] One of these glasshouses was excavated in 1860. Godfrey, *Development of English Glassmaking*, pp. 35, 141; E. Kell, 'On the Discovery of a Glass Factory at Buckholt', *The Journal of the British Archaeological Association*, 17 (1861), 55–58.

[28] SRO, SC2/6/5, f. 64.

[29] Kenyon, *The Glass Industry of the Weald*, p. 215.

[30] According to Godfrey, 'Two of the Normans at Buckholt soon appeared on the estates of Knole House in Kent, where they were joined by an Italian and a glassmaker of uncertain origin, while one of the Lorrainers, Jan du Tisac, seems to have moved to Ewhurst, where he appears as John Tysac [*sic*] a few years later'. The evidence cited does not seem to support convincingly the migration of the Buckholt glassworkers. At Knole there were four glassworkers (Valyan, Ferris, Mr. Brussell/Bousell, Oneby) in 1587; only Valyan could be tentatively identified with Pierre Vaillant although there is no evidence to show that he came to Knole from Buckholt. In view of the similarity of the names of the glassworkers care needs to be taken in tracing their migration. Godfrey, *Development of English Glassmaking*, p. 35; T. Barrett Lennard, 'Glass-making at Knole, Kent', *The Antiquary*, 41 (1905), 127–29; S.E. Winbolt, *Wealden Glass. The Surrey-Sussex Glass Industry, (A.D. 1226–1615)*, (Hove, 1933), p. 20.

[31] SRO, SC2/6/5, f. 83; *The Hampshire Lay Subsidy Rolls, 1586*, ed. C.R. Davey, (Hampshire Record Series, 4, 1981).

the 'new draperies' they were important in introducing new techniques. The lack of information about other occupations in the Southampton community could either be the result of insufficient surviving evidence or could be because the community was predominantly composed of merchants and those involved in textile production. The pursuit of 'unauthorised trades' certainly does not seem to have been a serious issue in Southampton as it had been in Sandwich.[32]

---

[32] See below pp. 162–63.

THE FRENCH-SPEAKING REFORMED CHURCH

Religious issues were an important part of the negotiations for the establishment of the Southampton community. Robert Horne, Bishop of Winchester, had attempted in his appeal to Sir William Cecil for the establishment of that community to identify the faith of Cecil and himself with that of the refugees. He wrote: 'As the zelous care that hath bene hitherto in you [Cecil] to preserve emonge our countriemen in this realme both the truth in religion and the fauters therof, is well knowne to all and in thankfull wise acknowledged of the godlye, althoughe no lesse misliked of the others, yeven so I doubte not your charitable affection stretchethe forth yt selfe same cause towardes all others beinge subiectes as we are to Christe in his kingdome, although by cyvill policyie they be strangiers to this kyngdome'.[1] Horne had been actively involved in attempting to establish the Religious Settlement in his diocese and was aware of the development of the Reformed churches of the Channel Islands which only became part of the diocese in 1568.[2] It is possible that Horne may have seen the establishment of the French church as providing a model for the reform of what remained a largely conservative county. The Edwardian church in London of John à Lasco had certainly aimed to serve as a model for further reform of the English Church but Elizabeth had not wanted the re-founded churches to perform such a role and so had curbed their independence.[3] However in spite of this, the foreign churches had during the 1560s come to serve as an example for the English Puritans.[4] Horne may have hoped that the French Church would exercise a similar role in his diocese.

Initially the Reformation only made halting progress in Southampton. In *c.* 1548 the Protestant minister Thomas Hancock visited the town but was told by Sir Richard Lyster that 'yf I shold teache such doctrine as I tawght at Sarum the towne wold be divided, and soo sholde hytt be a way or a gapp for the enemy to enter in, and therfor he commawnded me that I shold not preache ther'. However Hancock heard another minister preach at St. Michael's church and attack Lyster for allowing 'the images in the church, the idol hanging in a

---

[1] PRO, SP12/43/16.

[2] Fritze, 'The role of the family and religion', 265–66, 271, 276–79; Northamptonshire Record Office, Finch-Hatton Papers FH312, p. 310; de Schickler, *Les Eglises du Refuge*, II, pp. 377–78; see below, p. 102.

[3] F. Norwood, 'The Strangers' "Model Churches" in Sixteenth-Century England', in F.H. Littell, (ed.), *Reformation Studies*, (Richmond, Va., 1962), pp. 186, 194–96; Pettegree, *Foreign Protestant Communities*, pp. 67, 74–76, 136.

[4] Pettegree, *Foreign Protestant Communities*, pp. 272–75; Collinson, 'The Elizabethan Puritans and the Foreign Reformed Churches', pp. 262–63.

string over the altar, candlesticks and tapers on them upon the altar, and the people honouring the idol'.[5] There were other disturbances in the Southampton area at this time.[6] Conservative piety continued to be expressed in the wills drawn up by some of the town's leading citizens and included bequests to the Franciscan friary which had apparently been re-established during Mary's reign.[7]

The prevailing conservatism within the town retreated only gradually during Elizabeth's reign. The churchwardens accounts only survive for one of the town's five parishes, that of St. Lawrence. These reveal how slowly the church came to conform with the 1559 royal Injunctions.[8] The *Paraphrases* of Erasmus were not purchased until May 1567, two years later the Book of Prayer and Homilies was bought and a copy of the Bishop's Bible was purchased in London in 1572. There were also structural changes in the church; 6*d* was paid in 1570 to 'take down ye p'tycion of ye quere'. There were further payments in 1572 for 'whytting and plastering the churche' and for the 'wrytinge of the great table' [Ten Commandments] and other suitable religious texts on the church walls.[9] Some of the plate belonging to the town churches dates from this period, although some Edwardian pieces have also survived.[10] Coincidentally Richard Etuer, a member of the French Church, served as a churchwarden of St. Lawrence's church for part of this time of change.[11]

However the advance of Protestantism was far from smooth and conservative religious practices persisted. The churchwardens of St. Lawrence's had sold the 'olde byble' and also sold 'a painted clothe with the x comande'.[12] There was a presentment to the Court Leet in 1576 concerning the continued use of wafers at communion by the ministers of All Saints, St. Lawrence and St. Michael's. This charge was repeated against the minister of All Saints in 1581.[13] A sense of the frustration of the reformers and the tensions which existed in the town, found expression in an anonymous memorandum in 1582:

In religion we are cold, to god we be unthankfull, to his word we yeeld no obedience: which may well be proved hereby. First let everie man examine

---

[5] J.G. Nichols, (ed.), *Narratives of the Days of the Reformation*, (Camden Society, 77, 1859), p. 76.

[6] Fritze, 'Faith and Faction: Religious changes, national politics and the development of local factionalism in Hampshire, 1485–1570', (unpublished Ph.D. thesis, Cambridge University, 1981), pp. 237–40.

[7] Platt, *Medieval Southampton*, pp. 212–13; A.A. Ruddock, 'The Greyfriars in Southampton', *PHFC*, 16 (1944–47), 146–47. The only indication of the refounding of the Friary comes from testamentary evidence.

[8] For the impact of the 1559 Injunctions on churches, see R. Hutton, 'The local impact of the Tudor Reformation', in C. Haigh, (ed.), *The English Reformation Revised*, (Cambridge, 1987), pp. 133–36.

[9] SRO, PR4/2/1 St. Lawrence's Churchwardens Accounts, ff. 11, 14.

[10] Platt, *Medieval Southampton*, p. 212.

[11] Etuer was elected as churchwarden for a year in July 1570 and again in May 1572. In August 1573 he was paid 3*s* 6*d* for 'a carpet for the table'. SRO, PR4/2/1, ff. 12, 13, 15v.

[12] SRO, PR4/2/1, f. 13.

[13] *Court Leet Records*, pp. 139, 204.

him selfe how much he hath profited and gone forward in religion for these xx[tie] yeares last, what thankfulnes he hath yielded unto god ... we have receaved his word at the mouthes of his ministers: then consider what Atheist or Papist is kept from the best offices in the towne for want of relligion; (yf he could get ryches to mainteine a pompe) that hath not been accompted worthie and sufficient to beare the office of Queenes Majestys Lieutenant in this towne. And what accompt we make of the Ministerie doth well appeare by the provision wee make for their intertainement; have the Preachers anie other alloweance or maintenance in this towne, otherwise than popish priests or reading ministers should have in their places: nay, what kicking and pricking hath here been against the preachers; I will not say against their lyves but against their doctrine also. Have they not been brought before the Mayor to render accompt of their doctrine, and to answere unto certaine articles obiected against them, by one which in such cawses is commonly used for the Maiors mouth: have the preachers not been belyed and rayled uppon behind their backes upon credit of wicked and slanderous libells made and devised against some of them no doubt eyther by Atheists or papists. These and manie other things doe sufficiently proove our slacknes in relligion, which being grannted howe we can look that god should blesse and prosper our towne seeing we make so small accompt of him & his word.[14]

Richard Biston who was the Mayor of Southampton in 1581–82 may have been the object of this attack. Biston had become embroiled in a quarrel with the minister of Holy Rood, Henry Hopkins.[15] The minister complained that Biston 'carpeth at everie sermon which I make, so that there is no good point in nature, by grace, to be reformed through the word of God'. 'At my Lord of Winton's table he fell to his accustomed rayling against mee, notwithstanding my lord had thrise requested him to hold his peace and was glad to rise from his table sooner than hee was accustomed'.[16] Hopkins had also managed to antagonise other influential men in the town such as John Crooke, twice Mayor and the town's M.P. in 1571, through alluding to a rumour that Crooke's son-in-law Edmund Caplin had carried a candle in a procession while overseas. The minister did however admit he had a 'plaine kynd of speach in teaching which God hath imparted to me mixed yet I hope with modestie as becometh such a one who laboureth for edification and not for destruction'.[17]

However in spite of these tensions evangelical protestantism began to emerge with some of the customary features of sabbatarianism, lecturers and alterna-

---

[14] PRO, SP12/156/43.
[15] PRO, SP12/288/37. The document in which this quarrel is related, has in the past been overlooked but it is unfortunately undated. However the minister of Holy Rood was Henry Hopkins who had been presented to the benefice in 1574 by John Caplin. Since he had served the parish for nine years when this account had been written, it can be dated to 1583. HRO, 21M65, A1/26, f. 100v.
[16] PRO, SP12/288/37.
[17] PRO, SP12/288/37.

tive means of financing the ministers.[18] From 1580 onwards presentments were made to the Court Leet concerning church attendance; one such complained about the large numbers of people who frequented the taverns and gambled during the sermon and at service time.[19] There were also complaints made about trading and gaming on Sundays, with fines being imposed for such offences. The clothiers and shearmen of the town were also accused of failing to observe the sabbath in 1613.[20] In 1604 there was a complaint that 'the notorious sinne of dronnkennes to be so Comon in this Towne as except some spedye reformacon be taken'.[21]

About 1607 Thomas Hitchcock was appointed as the town lecturer and was confirmed in this position in 1611.[22] However after his death in 1612, the responsibility for the sermons fell to the town's ministers. The lectures were held at Holy Rood church and were financed through voluntary contributions.[23] There does not seem to have been any attempt by the town corporation to secure the finances of the ministers, one of the issues addressed in the anonymous memorandum in 1582. The Corporation did however occasionally provide some clerics with a livery or financial help.[24]

It is therefore against this background of gradual religious change that the French church was established in Southampton. The negotiations for the establishment of the community had been largely taken up with the provision of a suitable place of worship and upon the form of church government that they would adopt.[25]

Bishop Horne assigned the refugees to the chapel of St. Julien at God's House Hospital which was located in the South Eastern corner of the parish of Holy Rood, close to the town walls. The owners of the Hospital, The Queen's College Oxford, do not seem to have been consulted or to have given the refugees permission to use of the chapel, which resulted in several disputes in the nineteenth century.[26] The college's acquiescence may have been a further sign of the relaxed administration of their estates at this time. The 1560s was a decade of uncertainty for the colleges at Oxford and Cambridge, anxious about their future after the earlier dissolutions of religious houses and

---

18 P. Collinson, *The Religion of Protestants. The Church in English Society, 1559–1625*, (Oxford, 1982), pp. 170–77. For his essay on 'The Protestant Town', see P. Collinson, *The Birthpangs of Protestant England. Religious and Cultural Change in the Sixteenth and Seventeenth Centuries*, (Basingstoke, 1988), pp. 28–59.

19 *Court Leet Records*, pp. 189, 266, 282, 305, 358, 436, 454.

20 *Court Leet Records*, pp. 370–71, 384, 401, 456.

21 *Court Leet Records*, p. 408.

22 *Assembly Books*, III, pp. 25–26.

23 HRO, Wills 1612/Ad/51; *Assembly Books*, III, p. 60, IV, p. 17.

24 *The Southampton Mayor's Book of 1606–1608*, ed. W.J. Connor, (SRS, 21, 1978), pp. 55, 99, 100, 107–8; *Assembly Books*, I, p. 101.

25 See above pp. 33–34.

26 SRO, D/FC 3/8; *The Minute Book of the French Church*, pp. 3, 113–15.

corporations.[27] The proposal to strip God's House of its chaplain in order to provide the parish of Holy Rood with another minister must have enhanced these fears.[28] However during the vigilant stewardship of Francis Mylls and the construction of almshouses between 1588–93, it is unlikely that the College could have remained unaware of the use made of the chapel by the refugees.[29]

The Hospital was described by 1585 as being in a ruinous condition. Repairs to the chapel had had to be undertaken in 1567–68 when the College paid for the reglazing of all the windows.[30] Stained or painted glass had been placed in the chapel in the fourteenth century which would have been offensive to the Calvinists as would the painting of the image of the Virgin Mary and the tabernacle placed there in the early sixteenth century. It is not clear whether these were removed with the arrival of the French community or at an earlier date by committed Protestants within the town.[31] The refugees however did not have exclusive use of the chapel as it seems to have still been used by the occupants of the almshouses. Small payments were regularly made by The Queen's College for bread and wine to be used at the chapel.[32]

The second area of discussion concerned the church order or Discipline, which defined the structure and government of the Reformed church. The refugees, according to a letter sent by Bishop Grindal to Cecil, agreed that:

> . . . for the ordre of theyr churche, they will agree in doctryne and rites withe the frenshe churche in London and geve a confession of theyr fayth to the bisshop of Winton [Horne].[33]

Grindal clearly expected the refugees in Southampton to adopt the Discipline of the French congregation in London. This had been devised by Nicholas des Gallars in 1561 drawing upon the earlier *Forma ac Ratio* of John à Lasco as well as the Genevan Church order.[34] Although the London Church had assisted in the composition of the refugees' appeal to the Queen, it is not certain that the refugees did adopt des Gallars' church order.

There were a number of influences on the emerging church which may have led to the adoption of a different church order. The exiles were predominantly Walloon and the initial settlers had, as we have seen, well-established links with

---

[27] *A God's House Miscellany*, ed. J.M. Kaye, (SRS, 27, 1984), pp. 35–38. The problems that had resulted in the poor state of the College houses were discussed in a letter written in 1599, *God's House Miscellany*, pp. 55–56.

[28] Platt, *Medieval Southampton*, p. 212.

[29] *God's House Miscellany*, pp. 33, 35, 36, 39, 42–43, 52–53, 56; *The Cartulary of God's House, Southampton*, ed. J.M. Kaye, 2 vols. (SRS, 19–20, 1976), I, pp. lxxxi–lxxxii, lxxxv.

[30] The Queen's College Archives, Oxford, GHA Box 4 (7); *God's House Miscellany*, p. 53.

[31] *Cartulary of God's House*, I, p. lxxviii.

[32] The Queen's College Archives, Oxford, GHA Boxes 4 & 5.

[33] PRO, SP12/43/29.

[34] N. des Gallars, *Forma Politiae ecclesiasticae nuper institutae Londini in coetu Gallorum*, (London, 1561); N. des Gallars, *Forme de police ecclesiastique instituée à Londres en l'Eglise des François*, ([London], 1561); Pettegree, *Foreign Protestant Communities*, pp. 163–64.

the Reformed movement in the Southern Netherlands. Guillaume Coppin and more significantly Jehan le Mesureur had been members of the consistory of the Valenciennes church. Walerand Thevelin had been a minister in the Netherlands but he does not seem to have arrived in Southampton until 1568.[35] Although little is known about the organisation of the Walloon churches, they do seem to have followed very much the same lines as the French Reformed church although some aspects of the church structure were omitted as being inappropriate for the Low Countries.[36]

The Channel Islands may have also influenced the church order adopted by the community. Nicholas Baudouin, who had brought about the Reformation on Guernsey, was in Southampton in October 1567 where he preached to the new community.[37] Permission was granted in August 1565 for the parishes of St. Peter Port on Guernsey and St. Helier on Jersey to adopt the Reformed manner of worship, following the order of the French Church at Threadneedle Street.[38] Baudouin had however already established a Calvinist church on Guernsey and a consistory of elders and deacons had been elected by 1563.[39] The churches had adopted their own church order and objected when Horne suggested in 1569 that they should conform to the Threadneedle Street Discipline.[40] The Islands were transferred to the jurisdiction of the Bishop of Winchester in 1568, although links had been established earlier. It seems likely that Baudouin was the delegate sent by the colloquy of the Channel Islands to see the Bishop at the end of September 1567.[41] Baudouin's appearance in Southampton at this crucial moment is tantalising and he may have played an important role in establishing the community.

By no means all the stranger churches conformed to the des Gallars Discipline and slight variations emerged in the religious practices of the exile congregations.[42] From 1582, the London Church pressed for the adoption of a single Discipline in all the French churches in England. This was finally agreed in 1588 but even after its adoption some variation in the practices of the French churches continued.[43]

The adoption of a single Discipline by the churches established a degree of unity between them. This was further emphasised by a new section of the Discipline concerning the holding of colloquies, '*a fin d'entretenir la pureté de*

[35] See pp. 6, 10, 12, 117.

[36] F.R.J. Knetsch, 'Kerkordelijke bepalingen van de Nederlandse synoden "onder het kruis" (1563–64), vergeleken met die van de Franse (1559–1564)', in J. Fabius, A. Spaanse, J. Spaans, (ed.), *Feestbundel uitegeven ter gelegenheid van het 80 – jarig bestaan van het Kerkhistorisch Gezelschap S.S.S.*, (Leiden, 1982), pp. 29–44.

[37] Hessels, *Ecclesiae Londino-Batavae Archivum*, III, pp. 2555–56.

[38] De Schickler, *Les Eglises du Refuge*, II, pp. 375–76.

[39] Northamptonshire Record Office, Finch-Hatton Papers FH312, p. 306.

[40] Northamptonshire Record Office, Finch-Hatton Papers FH312, p. 312.

[41] Northamptonshire Record Office, Finch-Hatton Papers FH312, p. 310; de Schickler, *Les Eglises du Refuge*, II, pp. 377–78.

[42] Spicer, 'The French-speaking Reformed community', pp. 185–86.

[43] *Actes des Colloques*, pp. 3, 5, 9, 13, 14; Spicer, 'The French-speaking Reformed community', p. 186.

vie et doctrine, et ensemble lordre et vnion des eglises.[44] Colloquies had only gradu-ally emerged in England, although the Synod of Emden had decreed in October 1571 that 'separate annual meetings shall be held each year for all the churches scattered through Germany and East Friesland, for all the churches in England and the churches "under the Cross" '.[45] The churches had appealed to the Archbishop of Canterbury, the Bishops of London and Winch-ester and the Dean of Westminister, to be allowed to establish *classes* but the authorities refused permission for such meetings.[46] This decision was in spite of the fact that the Reformed churches of Guernsey, Jersey and Sark had met regularly for a synod since 1564.[47] When the first colloquy of all the French churches in England did meet in May 1581, it was proposed that they should meet annually and in 1587 it was suggested that they should convene in London each year.[48] The representatives of the French churches met annually until 1590, except 1585, and after that date less frequently but their meetings were not confined to London.

Some of the functions which one would expect to be carried out by the colloquy were already fulfilled by the Superintendents, the diocesan bishop for each community. One of these responsibilities was initially to confirm the appointment of a new minister although by 1588 the Bishop merely had to be notified about an appointment.[49] Des Gallars' Discipline gave the Bishop further powers which do not appear in the 1588 discipline:

> *Et quand ils ne pourront estre obeiz en faisant leur devoir, que le tout soit rapporte a l'Euesque pour y mettre ordre, & qu'ils soit prie que les rebelles apres auoir este chastiez, soient renuoyez au consistoire pour proceder contre eux, selon l'ordre Ecclesiastique.*[50]

Excommunications in London were carried out with the approval of the Superintendent and a similar situation existed in Southampton; the Bishop of Winchester, Robert Horne, confirmed the excommunication of Nicholas du Chemin in 1571.[51] This was a power which was exercised by the classis in the Netherlands.[52] Edmund Grindal took a close interest in the affairs of the London church, for example mediating in disputes, and it is possible that Horne may have had a similar interest in the affairs of the Southampton

[44] 'Discipline of the French Churches in England, 1588', in Moens, *The Walloons and their Church at Norwich*, p. 301.

[45] A.C. Duke, G. Lewis & A. Pettegree, (ed.), *Calvinism in Europe 1540–1610. A collection of documents*, (Manchester, 1992), p. 158.

[46] Pettegree, *Foreign Protestant Communities*, p. 269; *Actes du Consistoire, II*, pp. 61, 69.

[47] Northamptonshire Record Office, Finch-Hatton Papers FH 312, pp. 306, 307.

[48] *Actes des Colloques*, pp. 2, 12.

[49] Des Gallars, *Forme de Police*, f. 7; Moens, *The Walloons and their Church at Norwich*, p. 287.

[50] Des Gallars, *Forme de Police*, f. 15v.

[51] *Actes du Consistoire, I*, pp. xvi, 33, 108, 115; *Actes du Consistoire, II*, pp. 11–12, 49.

[52] *Livre Synodal contenant les Articles résolues dans les Synodes des Eglises Wallonnes des Pays-Bas*, 2 vols. (The Hague, 1896), I, pp. 55, 69, 81.

church.[53] In 1584 a delegation was sent from the French Church which included Walerand Thevelin, Mathieu Sohier, Guillaume Hersent and Pierre le Gay to congratulate Horne's successor, Thomas Cooper, on his appointment as Bishop of Winchester. They asked the Bishop to continue to look favourably on maintaining their church as his predecessor had done.[54]

The provincial churches therefore seem to have enjoyed a degree of independence before the adoption of the single discipline and the regular meeting of colloquies. The churches occasionally sought advice from London or else other churches might request assistance or information.[55] The colloquies however became more influential and the refugee churches came to be bound by their decisions. The brethren of Southampton were urged by the Colloquy in 1581 to visit Rye *'pour coriger tels vices qu'ils rangent a la Discipline comme les autres Eglises'*. In 1610, the church was rebuked for failing to introduce *mereaux* (tokens) for those who were to be admitted to the Lord's Supper after this had been agreed upon by the colloquy.[56] The decline of the church's independence clearly coincided with the congregation's increasing financial dependence on the Threadneedle Street Church.[57]

The exile churches had long standing links with the continental churches, these contacts seem to have been closer with the Walloon churches in the Netherlands than with the Reformed churches in France. Anthoine Lescaillet represented the Walloon churches at the Synod of Dordrecht in 1578 and at Middelburg in 1581.[58] There is no record of a minister being sent to the meetings of the French National Synods; their contact with the exile churches was limited and generally confined to the French church in London.[59] The French-speaking provincial churches generally looked to the Netherlands whereas in London the French influence was much stronger.[60] The colloquies sought to establish their position *vis à vis* the continental churches, with appeals that these churches should not recognise those who returned to the continent without a testimony from their churches. The colloquy even wrote to the Synods of France and the Low Countries *'pour rafrêchir la memoire de l'union que nous avons avec eus en Doctrine et gouvernement de l'Eglise'*.[61]

---

[53] For Grindal's involvement in the affairs of both the French and Dutch churches, see Pettegree, *Foreign Protestant Communities*, pp. 150–51, 154, 157, 161–63, 171–72, 178, 245–49, 271.

[54] *Registre*, p. 133.

[55] CDRO, U47/A1, pp. 98, 107, 112; *Actes du Consistoire, II*, pp. 32, 76–77; Hessels, *Ecclesiae Londino-Batavae Archivum*, III, pp. 709–10.

[56] *Actes des Colloques*, pp. 1, 41.

[57] See below pp. 112, 164.

[58] *Livre Synodal*, I, p. 82; F.W. Cross, *History of the Walloon & Huguenot Church at Canterbury*, (HSQS, 15, 1898), p. 71.

[59] J. Quick, *Synodicon in Gallia Reformata: or the Acts, Decisions, Decrees and canons of those Famous Councils of the Reformed Churches in France*, 2 vols. (London, 1692), I, pp. 124–25, 185, 203. On the links between the exile churches and the continental Reformed churches, see Spicer, ' "A Faythful Pastor in the Churches" ', pp. 202–4.

[60] On the French influence in the exile churches see Pettegree, *Foreign Protestant Communities*, pp. 161–62, 163–64, 265; Spicer, ' "A Faythful Pastor in the Churches" ', p. 204.

[61] *Actes des Colloques*, pp. 7–8, 35.

In Southampton the church was governed by the consistory which maintained discipline within the community. The consistory had been formed
before the first administration of the Lord's Supper in December 1567 and
may have existed as early as September 1567 when Robert Horne referred in
a letter to the 'minister and eldres of that churche'.[62] There is only a partial
record of the membership of the consistory but initially there seem to have
been five elders and two deacons.[63] The number of deacons may have
increased because in 1589 there is a reference to 'two *of the* deakens of the
frenche churche'.[64] By the early eighteenth century there were three deacons
and four elders, who were both members of the consistory until the office of
deacon was abolished in 1706.[65] Besides the consistory there is a single reference to a '*Lecteur*' in Southampton in 1618.[66]

The consistory was composed of the most prominent members of the exile
community. At different times the leading refugee merchants (Arnoul le
Clercq, Mathieu Sohier, Jean le Mercier, Pierre le Gay and Jean Hersent) were
all members of the consistory. They had the wealth and status to provide the
community with the necessary leadership through the consistory.[67] However
this fairly oligarchical composition should perhaps be expected in such a small
community. There was also a remarkable degree of consistency in the composition of the consistory; for example, Guillaume Hersent is recorded as being
a member of the consistory in 1573, 1580, 1584 and his son Jean Hersent was
recorded as a member in 1589, 1598, 1606, 1610 and 1615. The initial members of the consistory were predominantly Walloon: Jehan le Mesureur (who
had been a member of the Valenciennes proto-consistory in 1561), Arnoul le
Clercq, Mathieu Sohier all originated from Valenciennes and were in fact cous-
ins. Marc le Blanc who was a deacon also came from Valenciennes while
Anthoine Jurion, an elder, came from Hainaut. Although the departure of le
Clercq and Sohier from Southampton in *c.* 1583 undoubtedly resulted in some
changes in the composition of the consistory, the Walloon influence continued.
By 1589, Pierre le Gay, Jean le Mercier and Vincent Nérin of Valenciennes
had become members of the consistory.[68] Although the Walloon character of
the consistory was retained through such figures, French refugees did become
members of the consistory. The earliest being Gaspard Desert of Dieppe who
was recorded as an elder in 1573; the Hersents, Estienne Latelais and Claude
Moutonnier are further examples.[69]

The purpose of the consistory was '*entretenir bon ordre es saintes assemblées,
faire les admonitions et corrections ecclesiastiques*'.[70] Few members of the South-

---

[62]   PRO, SP12/44/8.
[63]   SRO, TC Box 1/40; Hatfield House, Salisbury MSS, CP64/38.
[64]   HRO, Wills 1589/B/39.
[65]   *The Minute Book of the French Church*, pp. 15, 30–31.
[66]   *Registre*, p. 112.
[67]   See above pp. 37–39, 54, 66.
[68]   Nérin had in fact married Catherine des Plus, the neice of Mathieu Sohier and the widow of
       Anthoine Jurion's son Abraham. *Registre*, pp. 85, 88.
[69]   Spicer, 'The French-speaking Reformed community', pp. 207–10.
[70]   Moens, *The Walloons and their Church at Norwich*, p. 289.

ampton community exempted themselves from their jurisdiction. The *Registre* records the names of those who were admitted to the Lord's Supper and therefore subject to the discipline enforced by the consistory. However a minority, who were not prepared to be admitted to the Lord's Supper, did attend services at St. Julien's. In 1593 the Corporation examined one Michael Collens as to 'wherfore he goeth not orderly to the french church as he ought to do'. Collens admitted that he only occasionally went to the French church but was prevented by his conscience from receiving communion. Collens was suspected of having mass celebrated in his house and had in his possession a 'french testament after the Papists translation'.[71] The case of Michael Collens and his wife is interesting because it shows that people attended the church's services but were not prepared to submit to its discipline. While a number of hangers-on, or *liefhebbers*, may be expected in London with its large foreign population, it would be surprising if there were many in a community as small as Southampton.[72] A few however do appear in the records. A widow who had lived in Southampton for more than seventeen years was described in 1606 as being 'chiefly of the French church' but there is no reference to her being admitted to the Lord's Supper.[73]

Those who failed to observe the censures of the consistory and acknowledge their errors were barred from attending the Lord's Supper. In spite of the loss of the consistory book, several references to such offenders can be found in the *Registre*. Jan Pora was barred on two consecutive occasions for drunkenness, having also been suspended earlier for his '*legierté et mauuais propos contre Dieu*'. Robert Cousin was barred for failing to acknowledge that he had deceived Cornelis Poingdextre by selling him a horse with poor eyesight. Attendance at the Lord's Supper was withheld from Martin Lietart for beating and hurting his wife.[74] Those who still refused to conform to the discipline of the church could be excommunicated, a process which involved the church's Superintendent, the Bishop of Winchester.[75]

However the censures of the consistory were not always accepted by the members of the congregation and some cases, such as that of Nicholas Provost, were discussed by the colloquy. Provost had been summoned to appear before the consistory but he refused to recognise his fault publicly before the church. His attack upon the consistory led to charges of rebellion. The colloquy stated that Provost was to be formally denounced before the church and if he persevered in his rebellion he was to be suspended from the Lord's Supper; ultimately, if he continued, the affair was to be placed before the town authorities.[76] In another case the schoolmaster Nicholas du Chemin was suspended from the Lord's Supper on three occasions and by 1571 he had been

---

[71] *Examinations and Depositions, 1570–1594*, p. 97.
[72] Pettegree, *Foreign Protestant Communities*, pp. 66–67, 78.
[73] *Southampton Mayor's Book*, p. 50.
[74] *Registre*, pp. 4, 5, 6.
[75] See above p. 103; *Actes du Consistoire, II*, p. 11–12, 49.
[76] *Actes des Colloques*, p. 11.

excommunicated by the church.[77] Disputes also appear to have arisen within the consistory itself. Two of the elders, Claude Moutonnier and Jean Catelain, and the deacon Vincent Nérin, together with one Richard Robert, were suspended from their offices and prevented from participating in the Lord's Supper. They appealed to the colloquy in 1598 against this punishment, although Claude Moutonnier had already left with his wife to join the church at Caen.[78]

An important area of discipline was the admission to the Lord's Supper of those who had attended Mass before their flight to Southampton. Some people, in the face of persecution, abjured their Reformed faith, either formally or by attempting to establish their Catholic orthodoxy through making donations to the Catholic parish churches or rebaptising their children.[79] The Reformed Church however took a strict view towards such abjurations. The 1559 French Discipline stated that 'those who abjured their faith under persecution should not be admitted to the church until they have made an act of public repentance'. This view was repeated by the Walloon synod in 1564 and elaborated further in 1578.[80] The London churches had had to face the problem of those who had conformed during Mary's reign when they were re-established in 1559.[81] The issue of attendance at Catholic services was later debated by the colloquies and resulted in changes being made to the Discipline.[82]

In Southampton those who had attended Mass before their arrival were noted in the *Registre* and were required to recognise their fault publicly before they were admitted to the Lord's Supper. In the period from October 1572 to October 1580, forty-five people who were admitted to the Lord's Supper confessed to attending Mass.[83] The majority of those who confessed were admitted in the wake of the St. Bartholomew's Day Massacre. They presumably attempted through their attendance to conceal their Protestant sympathies, until they were able to flee the country. The numbers increased again at the end of 1576 and in 1577 although the reasons for this are not quite so clear. The generous terms of the Peace of Monsieur which brought to an end the Fifth Civil War in 1576, had resulted in the formation of the Catholic League in order to destroy heresy. Protestantism had been outlawed in February 1577 with the outbreak of the Sixth Civil War but Henry III undermined this by ordering local officials to protect the Huguenots within their jurisdictions. 'During this civil war Rouen's Protestants do not seem to have been molested, burdened with special taxes, or otherwise harassed as they had been during

---

[77] *Registre*, pp. 4, 5; *Actes du Consistoire, II*, pp. 11–12.
[78] *Actes des Colloques*, pp. 36, 37, 38–39.
[79] Benedict, *Rouen during the Wars of Religion*, p. 130; *Abjurations de Protestants faites à Bayeux; Guerre de religion, 1570–1573*, ed. E. Anquetil, (Bayeux, n.d.).
[80] Duke, *Calvinism in Europe*, p. 75; *Livre Synodal*, I, pp. 9, 61.
[81] Pettegree, *Foreign Protestant Communities*, pp. 127, 131–32.
[82] *Actes des Colloques*, pp. 6–7, 10.
[83] PRO, RG4/4600, ff. 7–9v, 11–12, 14; Spicer, 'The French-speaking Reformed community', pp. 213–14.

earlier periods of conflict'.[84] The origins of only one of these refugees can be identified, Nicholas Bouton from the Pays de Caux, Normandy.[85] Perhaps Protestants in the rural areas were less fortunate.

Marriage was another area of concern for the consistory. The procedures for the betrothal, the reading of the banns and the wedding were all carefully defined by des Gallars' Discipline and later by the Synod of Emden in 1571. In particular the need for obedience to one's parents and the need for their consent in the case of minors was emphasised. Marriages contracted without permission were declared void.[86]

The Southampton consistory had to deal with several disputes concerning betrothals. In 1580 Jan le Vasseur and Perronne Jorre were betrothed in the house of the Mayor, Bernard Courtmill, in the company of the Archbishop's Lieutenant, Mathieu Sohier, Richard Etuer and Jan Ric. The couple made their promises of marriage after the invocation of the name of God by Walerand Thevelin, then their banns were to be read on three Sundays, following the established custom. However when the marriage took place three months later, the entry commented '*deuant que le presche fut acheué s'en fuit hors le temple, et la Ville, et le pais, Abandonnant sa femme. Mariage fet par Justice et force du costé de Jan*'.[87] In another case, Nicholas du Chemin was involved in a dispute over his betrothal to the daughter of Henry le Sueur. Du Chemin had made his promises of betrothal without either the minister, an elder or deacon of the church being present.[88] The Southampton church was also clearly exercised by the problem of a young man who wanted to marry a woman already betrothed to another. He had boasted about impugning her honour and the representatives of Southampton asked the colloquy for their advice in 1584 about how to discipline the man.[89]

The church kept detailed records about the granting of parental consent for marriages, although the information is erratic after 1587 and ends in 1594. The need for parental consent caused particular difficulties in exile communities where the parents had not also fled. In some cases permission for a marriage had been granted to a close relation or a letter of approval was sent.[90] Occasionally the Dutch church in London was prepared to waive the need for parental consent due to the difficulties in communication with the continent but this was only after serious efforts had been made to obtain the necessary consent.[91] The granting of permission to marry was recorded for the 95 marriages which were celebrated between 1567 and 1587 in Southampton.

---

[84] Benedict, *Rouen during the Wars of Religion*, pp. 132–33.
[85] *Registre*, pp. 13, 87.
[86] Des Gallars, *Forme de Police*, ff. 20–20v; *Livre Synodal*, I, p. 18.
[87] *Registre*, pp. 86–87.
[88] *Actes du Consistoire, II*, pp. 11–12, 49. See also Pettegree, *Foreign Protestant Communities*, p. 185.
[89] *Actes des Colloques*, p. 8.
[90] *Registre*, pp. 83, 84.
[91] Pettegree, *Foreign Protestant Communities*, p. 226.

Twenty-three grooms and twelve brides claimed that they were orphaned and in another two cases it was noted that it was not known if the mother was alive.[92] On yet another occasion *'la mere d'iceluy ne consentoit en mariage en haine de la religion'*.[93]

In 1585 a couple married in the English church, and in 1588 another couple also married outside the French church.[94] This may have prompted the advice sought by the Southampton consistory from the colloquy in 1589. The colloquy responded that where a couple had married outside the church, without the consent of their parents, they should be required to provide proof of their marriage and recognise their faults before the consistory. However if the couple failed to recognise their error they were to be suspended from the Lord's Supper.[95] The consistory in Canterbury was particularly troubled by one couple who refused to recognise their error.[96]

The responsibility for visiting the sick and the dying was not the exclusive concern of the community's minister; it was a duty which was shared with the consistory. Attending the dying could involve the minister or other members of the consistory in the drawing up of a will or acting as witnesses. This was not always straightforward. The minister Philippe de la Motte, together with Estienne Latelais and Jean Hersent, who may have both been members of the consistory at the time, were called with two others to the bedside of Cecille Seulin, who died in June 1596. On that occasion the dying woman expressed her concern about her son Daniel Seulin and his debts. So she made a will in the presence of the witnesses, whom she made executors of her estate, on behalf of her grandchildren, thereby excluding her son Daniel Seulin. When the will was susbsequently challenged in the Court of Star Chamber by her stepson Peter Seulin, the witnesses were forced to defend their position.[97]

The discipline and role of the consistory also had a more secular element. The colloquy of the French churches ruled in 1584 that quarrels should be disciplined within the consistory, if there was no bloodshed or scandal and the parties were prepared to be reconciled.[98] However it was not always possible for these petty disputes to be dealt with by the consistory. In the stranger communities established in Norwich and Canterbury another element of church government emerged, the *Hommes Politiques*. In Norwich, they were intended to handle petty disputes within the community and also assumed responsibility for the care of orphans, and often their concerns overlapped with

---

[92] In six cases the marriage partners were described as being at liberty to marry and another forty-two partners were widowed and so did not need parental consent. Spicer, 'The French-speaking Reformed community', pp. 214–15.

[93] *Registre*, p. 88.

[94] *Registre*, pp. 88, 89. In the second marriage, Jan Christmus was described as *Anglois*.

[95] *Actes des Colloques*, p. 17.

[96] CDRO, U47/A2, ff. 9v–10, 11v–12.

[97] PRO, STAC 5 83/3; *Registre*, p. 106. The family relationships are explained in the will of Gilles Seulin, PRO, PCC Prob. 11/88.

[98] *Actes des Colloques*, p. 8.

those of the consistory.[99] There does not seem to be any similar institution to deal with secular affairs in Southampton but this may reflect the limited size of the community. The town authorities were able to deal with the problems that arose between the members of the community as well as those with the natives of Southampton. For example, in July 1574 20s was received from 'a ffrenchman that lay with a ffrench woman', while in June 1577 three Frenchmen were fined 5s for fighting and drawing blood.[100]

The consistory also represented the refugees by acting as a spokesman for their interests. The two surviving letters written by the consistory relate to secular issues. At the end of 1589 the consistory wrote to the town authorities emphasising the poverty of the community and therefore its inability to meet the financial demands made by the corporation.[101] On another occasion in 1598 the consistory protested to Sir Robert Cecil about the claims made by Rachel Terrie, a member of the stranger church, to have the monopoly in the pressing of serges produced in Southampton.[102] These are only isolated examples of the consistory acting on behalf of the French community in secular affairs, but this was probably quite common.

Besides dealing with matters of discipline and admissions to the Lord's Supper, the consistory also had various financial and social responsibilities. As in other communities, the Southampton church probably had two funds, one to maintain the minister and the other to fulfill the church's obligations to the poor and needy.[103] The deacons collected and distributed poor relief while the elders were responsible for the maintenance of the ministry.[104]

Some impression of the potential sources of revenue can be obtained from the fragmentary survival of several financial records from other com-

[99] R. Esser, 'Social Concern and Calvinistic Duty: The Norwich Strangers' Community' in *Het Beloofde Land. Acht opstellen over werken, geloven en vluchten tijdens de XVI*e *en XVII*e *eeuw*, (Dikkebus-Ieper, 1992), pp. 173–84; A.M. Oakley, 'The Canterbury Walloon Congregation from Elizabeth I to Laud', in I. Scouloudi, (ed.), *Huguenots in Britain and their French Background, 1550–1800. Contributions to the Historical Conference of the Huguenot Society of London, 24–25 September, 1985*, (Basingstoke, 1987), pp. 60–61.

[100] SRO, SC5/3/1, ff. 143v, 161.

[101] SRO, TC Box 1/40.

[102] Hatfield House, Salisbury MSS, CP64/37–38. Also see pp. 78–79, 114.

[103] *Actes du Consistoire*, I, p. 14; Moens, *The Walloons and their Church at Norwich*, p. 293; Pettegree, *Foreign Protestant Communities*, p. 202.

[104] According to the Discipline of the French churches, the deacons handled all the church's finances but this differing division of responsibilities seems to have been made in Southampton and elsewhere. PRO, PCC Prob. 11/88 Gilles Seulin, Prob. 11/67 Robert Cousin; Guildhall Library, London, Commissary Court of London, 1593 Reg. 18, f. 60 Christiana de Preseau; CDRO, U47/B1; Moens, *The Walloons and their Church at Norwich*, p. 293; B. Magen, *Die Wallonengemeinde in Canterbury von ihrer Gründung bis zum Jahre 1635*, (Frankfurt, 1973), p. 88.

munities.[105] Money was raised through collections at services while further funds could be raised from house to house collections. Wealthy members of the community may also have loaned sums to the church; Anthoine Jurion was owed 18s by the church when he died in 1578.[106] Further revenue was raised in Norwich from a third of the fines imposed on cloth that was not sold in the market halls; money was also raised through the cloth industry in Sandwich. The London community benefited from a levy imposed on cloth bought by foreign merchants at Blackwell Hall.[107]

Gifts and legacies provided another important source of revenue; sixty percent of the 250 wills drawn up by members of the London community between 1550 and 1580 included some sort of bequest to the poor.[108] Some references to this form of revenue have survived for the French church in Southampton. Approximately twenty wills were drawn up by members of the church while living in Southampton during the period 1567–1620.[109] In view of the comparatively small size of the Southampton community, this is a not inconsiderable number. Bequests were also made by people who had been members of the Southampton community and had later migrated to London, such as Chrestienne de Preseau who wrote fondly in her will about the time she had spent in the town.[110] Richard Etuer remembered not only the Southampton Corporation in his will but made a generous bequest to the French community.[111] A few bequests were made by Channel Islanders such as Thomas de Lecq, and also a small number by natives of Southampton.[112]

The legacies can be divided into three main groups: bequests to the poor, to the church as a whole, or gifts for the ministry/minister.[113] In the latter case it is not always possible to distinguish between personal bequests and those for the maintenance of the ministry, although in some cases where the minister is not actually named the latter may be the case. There is also the added complication in a community as small and endogamous as that in Southampton that the minister could actually be related to the testator as was the case with Martine des Maistres who was the grandmother of the children of Philippe de la Motte and Timothée Blier, the main beneficiaries of the will.[114]

[105]   HLL, MS/J 27; French Protestant Church of London Archives, Soho Square, DL/MS 194; W.J.C. Moens, 'The Relief of the poor members of the French Churches in England', HSP, 5 (1894–96), 321–42; A. Spicer, 'Poor relief and the exile communities' in B. Kümin, (ed.), Reformations Old and New. Essays on the Socio-Economic Impact of Religious Change, c. 1470–1630, (Aldershot, 1996), pp. 243–48.

[106]   HRO, Wills 1578/B/53.

[107]   HLL, MS/J 27, f. 2v 'S'ensuisant les receptes des baies quy penny a la baie done au pouvre de l'eglise de Sandewye franchoise'; Moens, The Walloons and their Church at Norwich, p. 260; Pettegree, Foreign Protestant Communities, p. 209.

[108]   Pettegree, Foreign Protestant Communities, pp. 198, 201.

[109]   Spicer, 'The French-speaking Reformed community', p. 218.

[110]   Guildhall Library, London, Commissary Court of London 1593 Reg. 18, ff. 60–62v.

[111]   PRO, PCC Prob. 11/102 Richard Etuer.

[112]   Spicer, 'The French-speaking Reformed community', p. 218.

[113]   Spicer, 'The French-speaking Reformed community', pp. 219, 220, 221.

[114]   HRO, Wills 1615/A/24.

Some of these bequests were particularly generous. In 1584 Robert Cousin left 40s to the French church, 20 gold crowns for the poor and 40s to the minister Walerand Thevelin. In 1615 Jean Hersent left £5 to the poor and to the ministers. He bequeathed £5 to Philippe de la Motte and 50s to Timothée Blier.[115] In London bequests generally ranged between 5s and £5; bequests in Southampton also fall within much the same range with the smallest being 3s and the largest £20.[116]

It is more difficult to identify gifts, as distinct from legacies, that were made to the church. The accounts of the Marian exile Robert Nowell reveal that he donated £10 to the French church in 1569.[117] It is possible that the church could have also benefited from the collections made by the Kirk of Scotland for the exiled French churches.[118] A gift of 6d from the Southampton Corporation was recorded in 1581–82.[119]

By the early seventeenth century the community had begun to experience severe financial difficulties in raising sufficient funds, which was no doubt in large part related to the decline in the size of the community itself. As early as 1589 the church had protested to the Southampton authorities that they were too poor to meet the dues demanded by the Corporation, especially as they had recently provided aid for the relief of Geneva.[120] It is unclear whether this appeal was the result of genuine hardship or whether it was merely an attempt to avoid paying further taxes. These financial difficulties may have resulted in de la Motte's involvement in the cloth trade and Blier's move to Titchfield.[121] In 1610 the church complained to the Colloquy that they were unable to sustain the ministry in Southampton and repeated their plea in 1615 and 1619.[122] The church at Rye had requested assistance from the other churches in 1583 and 1584.[123] In 1610 the other French churches were urged to assist the church in Southampton. By the meeting of the Colloquy in 1623 the Southampton congregation appeared to be dependent upon the other French churches for voluntary contributions.[124]

The maintenance of the ministry was one of the church's principal expenses. Ministers in the provincial churches generally earned less than their counter-

---

[115]   PRO, PCC Prob. 11/67 Robert Cousin, Prob. 11/125 Jean Hersent.

[116]   Pettegree, *Foreign Protestant Communities*, p. 201; Spicer, 'The French-speaking Reformed community', p. 220; Spicer, 'Poor relief and the exile communities', pp. 247–48.

[117]   A.B. Grosart, (ed.), *The Spending of the money of Robert Nowell of Reade Hall, Lancashire: Brother of Dean Alexander Nowell*, (Manchester, 1877), p. 103.

[118]   CDRO, U47/A1, p. 49; *Acts and Proceedings of the General Assemblies of the Kirk of Scotland from the year MDLX*, 3 vols. (Edinburgh, 1839–45), pp. 356, 379–80; *Register of the Minister Elders and Deacons of the Christian Congregation of St. Andrews . . . 1559–1600*, ed. D. Hay Fleming, (Publications of the Scottish History Society, 4, 7; 1889, 1890), p. 610.

[119]   SRO, SC5/3/1, f. 182.

[120]   SRO, TC Box 1/40.

[121]   See below pp. 121, 123, 164.

[122]   *Actes des Colloques*, pp. 52–53, 56, 58.

[123]   *Actes des Colloques*, pp. 5, 7. There seems to have been a collection at Canterbury to help the church at Rye. CDRO, U47/A2, f. 29v.

[124]   *Actes des Colloques*, p. 65.

parts in London. At Canterbury, the minister Anthoine Lescaillet was granted a salary of £24 per annum and by 1596 the minister's salary had increased to £48.[125] The minister in Southampton may have earned less than this, for the community there was much smaller and the minister's salary was raised through contributions from church members.[126] The exile ministers seem to have been in a better position than their English counterparts. The benefice of Holy Rood was worth only £24 per annum in c. 1583,[127] which seems to have been sufficient for Henry Hopkins but his successor Simon Pett experienced serious financial difficulties.[128] A comparison of the estates of Hopkins and the town's lecturer Thomas Hitchcock with that of Philippe de la Motte reveals his relative prosperity. Hopkins left moveable goods worth £90 17s 8d when he died in 1600, while Hitchcock's goods were valued at £83 6s 6d in 1612. De la Motte's will included bequests to the value of £163.[129]

Poor relief was the other principal area of church expenditure.[130] Initially the community was sufficiently wealthy to contribute towards the relief of the poor in other communities. The church sent £2 to the Walloon congregation in Sandwich in December 1568 and a further gift of £1 10s in November 1569.[131] In 1577 the community enquired about the state of the French church in Canterbury as they were considering a donation to the poor there.[132]

Provision for the poor was a pressing matter in Southampton in the second half of the sixteenth century. Like other urban centres Southampton became a magnet for the impoverished from the surrounding area; there were frequent complaints made to the Court Leet about the increasing number of undertenants which resulted in overcrowding and created 'great danger of infection and damage by fire'. There were orders issued for newcomers to leave the town and in 1574 the Court Leet first separated the list of undertenants from the record of 'stall & art' payments.[133] This problem was no doubt compounded

[125] Spicer, ' "A Faythful Pastor in the Churches" ', pp. 204–5.

[126] Des Gallars, *Forme de Police*, ff. 17v–18. The accounts for the end of the sixteenth century survive from the Canterbury church recording the house to house collection to pay for the ministry. CDRO, U47/B1.

[127] PRO, SP12/288/37. For the dating of this document, see above pp. 99n.

[128] Simon Pett succeeded Henry Hopkins at Holy Rood church in 1586–87 and from either 1588 or 1591 was also the minister of St. Michael's. He received a loan of £25 under Sir Thomas White's Charity in 1607 to help him in his trade as a clothier. He was provided with the money for a livery by the town in the same year. After his death in 1611 his wife and son experienced financial difficulties and were forced to sell his books. He became a burgess in 1603. HRO, 21M65, A1/26 f. 8v., A1/27 ff. 13v, 20v; SRO, SC3/1/1, f. 143v; *Southampton Mayor's Book*, pp. 99, 100, 107–8; *Assembly Books*, III, pp. xxi, 25, 56, 65, IV, pp. xvii–xviii.

[129] Spicer, ' "A Faythful Pastor in the Churches" ', p. 205.

[130] Spicer, 'Poor relief and the exile communities', pp. 248–51.

[131] HLL, MS/J 27, pp. 8, 49.

[132] CDRO, U47/A1, p. 81.

[133] SRO, SC6/1/10; *Court Leet Records*, pp. 236, 284, 298, 306, 369, 386, 402, 439, 455, 498, 519, 533. On poverty in Southampton, see *Southampton Mayor's Book*, pp. 25–30; E.A. Rothery, 'Poverty in Southampton, 1540 to 1560', (unpublished dissertation, Portsmouth Polytechnic, 1989). On migrant poor in Southampton, see *The Third Book of Remembrance*, IV, pp. xxii–xxiii. On urban migration generally and the impact on towns, see P. Clark, 'The migrant in Kentish towns, 1580–1640', in P. Clark & P. Slack, (ed.), *Crisis and Order in English Towns, 1500–1700*, (London, 1972), pp. 117–63.

by the policy of the Royal Court of Guernsey which sent youths to England who could not be employed on the island. In view of the close links between Southampton and the Islands, a number probably came to the port.[134] Regular collections for the relief of the poor in the town began after 1552.[135] Some members of the community are known to have contributed to the relief of the English poor, such as Adrian Saravia and Arnoul le Clercq in 1575.[136] However the French church operated its own completely separate system of poor relief; this explains the conspicuous absence of members of the community in the accounts of money that was distributed to the poor by the authorities.

The beneficiaries of poor relief were probably similar to those in London and Sandwich. There the indigent could be divided between those who had fallen temporarily into difficulties and those who required long-term assistance, such as the seriously ill or widows. Money was provided to allow the refugees to travel to other communities and to buy essentials. The deacons at Sandwich organised the baking of bread to support the poor and even had a store of mattresses, beds etc. which could be lent out.[137]

There is only limited information about the recipients of poor relief in Southampton. In 1570 Jerome Dentiere died after being cared for '*long tamps et au grand despens des poures*'. Jacob Dixt from Antwerp left a ship returning from Spain and was only passing through the town. However he fell ill and was cared for by the community for between eight and nine weeks before he died.[138] Rachel Terrie was helped by the church for one and a half years as her husband was in debt and living in La Rochelle. Relations were not easy between Terrie and the church. The consistory criticised her, commenting that she was 'a woman aloane, idle, and of noe abilitie', they also wrote about 'a grate oathe which she hath made that she will plucke up by the rootes the said Churche'.[139] These are just isolated examples of the relief that the community provided. There were probably heavy demands upon the deacons' funds during the plagues of 1583–84 and 1604. The separate arrangements of the English citizens of the town continued then and there is no reference to members of the French community amongst the beneficiaries of a special collection

[134] D. Ogier, 'The Reformation and Society in Guernsey *c.*1500–1640', (unpublished Ph.D. thesis, Warwick University, 1993), Ch. 7. There was certainly a complaint in the Court Leet in 1582 protesting that the strangers should be made to 'take towne borne childeren & other Englishe childeren, whereas now they take frentch & guarnzey childeren' as apprentices. However none of the names given in a list of people sent to England in 1606 appear in the *Registre*. Greffe Archives, Guernsey, 'Clameurs de Haro' vol. I – People sent to England, January and May 1606; *Court Leet Records*, p. 228. I am grateful to Dr. Ogier for the former reference.

[135] Spicer, 'Poor relief and the exile communities', p. 254.

[136] SC5/17/1; Spicer, 'The French-speaking Reformed community', p. 224.

[137] For example, 3*s* was paid to the wife of Gilles le Plus of Armentières so that she could travel from Sandwich to Southampton in June 1571. In December 1572 the London deacons gave the wife of Guillaume Coppin 2*s* to buy a blanket. HLL, MS/J 27, pp. 7, 122, 174; French Protestant Church of London Archives, Soho Square, DL/MS 194, f. 23.

[138] *Registre*, pp. 100–1.

[139] Hatfield House, Salisbury MSS, CP64/37.

made for the relief of plague.[140] The first person who seems to have benefited from the town's charity was Paul Latelais who in 1607 was loaned £25 by Sir Thomas White's Charity.[141]

Children who were orphaned or whose parents were too poor to care for them posed a serious problem for the town authorities. The Corporation attempted to lodge the orphans with other citizens or to apprentice them at an early age.[142] Another solution was reached by entering into agreements with newcomers to the town, permitting them to stay in the town if they cared for a particular child at their own expense.[143] The responsibility for such children within the French community fell upon the church's system of poor relief, unlike Norwich where orphans were the responsibility of the *Hommes Politiques*.[144] Georgette Loys gave the poor of the church 10s wishing that the consistory would care for her son.[145] More specific arrangements were made by Magdalen Mesnier for the provision of her six children. She bequeathed her whole estate into the hands of the church's two deacons, Jean Hersent and Vincent Nérin in order to care for the children until they had all come of age when the remaining estate was to be divided between the children. Mesnier wrote her will in 1589 and the deacons finally discharged their responsibilities in 1613.[146]

Apprenticeship provided another means for the care of children who were either orphaned or of impoverished parents, and in the early seventeenth century a Poor Child Register was kept by the Southampton Corporation.[147] The French community had, because of the terms governing its establishment, an obligation to take English apprentices. Even so in 1615 Judith de la Motte and other clothiers in the town offered to set the English poor to work.[148] Certainly almost 40 percent of the poor boys were recorded, in the Poor Child Register, as being apprenticed in the cloth industry, although this may be because it was the largest trade in the town.[149] Vincent Nérin, a deacon of the French church, took John Cordon as his apprentice until 1591 and he appears to have been

---

[140] SRO, SC5/3/1, ff. 189–90.

[141] Paul Latelais was the son of Estienne Latelais, born in Southampton in 1580. *Southampton Mayor's Book*, pp. 99, 100; *Assembly Books*, II, p. 85; *Registre*, p. 44. On Sir Thomas White's Charity, see Davies, *A History of Southampton*, p. 300.

[142] Rothery, 'Poverty in Southampton', pp. 25–27.

[143] E.g. Charles Poingdextre and his wife were allowed to remain in Southampton in 1577 on condition that they cared for one Elizabeth Darvall at 6d per week for a year, then to maintain her at their own expense until she was apprenticed to them for twelve years. *Examinations and Depositions, 1570–1594*, p. 51.

[144] Esser, 'Social Concern and Calvinistic Duty', p. 177.

[145] HRO, Wills 1583/B/13.

[146] HRO, Wills 1589/B/39, 1613/A/81.

[147] *Calendar of Southampton Apprenticeship Registers*, pp. xlii–l. The Poor Child Register appears on pp. 61–108.

[148] *Assembly Books*, IV, p. 3.

[149] Of the 100 boys for whom a trade was recorded, in the period 1609–1645, 36 were apprenticed in the cloth industry. The next largest group were handicrafts with 35 apprentices. *Calendar of Southampton Apprenticeship Registers*, p. liv.

an orphan although he was certainly not impoverished.[150] As has already been noted the strangers may also have taken boys from Guernsey as apprentices.[151]

Education was an important concern for the stranger churches, in particular instructing the young in the catechism. Whether the Southampton community went beyond this to finance and develop any formalised system of education, is far from clear. It is possible that the congregation did not employ a schoolmaster. In London, the members of the Dutch congregation preferred until the 1570s to send their children to the local English schools or independent schoolmasters in the community.[152] There are occasional references to French schoolmasters in Southampton and in October 1576, Anthoine Ylot alias M. du Plantin was admitted with seven of his students![153] Nicholas du Chemin was described in 1571 as having been 'mestre descolle a Hampton', suggesting that he had actually taught in the town although he was subsequently excommunicated by the Southampton consistory.[154] Certainly the most prominent schoolmaster in Southampton in this period was Adrian Saravia. He was employed by the Southampton Corporation as the Headmaster of the King Edward VI's school, then known as the Free Grammar School. Nijenhuis has speculated about Saravia having some sort of educational role in the town before he was appointed to the Free School.[155]

Ministers guided the faithful in the way of truth through preaching the Word of God and correcting faults, as well as through administering the sacraments. The role of the minister in Southampton would differ little from that in other communities. The minister would have regularly preached to the congregation but only occasional references have survived.[156] Initially the Lord's Supper was administered four times a year in the church but after 1583 these services were held monthly.[157] The minister also regularly conducted baptisms and marriages as well as recording the admissions to the Lord's Supper and deaths within the community. Besides their liturgical responsibilities, there are a few surviving glimpses of the minister's pastoral role. The minister sometimes acted as a *parrain* at a baptism and occasionally attended the dying and acted as a scribe for wills.[158]

[150] Cordin does not appear to have been a member of the French community as his name does not appear in the *Registre*. SRO, SC2/6/5, f. 167v; *The Third Book of Remembrance*, III, p. 46, IV, p. 8.

[151] See above p. 114.

[152] O.P. Grell, *Dutch Calvinists in Early Stuart London. The Dutch Church in Austin Friars, 1603–1642*, (Leiden, 1989), pp. 106–8.

[153] SRO, SC6/1/10, SC5/17/1; *Registre*, pp. 4, 12, 39.

[154] *Actes du Consistoire*, II, pp. 11, 12, 31.

[155] W. Nijenhuis, *Adrianus Saravia (c. 1532–1613). Dutch Calvinist, first Reformed defender of the English episcopal church order on the basis of ius divinum*, (Leiden, 1980), p. 32.

[156] *Registre*, pp. 17, 87, 104.

[157] *Registre*, p. 18; Spicer, 'The French-speaking Reformed community', pp. 185–86.

[158] *Registre*, pp. 40, 41, 43, 46, 47, 50, 51, 54; PRO, PCC Prob. 11/68 Gilles Seulin, Prob. 11/122 Isaac le Gay, Prob. 11/125 Jean Hersent; HRO, Wills 1569/B/81–84, 1578/B/53, 1583/Ad/10, 1606/B/46, 1611/B/65.

The Southampton church was served by four ministers during this period: Walerand Thevelin, Philippe de la Motte, Timothée Blier and Elie d'Arande. They came from different backgrounds and their careers exemplified the problems faced by the exiled communities.

The community's first minister was Walerand Thevelin; a Walloon, he had been actively involved in the Troubles of 1566–67. He came from Frelinghien sur le Lys near Armentières and may have been related to a certain Jacques Thevelin who was involved in the iconoclasm at Armentières and the construction of the Protestant temple in the village.[159] He was one of the wave of lay reformed preachers who only came to prominence during the Troubles, and were characterised by Phyllis Crew as being for the most part obscure priests or laymen mainly from the working class and of limited education.[160] In August 1566, Thevelin was chosen as the preacher in Tourcoing where he publicly administered the Lord's Supper in the market-place, attended by a 'grand nombre et avecq armes'.[161] He was one of the ministers present in October 1566 at the Synod of Ghent which discussed the possibility of buying religious freedom from Philip II, the so-called Three Million Guilders Request.[162] By September 1567 he had fled from the Netherlands and was subsequently banished by the Conseil des Troubles.[163] He had arrived in Southampton by July 1568, when the register appears in his hand; his wife, Elisabeth le Mahieu, was admitted to the Lord's Supper at about the same time.

Thevelin served the church until his death in September 1584 but apart from occasional references, his time as a minister remains shadowy. His ministry coincided with a period of rapid change for the Southampton church. The exodus from France in the wake of the St. Bartholomew's Day Massacre swelled the congregation but also significantly altered its composition. A number of exiled ministers passed through Southampton and it is likely that some may have assisted Thevelin with this burgeoning congregation. In particular, Thevelin was probably assisted in his pastoral work by Adrian Saravia.

Between 1571–72 and 1578, Adrian Saravia was the Headmaster of the town's grammar school. A former Franciscan friar from St. Omer, Saravia had played a prominent rôle in the affairs of the churches 'under the cross' and the London exile communities. He was involved in the composition of the Belgic Confession of Faith and had served with Orange in 1568–71 as an army chap-

---

[159] Beuzart, 'La Réforme dans les environs de Lille', 54. The relationship is however less certain than suggested in P.M. Crew, *Calvinist Preaching and Iconoclasm in the Netherlands, 1544–1569*, (Cambridge, 1978), p. 191. See Spicer, 'The French-speaking Reformed community', p. 43.

[160] Crew, *Calvinist Preaching and Iconoclasm*, pp. 162–63. See also, Spicer, ' "A Faythful Pastor in the Churches" ', p. 198.

[161] Beuzart, 'La Réforme dans les environs de Lille', 58–59.

[162] Stadsarchief Gent, Series 94 bis, reg. 9 ff. 253–56v. I am grateful to Dr. J. Decavele for providing me with a photocopy of this source.

[163] AGR, Conseil des Troubles 6, f. 229.

lain before coming to Southampton.[164] While Headmaster of Elizabeth College on Guernsey, Saravia retained his links with the Netherlands as well as being involved in the Island's religious affairs. In October 1565 he was chosen as a minister of St. Peter Port to assist Nicholas Baudouin not only with preaching but also with the administration of the sacraments.[165] It would be difficult to believe that Saravia was not similarly involved in the religious life of the community in Southampton, especially in view of the proximity of the Grammar School to the French Church, a material circumstance which has often been overlooked.[166] Even when later he became a canon at Canterbury, he preached occasionally in the French church there.[167]

Following Thevelin's death in September 1584, the community remained without a minister until May 1585.[168] During this period the Lord's Supper could not be administered but the consistory directed the church's affairs, organising a fast in October 1584, for example.[169] The church was also helped by the minister of Holy Rood, Henry Hopkins, who conducted several baptisms and a marriage service for members of the community.[170]

The vacancy at Southampton was discussed at the meeting of the Walloon synod in the Netherlands at Middelburg in April 1585. The meeting appointed a certain M. du Forest to the post with the proviso that he would return to the Netherlands when he was recalled, but for reasons unknown the post was actually assumed by Philippe de la Motte.[171]

De la Motte represents the next generation of Reformed ministers and the gradual move towards a more educated and professional ministry.[172] Although born in the Netherlands, he would only have been a child at the time of the Troubles.[173] An account written in 1743 provides a colourful description of de la Motte's career before he came to Southampton.[174] Certain elements in the story can be corroborated but other details concerning de la Motte's career in the Netherlands were confused and his escape from the authorities over the garden wall, Bible in hand, sounds too good to be true. Philippe de la Motte certainly studied in Geneva where he matriculated as a student of Theology at the Academy in June 1581.[175] He was confirmed in his ministry by the Walloon

[164] Nijenhuis, *Adrianus Saravia*, pp. 3–34.
[165] Northamptonshire Record Office, Finch-Hatton Papers FH312, p. 308.
[166] The Free Grammar School occupied a loft in Winkle Street opposite God's House from 1573 onwards. SRO, SC4/2/365.
[167] CDRO, U47/A3, pp. 26, 53.
[168] *Registre*, pp. 4, 8, 104.
[169] *Registre*, pp. 19, 127.
[170] *Registre*, pp. 46, 88.
[171] *Livre Synodal*, I, p. 110.
[172] Spicer, ' "A Faythful Pastor in the Churches" ', pp. 197–200.
[173] According to de la Motte's portrait he was 59 in 1615.
[174] The manuscript is in a private collection. However it was used in the nineteenth century by S. Smiles in his revised third edition of *The Huguenots: their settlements, churches and industries in England and Ireland*, (London, 1869), p. 361; *D.N.B.* entry on William de la Motte, (1775–1863).
[175] *Registre*, p. 89; Stelling-Michaud, *Le Livre du Recteur de l'Académie de Genève*, IV, p. 603.

synod in the Netherlands at Ghent in 1583, where he was examined as to his doctrine and his life.[176] De la Motte presumably did not return to Tournai which had been recaptured by Parma on 30 November 1581. He had acted as the secretary for the classical meeting of the Walloon Churches of Holland and Zealand held at Leiden at the end of October 1584, and the following month he was an unsuccessful candidate in the disputed election for the post at Leiden.[177] As the moderator of the classical assembly at Leiden was Adrian Saravia, he may have been responsible for drawing de la Motte's attention to the French church in Southampton.[178] Although the Synod directed de la Motte in April 1585 to serve the Walloon community in Ostend, he arrived in Southampton in May 1585 accompanied or joined shortly afterwards by his wife Jeanne de Massis and her family.[179]

In contrast to his autodidactic predecessor de la Motte affected the image of the learned divine. He usually signed his name in Latin and a portrait completed shortly before his death perpetuates this scholarly impression with de la Motte sitting working beside some books while the painting is adorned by several phrases in Hebrew.[180] He also began what has come to be known as the Delamotte diary. This in fact was a list of the Mayors of Southampton recorded from 1498 until his death in 1617 which formed the basis for a chronicle that de la Motte compiled on English history, interweaving events of national and local significance, and which later grew into a family diary.[181] He also appears to have taken an interest in Puritanism. Peter Caplin bequeathed to de la Motte the works of the Puritan minister Richard Greenham which he had borrowed together with others of Caplin's books still in his possession.[182]

The Calvinist churches on the continent frequently sought new ministers from the exile churches.[183] It is perhaps a reflection of de la Motte's reputation and abilities that he was approached to serve the churches at Aachen and, later, at Delft. The Walloon synod proposed that de la Motte should be sent to the church at Aachen in 1597.[184] While the minister agreed to take up the post,

[176]   *Livre Synodal*, I, p. 105.
[177]   Nijenhuis, *Adrianus Saravia*, p. 60.
[178]   *Livre Synodal*, I, pp. 108–9.
[179]   *Registre*, pp. 19, 104; *Livre Synodal*, I, pp. 110, 111; BL, Egerton MS 868, 'Delamotte Yearbook', f. 8.
[180]   Two versions of this portrait are known. One states that de la Motte was painted in 1615 when the minister was 59 and adds that he died in 1617. This portrait also has several Hebrew phrases and motifs included on it. The second version lacks these phrases and the date of death. The former is in a private collection while the latter was sold at Christies on 25 November 1960, lot no. 59. I am grateful to the National Portrait Gallery and the owner of the former de la Motte portrait for their assistance.
[181]   The entries range from Henry VIII's conquest of Tournai (which clearly would have been of interest to de la Motte) in 1513, to Henry's assumption of the title of Supreme Head of the Church in 1530 and the execution of Anne Boleyn, to plague in Southampton in 1562 and 1583, BL, Egerton MS 868, ff. 3, 4, 6, 8.
[182]   HRO, Wills 1609/A/15.
[183]   Spicer, ' "A Faythful Pastor in the Churches" ', pp. 202–3.
[184]   *Livre Synodal*, I, p. 166

the English colloquy was unenthusiastic. They criticised the Walloon synod of Holland for its lack of consideration and decided to delay de la Motte's departure for five months, until 1 September so that they could find a replacement for him. Only then was the colloquy prepared to provide de la Motte with a suitable testimony as to his religious doctrine and conduct. The colloquy decided that the French church in London should assume responsibility if a suitable replacement could not be found.[185] However by April 1598, de la Motte still had not taken up his post at Aachen and the Walloon synod, meeting at Zierikzee, decided to write to Southampton to urge them not to delay de la Motte's departure.[186] The church at Aachen was still awaiting a minister in September 1600.[187] A more peremptory resolution was agreed in May 1601 which advised the church in Southampton to find a replacement for de la Motte so that he could give effect to his call from Delft within two months.[188] Still de la Motte failed to return to the continent and so the synod requested that he should write and inform the synod of his reasons.[189] There is no record of his reply.

However in 1604 Timothée Blier was appointed to serve as the minister in Southampton '*a cause de l'infirmité de Mons' De La Motte*'.[190] Although de la Motte's illness was presumably serious, he appears to have recovered; he did not die until 1617. In fact his youngest child, Mathieu, was not baptised until April 1608.[191] Indeed it is possible that de la Motte may have resumed his ministry in Southampton because the entries in the *Registre* between June and November 1606 are once more in de la Motte's hand.[192]

Although, according to the family tradition, de la Motte had been apprenticed as a silkman, there is no evidence as to when he became involved in the cloth industry in Southampton. The 'stall & art' lists recorded the non-burgesses who traded within the town. Although one 'Philip lamote' was recorded in 1587 he made no payment. His name does not reappear in the lists until 1602, when the entry has been crossed through. De la Motte was however certainly trading by 1602 because he was fined in that year for incorrect weights and measures.[193] From 1604 onwards his 'stall & art' payments gradually increased: 1604, nil; 1611, 2s; 1613, 2s 6d; 1615, 5s.[194] De la Motte's name also began to appear in the Court Leet records: in 1604 he was presented for selling his goods retail and in 1615 because either he or his servants had thrown refuse over the town walls.[195] His wife, Judith de la Motte, was actively

[185] *Actes des Colloques*, pp. 37–38.
[186] *Livre Synodal*, I, p. 167.
[187] *Livre Synodal*, I, p. 175.
[188] *Livre Synodal*, I, p. 178.
[189] *Livre Synodal*, I, p. 179.
[190] *Actes des Colloques*, p. 47.
[191] *Registre*, pp. 55, 111–12.
[192] PRO, RG4/4600, ff. 19v, 42–42v, 79, 92.
[193] SRO, SC6/1/26–27. Other weights and measures offences were recorded in following years. SC6/1/30–32.
[194] SRO, SC6/1/19, SC6/1/28, SC6/1/31–32.
[195] *Court Leet Records*, pp. 413–14, 480.

involved in the trade and could have been his partner; they were both named in an apprenticeship agreement in 1611.[196] When Philippe drew up his will in May 1615 he commented 'I desire my wiffe to keepe her trade' and it seems that by that date, Judith de la Motte was established as one of the clothiers in the town.[197] She certainly continued to dominate the trade after her husband's death.

The late date of the surviving evidence for de la Motte's business is intriguing. It could be that earlier references just have not survived. The only early link between de la Motte and the cloth trade is a letter written by the minister and the consistory over contributions in 1589, which does not necessarily imply that de la Motte himself was a clothier at that date. Most of the surviving evidence appears to date from the early seventeenth century and in particular from after the date at which de la Motte retired from the ministry due to ill-health. It is possible that de la Motte may have been forced to become involved in the cloth trade because he could no longer exist on his minister's salary. Certainly ministers in other refugee communities such as Canterbury were beginning to experience financial difficulties.[198] It is also interesting to note that one Southampton cleric, Simon Pett, combined being the minister of Holy Rood and St. Michael's churches with being involved in the cloth trade.[199]

De la Motte appears to have become a respected member of the town and in 1608 became a denizen.[200] The family lived at West Hall, a substantial property in Southampton, and had the funds and self-esteem for a portrait to be painted of the minister. Some of the bequests made to de la Motte may be a reflection of the esteem in which he was held. When he was buried on 8 May 1617 the service was attended by the entire town Corporation.[201]

The appointment of Timothée Blier as the minister of the French church emphasised a significant change which had taken place in the character of the community. Although the composition of the community had become significantly more French than Walloon after 1572, the exiled congregation continued to look to the Walloon churches for ministers and guidance. However, the third minister to serve the Southampton congregation was a Frenchman. Timothée Blier, a native of Rouen, was the son of a London merchant and elder of the French church.[202]

---

[196] *Calendar of Southampton Apprenticeship Registers*, p. 2.

[197] PRO, PCC Prob. 11/130 Philippe de la Motte; *Assembly Books*, IV, pp. 1, 3, 37.

[198] Spicer, ' "A Faythful Pastor in the Churches" ', pp. 204–5. Also see above p. 112.

[199] See above p. 113.

[200] *Letters of Denization and Acts of Naturalization for Aliens in England and Ireland, 1603–1700*, ed. W.A. Shaw, (HSQS, 18, 1911), p. 12.

[201] *Registre*, pp. 111–12.

[202] The variations in the spelling of Blier and the presence of several people with the same name means that it is difficult to discover for how long Jacques Blier had been resident in London. He was probably the Jeames Blear who appeared in the 1599 lay subsidy return with his wife and daughters, Mary and Jane Blear (these names also appear in his will) who paid the poll contribution of 2s 8d. Jacques Bellier, a native of Rouen, had been elected as an elder of the French Church in July 1598. French Protestant Church of London Archives, Soho Square, AD/MS 4, p. 306; PRO, PCC Prob. 11/102 Jacques Blier; *Returns of Aliens*, III, p. 55.

Blier matriculated as a pensioner at Emmanuel College, Cambridge on 21 October 1599, a college which had been established in 1585 to train men for the ministry of the Church of England.[203] Initially the costs of his education were borne by the Threadneedle Street Church but the London consistory only viewed this as being a temporary measure. Pledges of financial support for Blier and another student, Daniel Tuvel, were made in July 1601 by the communities at Norwich (£10), Canterbury (£12), Southampton (£7 11s), and £3 from Jacques Blier, which were to be paid over two years.[204] In 1603, the London church resigned their rights to Timothée Blier, on condition that the three other French churches should pay for his maintenance until he was fit to serve a church. These churches would then decide where he could be employed to the best advantage.[205]

On 24 May 1604, Timothée Blier was confirmed and installed as the minister of the Southampton community because of Philippe de la Motte's ill-health. The colloquy agreed to allow this to continue temporarily until there was a greater need elsewhere. This did not however stop those gathered in London from sending a strongly worded letter to Southampton. The church was criticised for encouraging Blier to abandon his studies; the representatives of the Canterbury church had wanted Blier to complete his training at Montauban. Besides their failure to consult the other churches who had financed Blier's education, the Southampton church was criticised for the precipitate promotion of the minister as well as their failure to follow the correct procedures. Blier had been presented to his pulpit and a fast had been held but he had not received the imposition of hands.[206] The church was also attacked for conniving at Blier's marriage. However at this date, Blier had only expressed his intention to marry; when he did marry in July 1604 his spouse was Philippe de la Motte's sister-in-law.[207] The colloquy, in censuring the church in 1606 recognised its need for a minister and allowed Blier to continue at Southampton as a temporary measure but again attacked the church for failing to inform the other churches involved.[208] However there was little that the colloquy could do and Blier even acted as the secretary for the 1606 colloquy which censured the Southampton church, as well as at the subsequent colloquy in 1610. All the churches could do was to repeat that the appointment was only a temporary measure, no doubt especially because Philippe de la

---

[203] *Alumni Cantabrigienses. A biographical list of all known students, graduates and holders of office at the University of Cambridge, from the earliest times to 1900. Pt I From the earliest times to 1751*, compiled by J. Venn & J.A. Venn, 4 vols. (Cambridge, 1922–27), I, p. 167; C.M. Dent, *Protestant Reformers in Elizabethan Oxford*, (Oxford, 1983), pp. 152–54.

[204] French Protestant Church of London Archives, Soho Square, AD/MS 4, pp. 338, 344, 383. The accounts have survived for the house to house collections which were made in Canterbury. CDRO, U47/D.

[205] *Actes des Colloques*, p. 45.

[206] *Actes des Colloques*, pp. 47–48, 50.

[207] *Registre*, p. 92. Elisabeth des Maistres was the daughter of Balthasar des Maistres, as was Judith the wife of Phillippe de la Motte.

[208] *Actes des Colloques*, pp. 47–48.

Motte remained in Southampton until his death in 1617.[209] Eventually when it became clear that the arrangement was permanent, the colloquy decided that the Southampton church should be responsible in the future for the maintenance of the minister's widow and children if Blier's ministry continued in the town until his death.[210]

By 1610 the church was experiencing financial problems and protested their poverty to the colloquy in 1615.[211] It may have been these financial difficulties that led Timothée Blier to take up the living of the parish of Titchfield near Southampton, in 1616.[212] By this date the minister had a wife and four children to support.[213] Unfortunately there are no surviving records concerning Blier's appointment to the benefice, so it is not possible to discover whether the appointment of a Calvinist minister to an Anglican benefice aroused controversy or any debate as to the validity of his ordination. Adrian Saravia had been presented to the rectory of Tatenhill, Staffordshire, by January 1588 and does not appear to have been reordained. In fact Saravia discussed the issue of reordination in *Defensio tractationis* and concluded that reordination within the 'established' churches, i.e. the Church of England and the Protestant churches of the continent, was unnecessary. While he could attack the churches of the Channel Islands for behaving contrary to the Church of England, the refugee churches in which Blier was ordained were in fact a part of the continental Protestant church.[214] In 1620 the minister of the Italian community in London, Cesar Calandrini was presented to the rectory of Stapleford Abbots, Essex, and there were calls made at the time for his reordination. However these calls were rejected by the Bishop of Lichfield, Thomas Morton, who was prepared to accept the validity of ordination within the stranger churches.[215]

In the same year as his appointment to Titchfield, Blier received his letters of denization and went on to complete his studies at The Queen's College, Oxford (the owners of God's House, Southampton) where he received a Bachelor of Divinity degree in 1618 and bècame a Master of Arts by 1622.[216] Blier remained at Titchfield for the rest of his life, remarrying in 1624 after the death of his first wife.[217] Despite his move to Titchfield, Blier appears to have retained his links with Southampton and with the de la Motte family. In 1623 one Mary de la Motte was married at Titchfield as was 'Anne delamotte of

---

[209] *Actes des Colloques*, pp. 47, 50; *Registre*, pp. 111–12.
[210] *Actes des Colloques*, p. 53.
[211] *Actes des Colloques*, pp. 52–53, 56, 58.
[212] Nicholas Munn, the Vicar of Titchfield was buried on 26 July 1616. HRO, 37M73A PRI Titchfield, f. 321.
[213] *Registre*, pp. 54, 56, 58.
[214] Nijenhuis, *Adrianus Saravia*, pp. 110–14.
[215] Grell, *Dutch Calvinists*, pp. 63–66.
[216] *Letters of Denization and Acts of Naturalization, 1603–1700*, p. 23; *Alumni Oxonienses: The Members of the University of Oxford, 1500–1714*, ed. J. Foster, 4 vols. (Oxford, 1891), I, p. 139; HRO, 21M65, B1/31.
[217] HRO, 37M73A PRI Titchfield, pp. 413, 415; HRO, 21M65, B1/27–28, B1/31–34.

Southampton by lysonne [licence]' in May 1627.[218] Blier also kept a house in Southampton for a short while, as he made a 'scavage' payment in 1617.[219] Nor did the French Church forget their former minister, for his death in April 1649 was recorded in the *Registre*.[220]

Blier's successor in Southampton was Elie d'Arande who had assumed the post by 1619 when he represented the church at the colloquy held in Norwich. He was born in the Pays de Vaud and seems to have come from a family of ministers.[221] By 1603 he was the minister at Claye, Ile de France, according to a survey of all the French Reformed pastors, recorded at the Synod of Gap.[222] By 1607 had moved to Amiens and he served the church at Etaples from 1617.[223]

While little is known about d'Arande's ministry in Southampton, it is clear that the church at this time was divided by faction and dispute. The problems that faced the church were hinted at in a question directed to the colloquy held at Norwich, at which d'Arande acted as moderator. The church was asked for advice on how to recover the church's papers – '*Le livre de la Discipline, Les Actes des Colloques, & partie des Actes du Consistoire*' – and they were instructed to either apply the church's discipline to those who had the records or to seek assistance from the magistrates.[224] Regrettably there is little evidence about this dispute although the involvement of the town magistrates suggests that the malcontents may have left the church. The clearest evidence of problems within the church comes from the will which d'Arande wrote in 1624. Although he did not die until 1633, he was excused from attending the colloquy held in 1625 on health grounds.[225] The extent of the minister's frustrations and disillusionment are evident in the will, whose preface merits quotation *in extenso*:

> I doe alsoe protest in a good conscience and before god, that I have forced myselfe accordinge to my full power, to behave myselfe as a faythful pastor in the churches, where God hath binne pleased to be served by my ministry, as well by giveinge a pure and faythfull declaration of the Councell of God towards men for theire salvation as for the observinge of all the other dewties which doe binde those of our callinge to be faythfull laborers in the worde of the Lorde Our God. Itt is true that I have not seene soe much fruite of my ministry as I desired, nor such reste and advauncement of the said churches as I wished by the blessing of God uppon my faithfull labours, in regarde of the malignity of certaine personnes which perticularly in this

---

[218] HRO, 37M73A PRI Titchfield, p. 451.
[219] SRO, SC5/17/26.
[220] *Registre*, p. 115.
[221] HRO, Wills 1634/B/12; E. Haag & E. Haag, (ed.), *La France Protestante*, Second edition, 6 vols. (Paris, 1877–88), V, col. 105–6.
[222] Quick, *Synodicon in Gallia Reformata*, I, p. 251.
[223] Haag, *La France Protestante*, Second edition, V, col. 105.
[224] *Actes des Colloques*, p. 59.
[225] *Actes des Colloques*, p. 66.

ffrench church of Southampton have served as Instruments to the greate adversary to hinder the same. Itt is alsoe true that my imperfections may have binne in parte cause and perticularly in the defecte which I have allwaies perceaved in my selfe of sufficient science, ardur, prudence, constancy or wante of courage againste the difficultys and force of the maliciious and vigilency and dexterity to breake the bad dessignes of the perverse.

And as for the Offences which many and dyvers personnes have committed against me either through ignorance or mallice particularly in this ffrench church of Sowthampton wherein many which doe boaste themselves to bee the cheefest and mostlie apparente to have pretexte and couver for their damnable Avarice, envy, hatred of piety, ingratitude and malignity have layd to my charge stronge impudente secrete affrontinge and perverse calumniations and have troubled me by falce and secrete practices and have offended God in divers waies moste cruelly in my personne, I doe alsoe proteste in a good conscience that I doe forgive them.[226]

The church was in a wretched state by the time of d'Arande's death in 1633, there even seems to have been some doubt as to whether or not a minister would be appointed to replace him.[227] Even an influx of refugees from the Ile de Ré in 1628 could not restore the community's fortunes.[228] In 1635 the church was investigated by Archbishop Laud's commissary, Sir Nathaniel Brent. He discovered that there were fifteen heads of families (an estimated thirty-six members) and only the heads of six of these families were born overseas. As a result the remaining families were ordered by Archbishop Laud to attend the parish churches. The Southampton church was too weak to resist for long and within four months had submitted to the Archbishop.[229] D'Arande's replacement, Daniel Sauvage, served the church until his death in 1655 but the church faced increasing financial problems and the minister was notorious for his drunkenness.[230] The church also regularly pleaded their poverty to the meetings of the colloquies of the French churches.[231] The church's decline continued until the arrival of refugees from Louis XIV's France, from the 1660s onwards, revived in the church's fortunes.

It is difficult to assess the extent to which the French church exerted any influence upon the town's religious life or even served as a model for reform. Links were forged between the parish clergy and the French ministers, largely

---

[226] HRO, Wills 1634/B/12.
[227] HRO, Wills 1637/B/13.
[228] *Registre*, p. 35.
[229] PRO, SP16/291/66. On the conflict between the exile churches and Archbishop Laud, see de Schickler, *Les Eglises du Refuge*, II, pp. 3–63.
[230] Cambridge University Library, MSS Dd 3 64 ³⁷. Letter to the Archbishop of Canterbury from Daniel Sauvage; *Registre*, p. 115; Hessels, *Ecclesiae Londino-Batavae Archivum*, III, pp. 1986–88; *A Calendar of the Letter Books of the French Church of London from the Civil War to the Restoration, 1643–1659*, ed. R.D. Gwynn, (HSQS, 54, 1979), pp. 44, 52.
[231] *Actes des Colloques*, pp. 72, 82, 96, 116; *Calendar of the Letter Books of the French Church*, pp. 43, 76, 79.

through necessity. The churches all shared the town's cemetery for example. After Walerand Thevelin's death in 1584, the elders and deacons of the church could continue to organise fasts but the Lord's Supper fell into abeyance.[232] However the necessary services of baptism and marriage still needed to be conducted. The community seems to have relied upon the minister of Holy Rood, Henry Hopkins to baptise several infants and to conduct the marriage of a couple who were married outside the French church in January, 1585.[233] Hopkins appears to have held Reformed or Puritan ideas and so may have been sympathetic towards the French church. This sympathy does not appear to have extended as far as being admitted to the Lord's Supper or even making a bequest to the poor of the church. This was also the case with the town preacher, Thomas Hitchcock.[234]

As we have seen a very few Englishmen became members of the French church,[235] although others may have attended services without becoming members of the church. Some of these people may have been amongst those who made bequests to the French church; there are certainly several bequests from people whose association with the church is unclear.[236] Similar links between the churches and people of Reformed opinions developed in London.[237] The influence of the church was however inevitably linked with the character and abilities of the minister, the fractious d'Arande and drunken Sauvage were unlikely to command the same influence as the respected Philippe de la Motte.

As the refugees became integrated into their host community, the church increasingly became an anachronism. It ceased to serve the needs of a refugee community distinct from their hosts through religion, language and experience of exile. However the church, as an institution, survived to serve the needs of French Protestants in the late seventeenth century and eighteenth century.

---

[232] *Registre*, pp. 19, 127.
[233] *Registre*, pp. 46, 88.
[234] HRO, Wills 1600/B/26, 1612/Ad/51.
[235] See above pp. 20–21.
[236] PRO, PCC Prob. 11/72 Robert Bulbeck, Prob. 11/129 William Linche; HRO, Wills 1618/A/18.
[237] Collinson, 'The Elizabethan Puritans and the Foreign Reformed Churches', pp. 262–63, 269–70; Pettegree, *Foreign Protestant Communities*, pp. 212, 273–75.

CHAPTER SEVEN

THE REFUGEE COMMUNITY AND EVENTS ON THE CONTINENT

The refugees who settled in Southampton did not turn their backs on the continuing struggle of the Calvinist churches on the continent; as some of the original settlers were actively involved in the Troubles of 1566 in the Low Countries, this is scarcely surprising.[1] Furthermore the continual arrival of new refugees, especially during the early years of the community, served as a constant reminder of the difficulties faced by the Reformed church on the continent. The community's concern was expressed through the fasts and collections held by the French church, while some individual members also took an active role in events overseas.

Fasting provided the clearest demonstration of the community's support for their co-religionists. The initial fasts held in Southampton were the result of local concerns and initiatives, but gradually the Threadneedle Street Church took over responsibility for organising fasts in all of the French-speaking churches. Initially there were two fasts a year in Southampton (four fasts were held in 1574); gradually they became annual fasts and declined further in the early seventeenth century. No fasts were celebrated in 1602 and 1603, none between 1606 and 1614.[2] This decline indicates the gradual integration of the stranger communities and a consequent lessening in their interest in overseas affairs.

The reason for each fast was carefully recorded in the *Registre*. A fast was held on 25 September 1572 to commemorate events both in the Netherlands and in France. On that occasion the refugees celebrated Orange's invasion of the Netherlands from Germany, which it was hoped would deliver the country and its churches from the cruel tyrant, the Duke of Alva. Orange had crossed the Maas on 27 August 1572 and invaded Brabant. However Orange's initial success in the Netherlands was overshadowed by the Massacre of Saint Bartholomew's Day in France. The community prayed for deliverance for the Reformed of France after the Massacre of 'between twelve and thirteen thousand nobles and faithful', the pillaging of their goods and the suppression of preaching.[3] The daily arrival of refugees from France made the exile communities even more keenly aware of the plight of their co-religionists.

While events in France were not ignored, the reasons given for celebrating fasts in the period before 1589 were primarily concerned with events in the

---

[1] See above pp. 9–14.
[2] *Registre*, pp. 125–31; Spicer, 'The French-speaking Reformed community', pp. 282–92.
[3] *Registre*, p. 125; Spicer, 'The French-speaking Reformed community', p. 282.

Netherlands. For example in January 1582, the church prayed as Parma launched his campaign on Flanders and Brabant after having taken Tournai. The eventual fall of Dunkirk, Nieuwpoort, Veurne, Diksmuide and Bergues in July and August 1583, and then Antwerp in August 1585, also prompted the community to pray and fast. The community had also fasted in August 1576 for an improvement in relations between the Queen and Orange, which at that time had reached a low point due to the disruption of English trade by Zealand privateers.[4]

Between 1589 and 1599 the community's attention was held by events in Northern France which became the new theatre of war following the assassination of Henry III. The situation in the Netherlands improved as Parma's forces were diverted to France and as the northern provinces gradually strengthened their position against Spain. This interest in France was no doubt increased by English involvement in the conflict between Navarre and the Catholic League, in particular in the Rouen and Brittany campaigns. In November 1591, the community fasted and prayed at the start of the siege of Rouen; they prayed again in April 1592 for God's help as the siege was raised due to 'les adversaires de l'Eglise et de l'estat de France'.[5]

The focus for the fasts reverted to the Low Countries after 1599. The community fasted in July 1601 when Ostend was besieged by the Archduke; when the siege was raised in May 1604, the Southampton community fasted again.[6] The refugee community was also aware of the religious disputes in the United Provinces and the community fasted in 1617 and 1618 over these difficulties and again in 1620 after the Synod of Dort.[7]

Fasts were not solely concerned with events overseas; the community was prompted to fast and pray concerning English interests. In 1579 they fasted about the confusion caused by the arrival of the Duc d'Alençon and the negotiations concerning his marriage to the Queen. In 1589 they prayed for God's blessing on the expedition sent to Portugal. English intervention in Ireland also moved the community to fast and pray in 1597 and 1599.[8]

Issues of much more local concern also led the community to fast. The community fasted in February 1604 because of the outbreak of plague; although the first deaths due to plague in the French community do not seem to have been until June. A further fast was held in July 1604. Other outbreaks of plague in Southampton but also in London led the community to fast.[9] The community was also prompted to fast 'pour prier dieu Nous Garder Contre les

---

[4] Registre, pp. 126, 127; Spicer, 'The French-speaking Reformed community', pp. 283, 286, 287.

[5] Registre, p. 129; Spicer, 'The French-speaking Reformed community, p. 289.

[6] Registre, p. 130; Spicer, 'The French-speaking Reformed community', pp. 290, 291.

[7] Registre, p. 131; Spicer, 'The French-speaking Reformed community', p. 292.

[8] Registre, pp. 126–27, 128, 129; Spicer, 'The French-speaking Reformed community', pp. 285, 288, 289, 290.

[9] Registre, pp. 107–10, 130–31; Spicer, 'The French-speaking Reformed community', pp. 290, 291.

effects des signes de son ire de quoy avons esté menaché en la Commette'. Although the comet was first observed by the community on 8 October 1580, it is surprising that the fast was not held until 6 April 1581.[10]

Besides these fasts the refugees on three occasions held services of thanksgiving. The first such service was held on 3 December 1587 and celebrated the victory of Henry of Navarre at the battle of Coutras in which the King's forces were destroyed and the royalist commander the Duc de Joyeuse killed. The battle brought to an end the War of the Three Henries.[11] The second service of thanksgiving, in November 1588, celebrated the defeat of the Spanish Armada and therefore the overthrow of the plan for the conquest and the restoration of Papal tyranny. The final service, relating to foreign affairs, was held on 20 March 1590 when the community celebrated the rout of the League forces by Navarre at the battle of Ivry.[12]

Besides these public manifestations of their concern for events overseas, the French Church also responded to appeals from the continental Walloon churches. These looked to the refugee churches for funds for the maintenance of the ministry, for the training of new ministers; some continental churches even attempted to secure the services of refugee ministers, such as Philippe de la Motte.[13] Some of these appeals for assistance were directed through the French Church in London. There are occasional references to Southampton responding to these appeals: £3 was sent for the relief of the poor refugees at Wesel in November 1571.[14]

Appeals to the exile churches were not however confined to raising money for the continental churches. The refugees and other exile churches found themselves subject to repeated demands for assistance, from William of Orange, for the rebel cause in the Low Countries.[15] In the Spring of 1573 Orange sent the minister Lieven Calwaert to raise money for military operations. Calwaert was probably in touch with Orange's former army chaplain, Adrian Saravia, in Southampton, for the Prince subsequently wrote to Saravia thanking him for his assistance and urging him to continue to further the rebel cause. He also expressed disappointment that an earlier collection at Southampton and Rye had only raised £10.[16] In 1582 and 1589 appeals for help

---

[10]   *Registre*, p. 127; Spicer, 'The French-speaking Reformed community', p. 286; D.K. Yeomans, *Comets. A Chronological History of Observation, Science, Myth and Folklore*, (New York, 1991), p. 415.

[11]   *Registre*, p. 128; Salmon, *Society in Crisis*, p. 241.

[12]   *Registre*, p. 128; Salmon, *Society in Crisis*, pp. 259, 260.

[13]   See above pp. 119–20; Spicer, ' "A Faythful Pastor in the Churches" ', pp. 202–3.

[14]   *Livre Synodal*, I, p. 69; *Actes du Consistoire*, II, pp. 36, 57.

[15]   For example, 8 June 1572: William, Prince of Orange to the Foreign Churches in England. Hessels, *Ecclesiae Londino-Batavae Archivum*, II, pp. 412–19.

[16]   Nijenhuis, *Adrianus Saravia*, pp. 38, 270. In Orange's letter to Saravia, he refers to 'Santone' which Nijenhuis has identified as Sandown. This is in fact a corruption of Southampton or S. Hampton, which appears frequently in the French archives of this time as 'anthone' or 'antone'.

were made by Geneva. The Southampton community does not appear to have contributed to the initial appeal.[17] However in 1589 the seizure of Gex by Savoy and the coalition of Catholic powers prompted the city authorities to send another agent to raise money and the money raised made an inportant contribution to the city's finances.[18] The Southampton congregation appears to have contributed this time because the consistory, in a letter written late in 1589, claimed that 'having of late exhibited for the state of the Church of Geneva wherby we be quit soked of all substannce'.[19]

Southampton was not well situated for operations on the continent such as the prison-breaking raids organised by some of the other exile churches.[20] Leading figures within the Sandwich community helped to plan the public Reformed service held at Boeschepe in July 1562 and in 1567–68, the Sandwich, Norwich and London congregations co-ordinated and financed the activities of the Wood Beggars in the Westkwartier of Flanders.[21] Evidence of assistance from the Southampton community is fragmentary. In July 1568 Philip II's ambassador Guzman de Silva noted that 'many persons with arms were still being allowed to leave ... Many of these rebels are now making ready in London, Norwich, Sandwich and Southampton, and other places'.[22] In 1572 with the seizure of Den Briel and Flushing appeals for men and funds were made to the exile communities. The Orangist commissioner sent to Veere by the Governor of Walcheren, travelled to Norwich where the Dutch community contributed 125 soldiers who were despatched to the town. The London church raised £1,400 to equip 200 soldiers while some richer members of the congregation equipped further soldiers or provided money for ammunition to be sent to Flushing.[23] There is no evidence of appeals being directed to Southampton from Flushing, but one of Alva's spies reported on 30 August 1572 that four ships with supplies had left the Isle of Wight and Southampton area, implying that they were heading for the Low Countries.[24] Furthermore Adrian Saravia appears to have briefly served as a minister at

---

[17] *Registres de la Compagnie des Pasteurs de Genève*, ed. J-F. Bergier *et al.*, (Geneva, 1962–), IV, p. 214, V, p. 259.

[18] *Registres de la Compagnie des Pasteurs*, VI, pp. 155–57; E.W. Monter, *Studies in Genevan Government (1536–1605)*, (Geneva, 1964), pp. 40, 46.

[19] SRO, TC Box 1/40. The letter is undated but it was written to the Mayor Peter Stoner who was only appointed at Michaelmas 1589 and had died by January 1590.

[20] Pettegree, *Foreign Protestant Communities*, pp. 239–41.

[21] See M.F. Backhouse, 'The Official Start of Armed Resistance in the Low Countries: Boeschepe, 12 July 1562', *Archiv für Reformationsgeschichte*, 71 (1980), 198–226; M.F. Backhouse, 'Guerilla War and Banditry in the Sixteenth Century: the Wood Beggars in the Westkwartier of Flanders (1567–1568)', *Archiv für Reformationsgeschichte*, 74 (1983), 232–56.

[22] *Calendar of Letters and State Papers Relating to English Affairs, preserved principally in the Archives of Simancas, of the reign of Elizabeth*, ed. M.A.S. Hume, 4 vols. (London, 1864), 1568–79, p. 53.

[23] P. Bor, *Oorsprongk, begin, en vervolgh der Nederlandsche oorlogen*, 4 vols. (Amsterdam, 1679–84), I, p. 371; Pettegree, *Foreign Protestant Communities*, p. 254.

[24] *Calendar of Letters and Papers*, 1568–79, p. 407.

Flushing in 1572, as he later appealed for payment for his services. Could Saravia be one of the four ministers whom 'Casimbrot' recruited to preach in Holland? Saravia had been Orange's army chaplain and later spoke well of Leonard de Casembroot whom the Prince had appointed as Councillor in the Court of Holland.[25]

While evidence about the contacts between the Southampton community and the rebels in the Low Countries is sparse, rather more information can be gleaned from the links between the community and the privateers operating off the Hampshire coast. The Huguenot privateers sailed with letters of marque from the Queen of Navarre while the Sea Beggars were nominally under the authority of William the Silent, in his capacity as sovereign Prince of Orange. A survey of the state of shipping on the South coast made in 1570 reveals that at Meadhole on the Isle of Wight there were 'x sayle of shipps well trymed in warlicke order and aborde them as I can lerne CCC of their nations as well Marriners as others' and that the French captains were serving under the Queen of Navarre. At Portsmouth, an important Sea Beggar base, there were six ships from Emden and one from Zealand; the majority of the Sea Beggar captains came from the coastal provinces of Holland, Friesland, Zealand and Groningen.[26] Meadhole on the Isle of Wight had, since the Middle Ages, been a centre for piracy and in the sixteenth century people were attracted from a wide area to buy prize goods there. In 1570 the cargo of the *Flying Dragon* attracted merchants from London, Bristol and Southampton as well as people from the smaller towns of Hampshire, Sussex and Kent.[27]

Privateering flourished in this area because of the connivance of the local officeholders and the attitude of the local magnates. This was most clearly demonstrated in 1568 when the Spanish treasure ships sailing to the Netherlands were forced to seek protection in English waters from Huguenot privateers. One of these ships sought protection at Calshot Castle but after being attacked possibly by pirates in league with the Captain of the Castle, James Parkinson, it moved on to Southampton where the ship's captain suggested that his cargo of bullion should be unloaded for its better protection.[28] It has been suggested that both Sir Anthony Champernowne, the Vice-Admiral of Devon, and Sir Edward Horsey, the Captain of the Isle of Wight, were prepared to assist in the Huguenot seizure of bullion with a proportion of the

[25] *Calendar of Letters and Papers*, 1568–79, p. 407; *Actes du Consistoire, II*, p. 96; Nijenhuis, *Adrianus Saravia*, pp. 32–33, 127.

[26] PRO, SP12/71/54, SP12/71/57; M.J. French, 'Privateering and the Revolt of the Netherlands: The *Watergeuzen* or Sea Beggars in Portsmouth, Gosport and the Isle of Wight 1570–71', *PHFC*, 47 (1991), 171–80.

[27] Crawford, 'Mead Hole and Shoesflete', 112–15; B. Dietz, 'Privateering in North Western European Waters, 1568–1572', (unpublished Ph.D. thesis, University of London, 1959), p. 328.

[28] C. Read, 'Queen Elizabeth's seizure of the Duke of Alva's pay-ships', *Journal of Modern History*, 5 (1933), 445; Ramsay, *The Queen's Merchants*, p. 93; *Examinations and Depositions, 1570–1594*, pp. 7–8.

prize going to the crown, rather than allow it to continue to the Netherlands.[29] While Horsey later denied helping the Huguenot privateers and the Sea Beggar fleet, he was to be employed in France and the Low Countries in support of the Protestant cause.[30] Besides Horsey and Champernowne there were other important supporters of the Huguenot cause in the area. Robert Horne, the Bishop of Winchester, together with the Bishop of London petitioned the Queen in 1573 to help Orange and Montgommery and raised money for their cause. In fact the Queen sent Horne's nephew on a secret mission in November 1572 with letters to the Duke of Saxony, the Elector Palatine and the Marquis of Brandenburg.[31]

At the more local level, Southampton merchants such as Peter Stoner, Michael Knight and Arthur Pitt were involved in the purchase of prize goods at Meadhole.[32] Pitt was the owner and captain of the *Ash of Southampton*, a ship licensed by the Huguenots, which with another ship took wines from the *Bien Allant* in 1569 which were subsequently landed in Southampton.[33] The 'inhabytants of Newporte greately favor, receyve, maynetayne, and succour the sea Rovers, whiche then laye in Mede Hole' and the captains daily came to the town. Some of the Sea Beggars also went to Southampton. In fact a certain Sneek, one of de Lumbres' captains, stayed in the town when he was sick, and there are other instances of privateers coming to the town.[34]

Several prominent Huguenots such as the Comte de Montgommery passed through Southampton. Montgommery, a leading Huguenot noble, had fled to the Channel Islands after the Massacre of St. Bartholomew's Day. Although Montgommery failed to obtain support from the Queen, in April 1573 he organised a fleet for the relief of La Rochelle and in March 1574 used Jersey as a base for his attack upon Normandy. During this campaign, Montgommery was captured by the royalist forces after the fall of Domfront and taken to Paris where he was executed on 26 June 1574.[35] In December 1573 Montgommery had been in London and he seems to have travelled there via the Isle of Wight.[36] He may have passed through Southampton because there

[29] Ramsay, *The Queen's Merchants*, p. 94.
[30] French, 'Privateering and the Revolt of the Netherlands', 177; Hasler, *The History of Parliament*, II, p. 339.
[31] *Calendar of Letters and State Papers*, 1568–79, pp. 446, 468.
[32] PRO, HCA 13/18, ff. 281v–85.
[33] PRO, HCA 13/17, ff. 1–2; Dietz, 'Privateering in North Western European Waters', pp. 402, 438.
[34] PRO, HCA 13/18, ff. 269, 378. Also see below p. 135. It is possible that Sneek may have been one Claes Snick of Amsterdam. J.C.A. de Meij, *De Watergeuzen en de Nederlanden 1568–1572*, (Amsterdam-London, 1972), p. 326.
[35] E. Haag & E. Haag, (ed.), *La France Protestante*, First edition, 10 vols. (Paris, 1846–58), VII, pp. 471–80; A. Landurant, *Montgommery le régicide*, (Paris, 1988), pp. 200–27; de Schickler, *Les Eglises du Refuge*, II, pp. 386–88; W.T. MacCaffrey, *Queen Elizabeth and the Making of Policy, 1572–1588*, (Princeton, 1981), pp. 177, 180, 188; M. Cauvin, 'Dernière Expédition de Montgomery dans le Cotentin (1574)', *BSHPF*, 104 (1958), 201–7.
[36] Landurant, *Montgommery*, p. 215.

is a reference in the Mayor's Account Book to the provision of wine for the 'Counte Montagomerie'.[37] Montgommery's widow and her entourage were admitted to the Lord's Supper in 1575.[38]

In October 1570 Odet de Coligny, the Cardinal de Châtillon and brother of Gaspard de Coligny, stayed briefly in Southampton, intending to sail from there to La Rochelle. He was a leading Huguenot and actively lobbied on their behalf at the English court. He was also responsible for the operations of the Huguenot privateers in the Channel as well as equipping ships and collecting the prize dues from the captains.[39] There is no evidence in the *Registre* of any direct contact between the Cardinal and the French church in the town but then his stay did not coincide with a celebration of the Lord's Supper.[40] The town authorities did however take the opportunity of granting him the freedom of the town.[41] In a letter written from the town the Cardinal expressed his gratitude for the assistance of the Marian exile, Henry Kingsmill, who had served him as a diplomatic attaché.[42] Châtillon retained contact with the privateers through English and French agents, one of whom was a certain Jean Ferey. A merchant from Le Havre who was commissioned by Châtillon to collect prize revenues, Jean Ferey may be tentatively identified with the 'Jean Feré' admitted to the Lord's Supper in July 1570.[43]

The leading Huguenot privateer Jacques de Sores was also admitted to the Lord's Supper in Southampton in October 1573. He had fled with his family and servants to England in October 1568, arriving at Rye. Châtillon requested that de Sores be provided with ships, and this resulted in de Sores being backed by the Champernowne-Hawkins interest. He had been appointed by the Prince of Navarre as the *Lieutenant-général en mer*, heading the *armée marine* operating from La Rochelle in July 1569. He was active in the Channel and the Atlantic during the third of the French Wars of Religion. He fled to England after the St. Bartholomew's Day Massacre and on his return to La Rochelle was appointed the commander of Montgommery's fleet. At the end of September 1572 with another privateer he 'brought into the Isle of Wight four prizes, two hulks, one loaded with salt, and the other with tar, one Portuguese ship with

---

[37] SRO, SC5/3/1, f. 144.
[38] *Registre*, p. 11.
[39] Dietz, 'Privateering in North Western European Waters', pp. 57–58.
[40] Châtillon seems to have arrived in Southampton about 9 October 1570 and the Lord's Supper had been celebrated by the church on 1 October. E.G. Atkinson, 'The Cardinal of Châtillon in England, 1568–1571', *HSP*, 3 (1889–91), 244–45; *Registre*, p. 6.
[41] SRO, SC3/1/1, f. 85.
[42] Henry Kingsmill was a member of the family favoured by Bishop Horne as he developed a Protestant faction in Hampshire. Garrett, *The Marian Exiles*, p. 208; Fritze, 'The role of the family and religion', 267–87.
[43] Dietz, 'Privateering in North Western European Waters', pp. 58–59; Atkinson, 'The Cardinal of Châtillon', 288; *Registre*, p. 6.

fish ... and another little French boat with Brazil-wood'.[44] His connections with the Southampton church have previously been overlooked.[45]

It is difficult to discover the attitude of the French church in Southampton towards the Huguenot privateers. As a rule the unpredictable attitude of the Queen towards the Huguenot privateers and the Sea Beggars obliged the exile churches to tread carefully. It may however be significant that Jacques de Sores was admitted to Communion in Southampton whereas at Canterbury a certain Pierre du Brusle was suspended from the Lord's Supper for actions in the Netherlands 'akin to brigandage'. Certainly the church at Emden excluded from communion members of the congregation who were associated with the lawless Sea Beggars operating from bases in East Friesland.[46]

By its very nature, information concerning privateering is scarce but the protracted dispute involving Jean de Beaulieu, which began before the High Court of Admiralty in 1571, sheds some light on the links between the Sea Beggars and the refugee community in Southampton. The dispute before the High Court concerned four barrels of cochineal, belonging to the Spinolas, which had been loaded in Cadiz on a ship bound for Antwerp. The *Flying Dragon* was, however, intercepted by the Sea Beggars and taken by de Lumbres, the Sea Beggars' Admiral, to Meadhole for the sale of its cargo. The Privy Council granted a commission to Philip van Asselier to purchase the goods from the *Flying Dragon*. Asselier had 'full power and aucthoritie from the owners of certein spices and merchaundizes that of late was taken in a Flemishe shippe by one Lumbrey'.[47] The goods from this ship were to remain at Meadhole until Asselier arrived. De Beaulieu claimed to have been acting as an agent for Asselier and had bought 730 bags of 'smake'[match?] which bore a friend's mark. It was alleged that the missing four barrels of cochineal, later valued at £360, were taken from the *Flying Dragon* by Jean de Beaulieu in a boat during the night and were sold in Southampton.[48]

[44] Hardy, 'Foreign Refugees at Rye', 414; Dietz, 'Privateering in North Western European Waters', pp. 432–33; B. Dietz, 'The Huguenot and English Corsairs during the Third Civil War in France, 1568 to 1570', *HSP*, 19 (1952–58), 283, 289–93; *Calendar of Letters and State Papers*, 1568–79, p. 422.

[45] *Registre*, pp. 7, 9, 41, 101. Another possible privateer was Capitaine Jacques Maillart who fled to Southampton after the Massacres of 1572 with his fiancé Anne Berot. They were married in March 1573. He could be tentatively identified with the Captain Maillard who had been detained in the Channel in 1570. A 'Monsr. le Cap. de Caré' who was admitted at the same time as de Sores may also have been another Huguenot privateer. *Registre*, pp. 8, 9, 85; Dietz, 'Privateering in North Western European Waters', p. 400.

[46] Cross, *History of the Walloon & Huguenot Church at Canterbury*, p. 67; A. Pettegree, *Emden and the Dutch Revolt. Exile and the Development of Reformed Protantism*, (Oxford, 1992), pp. 163–64.

[47] *Acts of the Privy Council*, 1571–75, pp. 17–18.

[48] PRO, HCA 13/18, ff. 265v, 266v, 13/19, ff. 32v–34, 58–74v; *Select Pleas in the Court of Admiralty, Vol.II High Court of Admiralty (A.D. 1547–1602)*, ed. R.G. Marsden, (Selden Society, 11, 1897), p. 148.

The depositions in the case throw light on de Beaulieu's links with the privateers. De Beaulieu had become acquainted with several of the captains both at Meadhole and in Southampton. This had included contacts with a Captain Jolye (possibly Clément Jolly), Jacques Hennebert and Captain Landay.[49] De Beaulieu seems to have had particularly close links with the commander of the Sea Beggars, Admiral de Lumbres. De Beaulieu and de Lumbres appear to have met frequently on board ship off the Isle of Wight, and de Lumbres visited de Beaulieu's lodgings in Southampton where they 'both made merry' on several occasions.[50]

De Beaulieu was reputed to have supplied the Sea Beggar ships. According to one testimony, which was however disputed, de Beaulieu had provided de Lumbres with '12 tonnes of beer, 2 tonnes of flesh and certen bread' which was distributed between the *Flying Dragon* and de Lumbres' ship *The Raven*. Another witness, whose testimony was also challenged, claimed that de Beaulieu had provided money for members of de Lumbres' company in Southampton on several occasions. Nor was de Beaulieu the only member of the French congregation to assist the Sea Beggars, for de Lumbres employed Roland Petit from Tournai to purchase clothing and necessities for members of the company.[51]

The good relations between de Beaulieu and the Sea Beggar captains probably enabled him to act as an intermediary between the privateers and the owners of the seized cargoes. It was a profitable enterprise. On one occasion de Beaulieu and another advanced the 1,700 thalers required by three shipowners to redeem their vessels from Jacques Hennebert. He then held the ships as security until the capital sum was repaid over a two month period.[52]

Contacts between the Sea Beggars and de Beaulieu continued after the autumn of 1571 when Lumey van der Marck replaced de Lumbres as Admiral. De Beaulieu appears to have provided substantial financial support to the Sea Beggars. On 24 October 1571 de Beaulieu received a promissory note for £100 signed by Lumey and eleven other leading Sea Beggar captains.[53] Since £150 to £300 was reckoned sufficient to keep a ship of between 100 and 300 tons at sea for three months with a crew of fifty to ninety men, the amount

---

[49] PRO, HCA 13/18, f. 265, 13/19, f. 62. Clément Jolly was a prominent member of the Huguenot fleet at the Isle of Wight. Jacques Hennebert of Tournai, and Arnaud de Landres jhr., sieur de Fiennes, of Hainaut were both recorded as Sea Beggar captains between 1571 and April 1572. Dietz, 'Privateering in North Western European Waters', pp. 399, 418, 419, 428; de Meij, *De Watergeuzen*, p. 315.

[50] PRO, HCA 13/18, f. 265.

[51] PRO, HCA 13/18, ff. 265v, 266v, 13/19, ff. 68–68v, 73.

[52] Dietz, 'Privateering in North Western European Waters', p. 331.

[53] The promissory note was signed by Willem van der Marck (Lumey), Bartholt Enkens van Mentheda, Joriaen Wybrantss., Egbert Wybrantss., Hans Lodewycx, Jan Claess. Spiegel, Willem van Treslong Bloys, Gorddert van Wilts, Peter van Greycken, Scholt van Sparendam, kapitein Meynert Friess., Adries van Nieukercken. SA, Verzameling 'Autographes', nr. 18 f. 67. I am grateful to Dr. G. Marnef for supplying me with a photocopy of the original document.

lent by de Beaulieu was significant.[54] Furthermore, when Charles de Beaulieu, the brother of Jean, and himself an active supporter and agent of Orange in the Netherlands, attempted to recover the money, which his brother had lent, from the States of Zealand, he claimed that Jean de Beaulieu's loan had enabled Lumey to seize Den Briel.[55] There may have been some truth in this. In the autumn of 1571 Lumey was apparently preparing an attack on Den Briel and was at that time absent from the Sea Beggar fleet in the Netherlands and was also reported as being in London.[56] The bill of October 1571 could have been drawn up in London, where de Beaulieu had lodgings and six of the signatories were known to have been just off the English coast at that time.[57] The pillaging of coastal ships greatly annoyed the Queen and in March 1572 she expelled the privateers from the realm. Lumey and sixteen ships sold prizes and obtained supplies from the Isle of Wight.[58] Then on 1 April 1572 the Sea Beggars raided Den Briel and seized the town.

The dispute between Benedict Spinola and de Beaulieu over the disappearance of the cochineal from the *Flying Dragon* resulted in a judgment being made against de Beaulieu in the High Court of Admiralty in 1572. He was ordered to return the four barrels if they still existed, if not to pay £360.[59] However the dispute between them continued in the Court of Star Chamber. De Beaulieu alleged that the witnesses that had been paid by Spinola's agents to swear in the Admiralty Court that de Beaulieu had removed the cochineal from the *Flying Dragon* while it was off the Isle of Wight. Some of the witnesses had not even been on board the ship at the time of the taking of the *Flying Dragon*. These agents even persuaded Anthony Agache, de Lumbres' secretary, to testify against de Beaulieu, and he in his turn seems to have suborned some witnesses.[60] In April 1572, two witnesses declared that they feared for their lives if they should return to the Low Countries though they had been offered letters of safe-conduct which could be procured by 'the Italians' – presumably Benedict Spinola and his associates – from François de Halewyn, Seigneur de Sweveghem.[61] This Flemish noble performed a number of services for the Brussels government and was at that time in London acting as Alva's envoy to England in the negotiations with Elizabeth concerning the seizure of the Spanish treasure ships in 1568.[62]

---

[54] K.R. Andrews, 'The Economic Aspects of Elizabethan Privateering', (unpublished Ph.D. thesis, University of London, 1951), p. 16.

[55] F. Prims, *Beelden uit den cultuurstrijd der jaren 1577–1585*, (Antwerpensia, 15e reeks), (Antwerp, 1942), p. 202.

[56] De Meij, *De Watergeuzen*, pp. 83–84.

[57] PRO, HCA 13/18, f. 317v; de Meij, *De Watergeuzen*, pp. 83–84.

[58] J.B. Black, 'Queen Elizabeth, the Sea Beggars, and the Capture of Brille, 1572', *English Historical Review*, 46 (1931), 42.

[59] *Select Pleas in the Court of Admiralty*, pp. 147–48.

[60] PRO, HCA 13/19, ff.162v–63, 171–71v, 178v, 226v; STAC 5/B102/18.

[61] PRO, STAC 5/B102/18.

[62] Ramsay, *The Queen's Merchants*, pp. 158, 162.

After four years in the Admiralty Court the dispute remained unresolved. Jean de Beaulieu appealed against the sentence of the High Court of Admiralty, having proved the false testimonies of the witnesses in the Admiralty Court and also before the Court of Star Chamber.[63] The Privy Council decided on 11 March 1574 to submit the dispute between de Beaulieu and Spinola to arbitration under the Earl of Bedford, Francis Walsingham and Sir Walter Mildmay.[64] On 31 March William of Orange wrote to the Queen about the dispute between Spinola and de Beaulieu and requested that the judgment concerning the cochineal be reversed. Spinola evidently refused to submit to arbitration in the dispute and so de Beaulieu appealed directly to the Queen.[65] The matter had still not been resolved by July 1576 when an appeal for justice in this dispute was included in a list of four requests submitted to Elizabeth by Orange and the States of the Low Countries.[66] It seems that eventually de Beaulieu was forced to reach a settlement in which he paid 200 crowns, but the dispute had caused 'great loss of property and time'. De Beaulieu's brother Charles requested that Jean be recompensed when he agreed to serve the Queen in deciphering Spanish correspondence.[67]

While the dispute between de Beaulieu and Spinola remained unresolved, de Beaulieu continued to be actively involved with the Sea Beggars. The seizure of Flushing and the island of Walcheren by the Beggars had given them control of the Scheldt and so access to Antwerp. English merchants who sent cargoes to Antwerp were obliged to stop at Flushing where they had to pay customs duties and other dues at a higher rate than elsewhere in Zealand. Cargoes could be seriously delayed at Flushing or even impounded on occasions. Privateers operated from Zealand and intercepted shipping.[68] Orange was prepared to sell licences granting safe passage to English merchants trading with the Netherlands. The proceeds from these licences were collected by a certain Robert Leeman and possibly by Jean de Beaulieu. De Beaulieu had been appointed '*Controleur*' by Orange and the councillors and governors of Zealand.[69] It is unclear whether or not de Beaulieu was resident in London or Zealand at this time. His brother, Charles de Beaulieu, seems to have been based at Calais where he also sold licences. In September 1575 he was appointed by Orange and the provisional government of Zealand to provide passports for goods imported or exported to Flanders from Calais and other French ports.[70]

[63]   PRO, SP12/90/41.
[64]   *Acts of the Privy Council*, 1574, p. 353
[65]   PRO, SP12/90/41. The document is undated but in the Calendar of State Papers it is assigned to 1572. This would seem to be too early because the document refers to Bedford, Walsingham and Mildmay as arbitrators and they were appointed in March 1574.
[66]   PRO, SP70/130/828, SP70/139/740.
[67]   PRO, SP70/133/3, SP83/12/34–35; Spicer, 'The French-speaking Reformed community', p. 247.
[68]   Ramsay, *The Queen's Merchants*, pp. 174–76, 180–81.
[69]   Smit, *Bronnen tot de geschiedenis*, II, pp. 1134–38.
[70]   J.H. Kernkamp, *De Handel op den vijand 1572–1609*, 2 vols. (Utrecht, 1913, 1934), I, p. 64.

Privateering persisted in the Southampton area into the 1590s, attracting on occasion merchants and members of the local gentry, such as Sir Henry Ughtred, and became an important element of the town's commercial life.[71] There are however few references to the continuing links between the refugee community and privateering. A certain Sohier of Rye, perhaps the brother of Mathieu Sohier, combined trading with La Rochelle and the Spanish peninsula with spying and privateering. He was given letters permitting him 'to goe to the coast of Spaine to discover there the preparacon by sea which we thought a thinge verie necessarie for manie respects'. Sohier had however abused his letters of safe-passage by attacking several French ships and then using the letters to avoid arrest.[72] In 1577 a dispute arose concerning Machuel Massicot who was described as being a Southampton merchant stranger, who had redeemed a ship together with its cargo which had been taken by privateers to St. Helen's Point off the Isle of Wight.[73] Generally the refugee merchants, in particular Jean le Mercier, were more actively involved in the purchase of prize goods and also smuggling goods from Northern France.[74]

The migration of some of the most substantial refugee merchants away from Southampton probably reduced the community's capacity to continue to be actively involved in overseas affairs. True the outbreak of hostilities between England and Spain and later English intervention in Northern France had a direct impact upon Southampton. The Mayor and Corporation found themselves pressed by central government to contribute towards expeditions and the country's defence. These expeditions were however mounted by the English government unlike the clandestine operations of the Sea Beggars. Some expeditions even started from Southampton. In 1589 troops embarked from Southampton for the ill-fated Portuguese expedition and also for Willoughby's expedition to Normandy.[75] The Corporation was obliged to provide food and supplies for the troops before they sailed to Portugal and was eventually compensated from some of the prize ships which were taken.[76] The exile community was also involved in these expeditions, the merchant Esay Bernay being, for example, licensed to transport supplies to the expeditionary force at Dieppe in 1589.[77]

In April 1588 the government requested that Southampton should contribute two ships and a pinnace in order to meet the threat of the Spanish

---

[71] On privateering in the Southampton area and the related dispute over Southampton's Admiralty jurisdiction, see Thomas, 'The Seaborne Trade of Southampton', pp. 143–65, 189–93; *The Third Book of Remembrance*, III, pp. 89–102.

[72] PRO, SP12/45/33.

[73] SRO, SC2/6/5, f. 51. There is no reference to this man as a member of the French church but he was recorded as an alien living in the parish of All Saints Without in 1577 and made a 'stall & art' payment of 18*d* in 1577. SRO, SC6/1/3.

[74] See above pp. 56–59.

[75] MacCaffrey, *Elizabeth I. War and Politics*, p. 39; Wernham, *Expedition of Sir John Norris and Sir Francis Drake*, pp. 344–45.

[76] See above p. 57.

[77] *Acts of the Privy Council*, 1589, p. 172.

Armada.[78] The Mayor and Corporation complained that they were unable to provide these ships due to the decayed state of Southampton and they alleged that 'some few strangers of foreign countries are come to inhabit here, and they (God knoweth) but very poor, living with the labour of their hands'.[79] This letter seems to have been part of an attempt by the Corporation to avoid the exactions of central government rather than evidence of the decay of the town, as has been previously assumed.[80] In the event, the town provided and equipped a ship called the *Angel* to meet the threat of the Armada. The Corporation also supplied ten barrels of powder, twenty hundred weight of shot and one hundred weight of 'match' to the *Ark Royal* from the town's stores.[81] In spite of the claims made by the Corporation, the French community did assist in meeting the demands placed on the town by the Armada. According to a list drawn up later the French church supplied four barrels of powder and four and a half barrels of 'match'.[82]

The French community also contributed to a request made of the town by the Privy Council in 1595–96. Initially the town was to provide two ships but they again pleaded their poverty and it was agreed that the merchants of the Isle of Wight should also contribute to the costs of these ships.[83] The town seems to have supplied just one ship, the *Elizabeth of Hampton* which was financed by voluntary contributions. Eleven members of the French community were recorded as making donations, ranging from £6 given by Jean le Mercier to a mere 5*s* provided by Widow Seulin.[84] The *Elizabeth of Hampton* was one of the ships which sailed in the expedition to Cadiz in 1596.[85]

The decline in the frequency of fasts and in the contributions made to the town's obligations reflects the growing integration and increasing poverty of the French-speaking community in Southampton. However, by this time the theatre of war had moved away from the Southern Netherlands. This impression should not be allowed to overshadow the role that the community played in the early stages of the Dutch Revolt. The community as a whole contributed to the Reformed cause and to the appeals of William of Orange. However it was the contribution of Jean de Beaulieu which is particularly striking. Indeed his involvement with the Sea Beggars and financial support may have contributed to the sensational seizure of Den Briel in 1572.

---

[78] *The Third Book of Remembrance*, III, p. 113.
[79] J.K. Laughton, (ed.), *State Papers relating to the Defeat of the Spanish Armada Anno 1588*, (Navy Records Society, 1–2, 1894), I, pp. 155–59.
[80] Thomas, 'The Seaborne Trade of Southampton', pp. 12–13; *The Third Book of Remembrance*, III, p. 113.
[81] *The Third Book of Remembrance*, III, pp. 54, 113–14.
[82] SRO, SC5/2/1, p. 129 B; *The Third Book of Remembrance*, III, p. 113 n.3.
[83] *Acts of the Privy Council*, 1595–96, p. 162.
[84] SRO, SC5/2/2, pp. 19–21.
[85] W. Slyngisbie, 'Relation of the Voyage to Cadiz, 1596', ed. J.S Corbett, in J.K. Laughton, (ed.), *The Naval Miscellany*, (Navy Records Society, 20, 1902), p. 46.

CHAPTER EIGHT

THE EXILE COMMUNITY AND THEIR HOSTS

Legally the refugees who settled in Southampton were aliens because they had been born overseas and owed allegiance to a foreign prince. Aliens were subject to a wide range of restrictions under Statute Law and Common Law as well as other local regulations. As such the Southampton refugees were strictly speaking subject to the same restrictions as were imposed upon other aliens who had come to England for whatever reason. During the sixteenth century the position of the alien who had been recognised, in the interests of trade, as being a 'friend' was gradually clarified, so that by the end of the century strangers were permitted to bring personal actions in the courts, take leases and in some cases purchase property. They were however obliged to pay higher taxes and dues than their English counterparts. There were also restrictions on the activities of merchant strangers and on the ability of aliens to pursue certain law suits and to bequeath real property. The children of strangers were also subject to restrictions; even those born in England were still considered to be foreign and therefore liable to the higher rates of taxation. Attempts in 1580–81 to define the children of strangers born in England as English and in 1594 as 'denizens', failed to be enacted.[1]

The restrictions upon aliens could be diminished, though not eliminated, through obtaining either patents of denization or more rarely through Acts of Naturalization. 1,962 patents were issued during Elizabeth's reign, of which 1,669 were granted during the first twenty years. Letters of denization gave aliens a degree of economic protection from restrictive pieces of legislation affecting alien craftsmen, in particular those limiting their right to take leases and the number of aliens in their employ, although it is unclear how many of the Henrician statutes were still operative in Elizabeth's reign. After denization, denizens were also able to bequeath real property to children born in England. Patents of denization often took several months to be granted and could be expensive.[2]

Several refugees who were or had been members of the Southampton community bought letters of denization: Adrian Saravia, Pierre Thieudet, Guillaume Hersent, Henry le Sueur, Gaspard Desert, Bon Rapareiller, Philippe de la Motte and Timothée Blier.[3] It is however difficult to understand why they

---

[1] Based on: *Returns of Strangers in the Metropolis*, pp. 1–3.

[2] *Returns of Strangers in the Metropolis*, pp. 3–8.

[3] *Letters of Denization and Acts of Naturalization for Aliens in England, 1509–1603*, ed. W. Page, (HSQS, 8, 1893), pp. 77, 80, 123, 153, 202, 231; *Letters of Denization and Acts of Naturalisation, 1603–1700*, pp. 12, 23.

went to the trouble of obtaining these letters, unless it was for social prestige.

During the negotiations for the establishment of the Southampton community, the refugees had been able to obtain privileges which had exempted them from some of the restrictions on aliens. In particular it was agreed that the Southampton community should enjoy the same privileges as those which had been granted to Sandwich in 1561.[4] The Sandwich community was established by letters patent for 'the exercising only of trades of making says, bays and such other cloth or tapestry as has not been accustomed to be made in England . . . notwithstanding stat. I Rich. III or stat. 32 Hen. VIII'.[5] The 1483 Act had forbidden alien artisans from taking strangers as apprentices and from the retail sale of goods; according to the Act only permitted denizens might establish themselves as craftsmen. The 1540 statute allowed artisan denizens to lease property but aliens were not permitted to employ more than four alien servants.[6] The Southampton community was therefore, like the Sandwich community, not bound by this legislation although of course other less limiting restrictions were accepted by the refugees during the negotiations. Furthermore the Southampton refugees had been able to negotiate a lower rate of customs duties for a seven year period on goods produced by the new techniques, so that they did not pay the usual strangers' double rate.[7] As a result of this negotiated settlement, the members of the community as a whole enjoyed a number of the benefits of being denizens. The denizens and non-denizens were still liable to pay and did pay double the lay subsidy payment of the native inhabitants as well as a higher rate of local dues. Furthermore Pierre Thieudet does not appear to have benefited from the denizen's right to bequeath real property, as neither his will nor the inventory of his goods makes any reference to bequests of land or real property.[8] The only noticeable consequence was that Thieudet together with two other denizens, Gaspard Desert and Guillaume Hersent, were included in the town's muster list in 1583, unlike other members of the French community.[9]

While the exile community clearly enjoyed a privileged status, they were restricted at a more local level by the town ordinances. Southampton society was divided into three main groups. The burgesses constituted a small élite – there were only an estimated fifty resident burgesses in 1596 – whose political and commercial privileges were outlined in the town's ordinances. The largest group in the town were the freemen and commoners who were allowed to follow their trades within the town, subject to the annual payment of 'stall & art' dues, and had various civic responsibilities but were not involved in town government. In 1596, 413 people paid their annual 'stall & art' dues for license

---

[4] PRO, SP15/13/82.
[5] *CPR, Elizabeth*, II, p. 336.
[6] Pettegree, *Foreign Protestant Communities*, pp. 14–15. Prof. Pettegree also considers here how the patents of denization were used by the government as a means of controlling aliens.
[7] See above pp. 32–33.
[8] HRO, Wills 1611/B/65.
[9] SRO, SC13/2/7.

to pursue their trade in the town. The strangers constituted the third community in the town: they were excluded from town politics and were commercially restricted.[10] The term 'stranger' was employed to describe anyone who did not come from the liberties of Southampton, regardless of whether they were English or foreign.

Non-burgesses were liable to a number of local dues. They were obliged to pay petty customs on ships which did not come from the town or any of the 'free' towns, paid anchorage and keelage dues when they entered Southampton's waters, and wharfage and cranage when they unloaded goods at the town quay. Brokage also had to be paid on goods which entered the town or left it through the Bargate. 'Strangers' were also required to pay 'hallage' for the use of either the Cloth Hall or the Linen Hall.[11] Certain groups were however granted concessions which reduced the level of petty customs that they paid, for example the merchants of Salisbury were liable to a lower rate under an ancient agreement, whereas a concession was made to the 'Northern men' as recently as 1554.[12] The refugees as well as non-burgesses were therefore placed at a disadvantage in commercial affairs by such privileges. There were also a number of restrictions imposed upon 'strangers' in the town. For example, only burgesses were allowed to buy from and sell goods to 'strangers'.[13] This was usually referred to as 'foreign bought and sold'. Brokers acted as intermediaries between the burgesses and merchants, to ensure that burgesses had the right of first refusal on goods.[14] On one occasion the Mayor confiscated a pipe of wine from a French merchant, Estienne Michellet, under the 'foreign bought and sold' rule.[15]

However one section of the French-speaking community was more fortunate, the Channel Islanders. They enjoyed certain commercial privileges in Southampton, in particular they had been granted in 1515 permission to pay a lower rate of petty customs duties but this was revoked in 1553. Furthermore the Channel Islanders had the right to sell linen cloth to non-burgesses on two weekly market days although this concession was withdrawn in 1572. There had been protests in the Court Leet that the Channel Islanders only sold their cloth on these days, 'so that the Inhabytants of the towne cane not sell in manner any thing at all to ther great hinderance'. Both of these privileges,

---

[10] *The Oak Book of Southampton*, ed. P. Studer, 2 vols. (PSRS, 10–11, 1910–11), I, pp. 116–50 *passim.*; *Assembly Books*, I, pp. vii–xii; A.L. Merson, 'The History of Southampton: Southampton in the Sixteenth and Seventeenth Centuries', in F.J. Monkhouse, (ed.), *A Survey of Southampton and Its Region*, (Southampton, 1964), p. 224; Platt, *Medieval Southampton*, pp. 17–20.

[11] Thomas, 'The Seaborne Trade of Southampton', p. 28.

[12] *The Third Book of Remembrance*, II, pp. 51, 102 n.2.

[13] *The Oak Book*, I, pp. 123–24; *The Third Book of Remembrance*, II, p. 90.

[14] *The Oak Book*, I, pp. 135–36, 139–40.

[15] Michellet attempted to outwit the Corporation by tampering with the confiscated cask. *The Third Book of Remembrance*, IV, pp. 18–19.

however, were restored in 1574 after arbitration by Cecil and Sir Walter Mild-may.[16]

The refugee community did attempt to circumvent or evade the local dues which they were liable to pay. One subterfuge was the 'colouring' of goods, whereby a non-burgess avoided the extra dues which he was obliged to pay, by passing goods off as belonging to a burgess. This practice was however prohibited by the town's ordinances. Peter Janverain, who later came to attend the French church, was stripped of his privilege of being a burgess for 'colour-ing' the goods of a non-burgess in 1565.[17] Henry Giles was ceremonially disen-franchised and then restored to being a burgess as well as being fined 10s for 'colouring' half a tun of Gascon wine belonging to Guillaume Hersent in 1589. Hersent was also obliged to pay a fine of 10s.[18] By the early seventeenth cen-tury the evasion appears to have become more blatant. There were complaints between 1612 and 1614 that Jean Hersent and other Frenchmen failed to pay the necessary petty customs on wool which was brought into the town through the Bargate.[19]

It is unclear whether the sale of the 'new draperies' was regulated by the Corporation as it was in Sandwich and Norwich. The refugees at Sandwich were permitted by the Mayor and Corporation to sell their products at a market hall on Wednesdays to freemen of the town and on Saturdays to freemen and strangers. Cloths which had not been sold on market days could be sent to another market provided that they were not sent to London either by the maker or buyer.[20] The Book of Orders for the strangers at Norwich included specific orders to regulate the quality of the cloth produced and its sale. The strangers were permitted to 'sell the commodities of ther owne makynge (in the citie of Norwiche) to enie parson or parsons, Englyshe or straunger, withowte lett or interruption, so that they do it in the salehawle onelye: and that everi daie in the weke, at the after none, from one of the clocke tyll fyve savinge the sonddies and holie daies, which be kepte in the churche of Englande'.[21]

The arrangements for the sale of the cloth made by the refugees in South-ampton are unclear, though they seem to have used neither the Cloth Hall nor the Linen Hall. From the partial records of the Linen Hall it is clear that this was not the market hall for the sale of the 'new draperies'. The payments for

[16] *The Third Book of Remembrance*, I, pp. 27–28, II, pp. 39, 138–39; *Court Leet Records*, pp. 59, 69.

[17] Janverain was later summoned to appear before the Privy Council, with one Thomas Berrye, to answer charges of being 'comon collorers of strangers goods'. The case concerning goods belonging to inhabitants of St. Malo came to be heard before the High Court of Admiralty. *The Oak Book*, I, p. 122; *The Third Book of Remembrance*, II, pp. 96–97; *Acts of the Privy Council*, 1577–78, pp. 249, 273, 278.

[18] *The Third Book of Remembrance*, III, pp. 60–61.

[19] *Assembly Books*, III pp. 40–41, 43, 81; see above p. 75.

[20] Backhouse, 'The Strangers at Work in Sandwich', 76.

[21] It was however recognised that the refugees might require fewer sale days and, if necessary, that the laws could be modified. Moens, *The Walloons and their Church at Norwich*, p. 257.

hallage made by the refugees were limited and only made for small quantities of cloth. This was probably canvas which they had imported; according to an ordinance from the Corporation in 1553 strangers were obliged to sell canvas in that hall.[22] The refugees may have been required to sell their cloth in some other hall for in 1574 the Court Leet complained that Mathieu Sohier, Arnoul le Clercq and 'others that make serge and estamell not to sell the same by Retaile for we arre enformed that they doo sell many & dyvers tymes by retaile'.[23] The allegation was repeated in 1575. The complaints may relate to some unidentified regulations concerning the sale of the 'new draperies' or may simply reflect the more general hostility about the retail sale of goods by 'strangers".

There were frequent presentments made to the Court Leet about 'strangers' who breached the town ordinances through the retail sale of their goods and merchandise. It is interesting to note that the retail sale of goods was specifically prohibited in the letters patent which were granted to the Maidstone community in 1567. These stated that 'they may sell the wares made by them in gross only and not by retail'.[24] The following presentment made at Southampton in 1569 seems to have been generally directed against the French-speaking community:

> Item we present that ye Straungers Inhabittinge in this towne are more freer within this towne then any other englishemen, for they doo retayle all things in theare housses which no other englisse men may doo onles they doo agree with ye towne and also with them of ye Corporation, also they have set vp in ye towne a dyenge house, wevinge & fullinge which is a discomodytye & hinderaunce to ye welthe of ye same towne whearfor we dessyer your worships to see yt redressid'.[25]

Besides such general complaints being made about trading by non-burgesses, specific accusations were made against members of the French community, concerning the retail sale of goods. In 1574 the Court Leet protested about the 'hinderance & domadge of such as kepe Retaylinge shoppes within this towne'. Anthoine Jurion was engaged in the retail selling of silk and ribbon lace and Robert Cousin 'hathe lately solde canvas & hollands to forreners that come out of the contery'. The presentment was repeated in 1575 but in spite of this there was a further complaint in 1579 that 'the frentche men sells silke lace by retayle'.[26] Fines were imposed on the refugees for breaches of the town ordinances. Jean le Mercier was fined 40s in 1587 because he

---

[22] After 1553 strangers in the town were obliged to use the Linen Hall for the sale of canvas and non-burgesses were forbidden to 'recyve into there howsses eny maner of canvas nor of merchandyse, or suffer anye to be solde or retayled within their sayde howsses, but to be browght to the towne halle and ther to be solde'. *The Third Book of Remembrance*, II, pp. 41–42.

[23] *Court Leet Records*, pp. 106, 114.

[24] *CPR, Elizabeth*, IV, p. 40.

[25] *Court Leet Records*, p. 60.

[26] *Court Leet Records*, pp. 106, 114, 180.

'vsually cary his wares & merchandyse home to his howsse, warehowses & sellers & doth sell the same ffreely as a ffree burges of the towne, who being of him selfe a very great dealer ys besids supposid to have the dealying of many other straungers which is a great hinderance to the burgesses . . .' Fines were levied for similar offences in 1589 on Esay Bernay and Guillaume Hersent but these appear to have had no effect because the presentments were repeated the following year, with a heavier fine being imposed upon Hersent.[27] The Court Leet's proposal in 1594 that a storehouse be set up for strangers in the town, was presumably an attempt to curb the retail selling of goods.[28]

Such complaints continued to be made even into the seventeenth century. In 1604 the minister Philippe de la Motte was accused with several leading members of the French community (Pierre le Gay, Estienne Latelais, Jean Hersent, Balthasar des Maistres and Robert le Page) of the sale from their homes, both retail and wholesale, of linen, woollen cloth and groceries to burgesses and non-burgesses of Southampton. They acted 'as freelie as anie free Burgesse amongest us tendinge to the great damage and hindraunce of the Burgesses and Comoners free of those trades, and expressly against the auntient ordinaunces privilegs and free customes of this Towne'. They were each to be fined 20s for every time that they failed to use the Linen Hall.[29]

However even when the refugees did use the Linen Hall problems still arose. A presentment made to the Court Leet in 1581, and repeated in 1582, complained about the operation of the Linen Hall, in particular that 'the inhabitants of Sarx & of the Islands often tymes have the Keys to shewe theire wares & sell the same as well unto fforeners as unto free burgesses'. The free use made of the Linen Hall by strangers was criticised in 1587.[30] The apparent disorder in the Linen Hall may have been responsible for the theft of goods belonging to Esay Bernay and merchants for whom he was the factor in 1591. On that occasion Bernay was obliged to exonerate the Mayor and Corporation from any claim relating to these thefts.[31]

The concern of the Court Leet about these breaches of the burgesses' privileges may have been the result of jealousy and a degree of officious legalism. In London, the authorities also heard cases concerning breaches of the city ordinances while seeking to exploit the skills of the newcomers. The Sandwich community was seriously harassed by the town council which enforced a series of measures which restricted and discriminated against the strangers.[32] However in Southampton, presentments about breaches of the town ordinances were not confined to members of the French community.[33] The measures reflect the importance of the petty customs duties for the town's finances by

---

[27] *Court Leet Records*, pp. 257, 276, 278, 288.
[28] *Court Leet Records*, pp. 292, 297.
[29] *Court Leet Records*, pp. 413–14.
[30] *Court Leet Records*, pp. 217, 235, 262.
[31] *The Third Book of Remembrance*, IV, p. 9.
[32] Pettegree, *Foreign Protestant Communities*, p. 278; Backhouse, 'The Strangers at Work in Sandwich', 81–86.
[33] For example, *Court Leet Records*, pp. 292, 333, 488.

the early seventeenth century and a wish to maintain the exclusive position of the burgesses.[34] The concern to prevent the erosion of the town's privileges led the Corporation to pursue a legal action against a London merchant and in 1607 to obtain an Act of Parliament which confirmed a charter of Henry VI, in particular 'restrayninge all Marchants not beinge free of the Liberties of the said Towne, to buy or to sell any manner of Merchandize within the same Liberties therof'.[35] None of the French community contributed towards the legal costs for obtaining this statute.[36]

The Corporation was however prepared to sell licences to members of the French community to allow them to pursue trades from which they were excluded under the terms of the original settlement.[37] Furthermore licences were sold that permitted the refugees to breach the town ordinances. Mathieu Sohier paid 40s in 1582–83 'for licence to sell certaine myllstonnes' and in 1571–72, 10s was 'Re. of a frentche man for lysens to sell three tonns of ffrentche wynns which he could not sell in the Towne'. Pierre Thieudet paid 40s in 1572–73 'for lycencinge him to open his shoppe windowes'.[38] Probably the most significant concession was granted to Jean le Mercier who was fined in July 1587 'for that he had solde certaine canvais and raisons & browne paper beinge forraine bought and solde to Bartholomew yatt of newberrye and to divers other & for leaue to sell freelye tyll michelmas by the consent of the whole magestratts'. Mercier was fined £6 13s 4d; during the following mayor-alty, £6 13s 4d was received from Mercier 'for a fine'. These fines seem to have, in effect, acted as a licence to trade although the payments are not recorded in every year. This compounding is confirmed in 1588–89, when it was noted that le Mercier's payment gave him leave to buy and sell his com-modities as in Mr. Studley's time.[39]

The failure to enfranchise some of the most prosperous members of the French community may be responsible for their more flagrant breaches of the town ordinances by the early seventeenth century. In the fifteenth century, Italian merchants who had been prepared to settle in Southampton became burgesses and some of them had been elected to municipal office, one even becoming Mayor.[40] In spite of a presentment in 1550 that forbade men from Guernsey or Jersey from becoming burgesses because 'their occupinge & crafte will be the decaye of our occupinge', a handful of Channel Islanders became burgesses in the later sixteenth century. These included men who had connec-

---

[34] *Southampton Mayor's Book*, pp. 20–21.

[35] *Assembly Books*, I, pp. xxv–xxvi; *Statutes of the Realm . . . (1101–1713)*, ed. A. Luders *et al.*, 12 vols. (London, 1810–28), 4 James I, c. 10.

[36] SRO, SC5/2/2, f. 119.

[37] See above Chapter Two.

[38] SRO, SC5/3/1, ff. 138v, 147v, 184.

[39] SRO, SC5/3/1, ff. 203, 210v, 217, 224.

[40] Ruddock, *Italian Merchants and Shipping*, pp. 159–61, 183–85; James, 'Geographical Origins and Mobility', pp. 68, 303–8. Antonio Guidotti is a good example of an alien burgess from the early sixteenth century, although he did not hold municipal office. See Ruddock, 'Antonio Guidotti', 34–42.

tions with the French Church such as Peter Janverain, Richard Etuer, Denis le Roux, William Marinell, Isaac Herevill, John Clungeon and Peter Priaulx.[41] Some refugees reached positions of minor importance in the town. For example, James Desert from Dieppe, was appointed as a beadle for St. Michael's in 1613.[42] But no person of refugee stock became a burgess in Southampton until 1630 when Peter le Gay was sworn in, to be followed in 1634 by Joseph de la Motte.[43]

These men were well established in the town. Peter le Gay's grandfather and namesake had originated from Armentières and had become a member of the French Church in April 1569. His son, Isaac le Gay, had been born in Southampton and was baptised in 1573. Isaac le Gay's son Pierre (Peter) was baptised in Southampton in 1602 and was admitted to the Lord's Supper in December 1618.[44] Joseph de la Motte was also born in Southampton but was only a second generation refugee, being the son of the minister of the French Church, Philippe de la Motte.[45] Both men went on to become Mayors of Southampton, le Gay in 1647 and de la Motte in 1651.[46] There had been discussions in September 1615 about admitting Jean Hersent as a burgess. Although Hersent had been proposed as a burgess by a former Mayor William Nevey, the Assembly was not quorate and so he was not sworn as a burgess. His name does not seem to have been subsequently enrolled as a burgess.[47]

The failure of refugees to enter the ranks of the Southampton burgesses before the early seventeenth century is perhaps surprising when compared with the admissions of Italians in the fifteenth and early sixteenth centuries. However it should be remembered that the Italians had settled in Southampton for a long time; they had first arrived in c.1270. The Italian merchants developed close links with their host community, often becoming denizens and marrying into local families. In the 1520s, Antonio Guidotti married the daughter of Henry Huttoft, a prominent figure in Henrician Southampton.[48] Although they worshipped as 'national' groups, they did so in the same churches as the townspeople.[49]

Although there were some wealthy members of the French church such as Jean de Beaulieu, Mathieu Sohier and Arnoul le Clercq, they do not appear to have forged links with the burgesses beyond their business contacts. Besides,

---

[41]   SRO, SC3/1/1, ff. 81v, 83, 111v, 129v, 157v, 164.
[42]   In fact Desert protested at this appointment as the beadle and asked to be relieved of the office, which was agreed to upon payment of a fine of 40s. *Assembly Books*, III, p. 70.
[43]   SRO, SC3/1/1, ff. 192, 198v.
[44]   See above p. 13; *Registre*, pp. 5, 33, 41, 54; PRO, PCC Prob. 11/106 Pierre le Gay, Prob. 11/122 Isaac le Gay.
[45]   Joseph de la Motte was baptised in April 1602 and was admitted to the Lord's Supper at the same time as Pierre [Peter] le Gay in April 1618. *Registre*, pp. 33, 54; SRO, SC3/1/1, f. 198v.
[46]   Davies, *A History of Southampton*, p. 178.
[47]   *Assembly Books*, IV, pp. 26–27; SRO, SC3/1/1, f. 177v.
[48]   James, 'Geographical Origins and Mobility', pp. 307–8; Ruddock, 'Antonio Guidotti', 35.
[49]   Ruddock, *Italian Merchants and Shipping*, pp. 121–22, 128, 131–33, 159–61.

these merchants only remained in Southampton until the early 1580s.[50] The consistorial disapproval of marriages outside the French community clearly deterred integration and therefore the establishment of such familial ties.[51] However by the early seventeenth century such restraints had lost much of their force and several prominent figures in the town's government developed links with the French community. John Mayor (Mayor, 1600–1), William Nevey (Sheriff, 1602–3; Mayor, 1604–5, 1612–13), John Cornish (Sheriff, 1604–5; Mayor, 1606–7) all acted as godparents for children baptised in the French church between 1598 and 1610.[52] Mayor and Nevey both had connections with the Channel Islands and the latter only became a burgess in 1591.[53] Family links also seem to have developed between these men and the French community; John Cornish's brother William may have been the same William Cornish of the Isle of Wight who married Esther Pontus in 1596.[54] A Nevey married Daniel Hersent, the half-brother of Jean Hersent.[55] William Nevey was appointed an overseer of the will of Isaac le Gay, in 1613, and Jean Hersent in 1614.[56] With the development of such links between members of the community and leading members of Southampton society, it became possible for some of those with refugee origins to become burgesses.

It is clear that while the town and Corporation of Southampton were prepared to exploit the commercial benefits of the refugee community, they were no less concerned to uphold the town's ordinances and the privileges of the burgesses. The penetration of the refugees into this élite was inevitably a slow process. However while that élite sought to exclude the refugees, there does not seem to be any evidence of serious unrest or hostility towards the exile community.

The Southampton Corporation did not make any serious attempt to monitor the numbers of refugees entering the town. Furthermore no returns of aliens in Southampton survive, though it would be surprising if such returns were not made. The government appears to have conducted a general survey in 1571 for which returns survive for Harwich, Colchester, Great Yarmouth, Lynn, Dover and Sandwich.[57] Furthermore in 1572 Robert Horne, Bishop of Winchester and a promoter of the refugee community, wrote to the authorities in Portsmouth to enquire after the number of refugees there. Horne was responding to a request from the Privy Council that the Bishop write to 'all the offices of suche townes and portes adioyning unto us where any such stranngiers doe make their abode', so that they could report on the number of

---

50   See above pp. 50, 52.
51   See above pp. 108–9.
52   *Registre*, pp. 52, 53, 54, 55, 56. Some of the children of Isaac le Gay, Philippe de la Motte and Jean Hersent were amongst those sponsored.
53   *The Third Book of Remembrance*, III, pp. 74, 85; SRO, SC3/1/1, f. 108v.
54   HRO, Wills 1611/A/28; *Registre*, p. 91.
55   *Registre*, p. 113; PRO, PCC Prob. 11/125 Jean Hersent.
56   PRO, PCC Prob. 11/122 Isaac le Gay, Prob. 11/125 Jean Hersent.
57   PRO, SP12/78/8–10, SP12/78/13, SP12/78/19, SP12/78/29.

strangers who had arrived since 1 September 1572 and the numbers and destination of those who had moved on. There was clearly concern about the number of refugees who were entering the country in the wake of the Massacre of St. Bartholomew's Day. The Bishop or Council however doubted the sincerity of the refugees' motives commenting that 'many stranngers are repaired in to this Realme under pretence of the libertie of their co'science and for safetie of their lives . . . ffor that under the coulour thereof besides many resorte which have not like honeste meaninge towards the preservac'on of the state and quiet of our countrey'.[58]

Though no such letter or return of aliens has survived for Southampton it would clearly be surprising if a similar letter had not been sent to the Corporation. The town authorities did take steps in July 1573 to monitor those who joined the community, requiring them to produce a testimony that they were members of the Reformed faith, in order to exclude false brethren who might have come under the shadow of religion to spy.[59] The situation was fluid with refugees arriving and moving on, some of whom left Southampton after being admitted to the Lord's Supper but without receiving the sacrament. The Corporation clearly expected any Frenchman in the town to attend the services at God's House even if they did not become members of the church and be admitted to the Lord's Supper. As the examination of Michael Collens suggests, the town authorities viewed membership or attendance at the French church as a kind of litmus test for foreigners.[60]

Besides the complaints about breaches of the town ordinances, there does not seem to have been the same degree of hostility towards the French-speaking community as occurred in other towns where the exiles had settled. One presentment made to the Court Leet appears to have been inspired by xenophobia. In 1569 it was decided that the conduit heads be covered and locked for fear that some of the many strangers in the town might poison the water supply.[61] There were occasional brawls between the strangers and their hosts: in 1569–70 Walter Hawkins paid 15d for causing a Frenchman to shed blood; a dispute between Andrew Pcalc and a Frenchman led to bloodshed in 1575–76 and a fine of 2s 6d. In fact there seem to be more fights amongst Frenchmen than between English and French.[62] These seem to have been relatively petty matters; there were no major disturbances such as those which occurred or were threatened in London. Relations between the Italians and the townsfolk of Southampton had been on the whole similarly cordial in the fifteenth century.[63]

---

[58] BL, Cott. MS Vesp. F.XII, f. 191.
[59] *Registre*, p. 8.
[60] See above p. 106.
[61] *Court Leet Records*, p. 57.
[62] SRO, SC5/3/1, ff. 129v, 135v, 143v, 154v, 159, 159v, 160, 161v, 161, 168v, 170, 170v, 192, 210, 211v.
[63] Pettegree, *Foreign Protestant Communities*, pp. 14, 282–94; Ruddock, *Italian Merchants and Shipping*, pp. 149–53.

This apparent lack of tension between the refugees and their host community was no doubt in part due to the very small size of the community. In Sandwich it has been estimated that in 1574 the Flemish and Walloon communities made up more than half of the town's population.[64] Southampton was a much larger town than Sandwich and its stranger population much smaller. A population census held in the town in 1596 classed 297 people as being aliens, a mere seven percent of the town's total population of 4,200, though the size of the French Reformed community had certainly been diminished as a result of migration and integration.[65] This alien population probably also included a few aliens in the town who were not members of the strangers' congregation. An earlier indication of the relative strength of the alien population in Southampton can be gleaned from the lay subsidy returns for 1571. These record payments from 51 aliens, including some who were established in the town before 1567, compared with 141 payments from members of the English community.[66] However Englishmen with goods worth less than £3 were exempt from contributing to the lay subsidy unlike the aliens who were obliged to pay a poll tax. The refugee population inevitably increased in the wake of the Massacre of St. Bartholomew's Day, although the scale of this influx cannot be determined.[67] In August 1584, there were 186 members of the church's congregation; this was after the 1583–84 plague epidemic in which about seventy members of the community had died.[68]

The exiles in Norwich and London were criticised for causing overcrowding and so causing rents to rise as well as increasing the risk of plague.[69] There were certainly complaints in Southampton about the growing number of undertenants in the town but this does not seem to have been directly related to the French-speaking community.[70] The regular lists of undertenants record both English and alien undertenants. The list for 1579, the first detailed record, shows that there were 69 aliens out of a total of 189 undertenants.[71]

Although the refugees tended to cluster in the southern parishes of the town, no ghetto developed. The Count of Heads which was carried out in 1596 revealed that there were 121 aliens living in the ward of Holy Rood and 88 in the ward of SS. Michael & John. The remaining 88 aliens were spread throughout the remaining wards.[72] The majority of these aliens would have been mem-

[64] Backhouse, 'The Strangers at Work in Sandwich', 77–78. In 1571 the Flemish population in Sandwich was 1,900 and in addition there were 300 Walloons. The town's native population was about 1,600.
[65] SRO, SC3/1/1, f. 254v.
[66] *Central Hampshire Lay Subsidy Assessments, 1558–1603*, ed. D.F. Vick, (Farnham, 1987), pp. 32, 35, 36, 38.
[67] For an indication of the size of this influx, see *Registre*, pp. 7–9.
[68] *Registre*, pp. 19, 102–4.
[69] Pettegree, *Foreign Protestant Communities*, pp. 283, 284, 285; C.M. Vane, 'The Walloon community in Norwich: the first hundred years', *HSP*, 24 (1983–88), 132.
[70] *Court Leet Records*, pp. 236, 284, 298, 306.
[71] SRO, SC6/1/14.
[72] SRO, SC3/1/1, f. 254v.

bers of the French-speaking community. The lay subsidy returns provide a clearer impression of the distribution of the refugees. In 1571 the wealthiest refugees were scattered around the town: Jean de Beaulieu and Robert Cousin lived in the ward of Holy Rood; Emery Durant and Jan de Bavais in the ward of St. Lawrence and Gilles Seulin in the ward of All Saints. A similar pattern can be seen in the exile community at Norwich.[73] The wealthier members of the community seem to have lived amongst the wealthier native inhabitants, although there were exceptions: Mathieu Sohier and Arnoul le Clercq both resided in the ward of SS. Michael & John where some of the poorest members of the community lived. Twenty-seven aliens were recorded as merely paying a poll contribution in the lay subsidy. This ward also contained the highest number of undertenants and so presumably the cheapest accommodation.[74] There were also more substantial properties within the ward including the West Hall, which Mathieu Sohier leased at £12 per annum from 1570.[75] In fact, Mathieu Sohier was recorded as having six undertenants in this ward in 1578 and 1579.[76] By 1599 the wealthier members of the community were similarly scattered around the town but the poorer members of the community had also come to live in the ward of Holy Rood (24 aliens were recorded as making only poll contributions) as well as the ward of SS. Michael & John (15 poll contributions).

Relations between the refugee community and their hosts therefore seem to have been relatively cordial. Yet curiously when the Queen visited Southampton for several days in 1591, the refugees were for reasons unknown not able to gain access to the Queen in order to thank her for the protection which she had afforded the community and were obliged to express their thanks outside the town. The Queen '*respondit fort humainement louant Dieu de ce qu'il luy donnoit puissance de recueillir et faire bien aux poures estrangers, et disant qu'elle scauoit bien que les prieres desdits seruoyent beaucoup sa Conseruation*'.[77]

While the refugees were grateful for the Queen's protection and were on generally good terms with the local population amongst whom they lived, they retained a separate identity within the town. The refugees, for a number of reasons, only slowly became integrated into their host community.

The stranger communities, in spite of the persecution which had driven many members of their community to seek exile, retained close links with the continent. The churches, although theoretically under the superintendence of an English bishop, looked to the Walloon synods in the Netherlands (rather than the French churches) for ministers to serve in their churches. The communities as a whole provided money for the training of ministers and the poor

---

[73] R. Esser, *Niederländische Exulanten im England des 16. und frühen 17. Jahrhunderts*, (Berlin, 1996), pp. 147–48.

[74] *Court Leet Records*, p. 184. In 1579, 71 undertenants were recorded as living in the ward of SS. Michael & John, compared with 46 in the ward of Holy Rood, 11 in St. Lawrence's, 15 All Saints within the Bar, 16 in All Saints without the Bar and 11 in Bag Row and East Street.

[75] SRO, SC4/3/58.

[76] SRO, SC6/1/13–14.

[77] *Registre*, p. 131.

of the churches, as well as giving financial support to the activities of Orange and the Reformed cause.[78] Links with the Netherlands were also maintained at a more personal level. Initially these contacts could be expected to be relatively strong as the exiles left family and property overseas, and expected to return. In her will in 1569 Jehanne de Caignoncle expressed the wish to be buried in Valenciennes.[79] The Southampton exiles kept abreast of family news, friends and interests – particularly property that had been left behind – through personal correspondence.[80]

Exiles also remembered their relatives and property overseas when it came to drawing up their wills. Robert Cousin bequeathed to his sister living in Tournai £200 together with 'my bedd furnished, and the moictie of all the lynnen that serveth for to be used in my howse'.[81] Other refugees claimed property that they had left overseas and so continued to bequeath it in their wills, although their estates may well have been confiscated by the *Conseil des Troubles*. Gilles Seulin referred in his will to a farm in Hainaut and further references to property overseas were made by Guillaume Coppin and Mathieu Sohier in wills drawn up after they had migrated from Southampton.[82] Indeed Jane Seneschal gave her son power of attorney to recover property at Armentières in 1576.[83]

These bequests of property and personal links represent, to an extent, a belief that the refugees would eventually return to the Low Countries or France. For as long as the refugees believed that their exile was only temporary, they were unlikely to become integrated into the host society. The pace of integration only quickened once the strangers lost hope of returning to their native lands.

The French community acted to an extent as a separate entity within the town. The church maintained discipline amongst its members, as well as providing a system of poor relief and welfare. The regular celebrations of the Lord's Supper, which became monthly after 1583, reinforced their sense of belonging to a particular community since members of the host community were only exceptionally admitted to membership. This distinction would initially have been particularly pronounced because the Protestant Reformation only gradually found acceptance in Southampton.[84] The French church therefore hindered the process of integration and this was further discouraged by

---

[78] See Spicer, ' " Faythful Pastor in the Churches" ', pp. 202–4; see above pp. 129–30.

[79] HRO, Wills 1569/B/81–84.

[80] Verheyden, 'Une correspondance inédite', 180–82, 194–95, 209.

[81] PRO, PCC Prob. 11/67 Robert Cousin.

[82] PRO, PCC Prob. 11/55 Guillaume Coppin, Prob. 11/88 Gilles Seulin, Prob. 11/106 Mathieu Sohier.

[83] Her hopes about recovering the property may have been raised by the Pacification of Ghent, article 10 of which permitted people 'to take possession of all their seignories, estates, prerogatives, shares, credits which have not been sold or alienated, in the condition in which these possessions are at present'. SRO, SC2/6/5, f. 36; E.H. Kossmann & A.F. Mellink, *Texts concerning the Revolt of the Netherlands*, (Cambridge, 1974), pp. 129–30.

[84] See above pp. 97–99.

the institutional and personal links developed with other stranger communities.

A degree of unity existed with the establishment of regular colloquies in the French-speaking churches after 1581, although less institutionalised contacts had existed before that date. Less formal contacts were retained with members of the exile communities. Augustin de Beaulieu and Erasmus de la Fontaine dit Wicart, though resident in London, acted on several occasions as a *parrain* at baptisms in Southampton.[85] In 1602, Judith de la Motte acted as a *marrain* in London.[86] In other cases family members migrated from Southampton to other communities. Gilles Cousin, the brother of Robert, initially lived in Southampton where three of his children were baptised but by 1584 he had moved to Norwich.[87] Sometimes marriages caused refugees to move to other communities. Members of other communities occasionally passed through Southampton, where they might be admitted to the Lord's Supper.[88]

The measures enjoined upon the community by the French church served to emphasise further distinctions between the refugees and the townspeople. There is a clear difference in the choice of names given by the two communities. While names such as Anne, Jane, John, Mary and their variants were popular baptismal names amongst both communities, the refugees were encouraged to give their children Biblical names at baptism rather than pagan, Humanist names or names associated with saints or offices (e.g. Baptiste or Toussaint). Old Testament names such as Abraham, Daniel, Isaac, and Susanne were popular and children were also given the less common names: Jahel, Jepthe, Joel, Lea, Lydie and Zacharie. This preference for Biblical baptismal names is not reflected in the surviving parochial baptismal records. Christian names like Richard, Robert and William, which were common enough amongst the townspeople, were not chosen by members of the French church community before the early seventeenth century.[89]

While the selection of baptismal names served to emphasise the distinction between the two communities, the consistory's dislike of inter-marriage seriously hindered the process of integration. It is difficult to measure the process

85 *Returns of Aliens*, II, pp. 215, 223, 303, 389, 402, 428, 440, III, pp. 85, 109, 124, 125, 128, 129, 130, 133, 442; *Registre*, pp. 45, 47, 50.

86 *Registers of the French Church of Threadneedle Street, London, 1600–1639* , ed. W.J.C. Moens, (HSQS, 9, 1896), p. 46.

87 SRO, SC6/1/14, SC6/1/15, SC6/1/17; PRO, PCC Prob. 11/67 Robert Cousin; *Registre*, pp. 9, 42, 43, 45.

88 For example, Pierre Bauters who was a member of the Dutch community in London. He fled from Ghent in 1567 and was condemned by the *Conseil des Troubles*. He became a member of the Dutch church in London but was admitted to the Lord's Supper in Southampton in July 1569. He was described in 1584 as having 'lived for some years as a faithful member of their church, to the edification of many, without any crime or accusation'. *Registre*, p. 5; A.L.E. Verheyden, *Le Conseil des Troubles. Liste des condamnés 1567–1573*, (Brussels, 1961), No. 458; *Register of the Attestations or Certificates of Membership, Confessions of Guilt, Certificates of Marriages, Betrothals, Publications of Banns, &c, preserved in the Dutch Reformed Church, Austin Friars, London 1568 to 1872*, ed. J.H. Hessels, (Amsterdam-London, 1892), p. 2.

89 Spicer, 'The French-speaking Reformed community', pp. 231–33, 296–305.

of integration into and assimilation with their host community. Steady inter-marriage between members of the exile community and the host community may however be regarded as a useful index of the pace of integration. How-ever, while a degree of intermarriage between members of an exile community might be expected, the French Church probably disapproved marriages between refugees and members of the host community.[90] An analysis of the marriage registers of the church reveals not only the slow process of intermar-riage into the host community but also other interesting marriage patterns within the community. Although the community was French-speaking, it was clearly divided between refugees from the Southern Netherlands, those from France and those from the Channel Islands and these divisions are also reflected in the patterns of marriages within the church. Indeed the process of integration between these groups was almost as slow as the integration into their host community.

During the early years the community was remarkably homogenous with a large population from the French-speaking Southern Netherlands. The refu-gees from the Low Countries married amongst themselves and the same was also true of the refugees from France. The concentration of Low Countries refugees was gradually diluted with the influx of refugees from France, particu-larly in the wake of the St. Bartholomew's Day Massacre. The first marriage between a French exile and a refugee from the Low Countries took place in 1570 but there were only eleven such marriages between 1567 and 1606, com-pared with 27 marriages between refugees from the Low Countries and 51 marriages between refugees from France. The first marriage of an exile to a Channel Islander did not take place until 1578 but there were only 16 such marriages before 1606. As the integration between the different groups of French-speaking refugees was in itself gradual, we should not be surprised that links between the strangers and their host community developed still more slowly.[91]

Marriages outside the community were exceptional. The first such marriage took place in 1577 when Caterine Midy from Artois married Thomas le Grand of Southampton. However Thomas le Grand and several others who married into the community (Thomas Renet of the Isle of Wight, Guillaume Formoyle of Hampton and William Cornish of the Isle of Wight) were all admitted to the Lord's Supper.[92] Although Marguerite Schepman of Romsey was not admitted to the Lord's Supper, her children were baptised in the French church between 1586 and 1600.[93] It is however important to distinguish between English partners and those who were second generation refugees who were born in Southampton and so described themselves as being natives of the town.

---

[90]   Pettegree, *Foreign Protestant Communities*, pp. 303–4.
[91]   Spicer, 'The French-speaking Reformed community', pp. 268–71.
[92]   *Registre*, pp. 13, 21, 22, 26, 86, 89, 90, 91.
[93]   *Registre*, pp. 47, 48, 53.

Five marriages were recorded as having taken place in the parish churches.[94] The first such marriage took place in 1585 and may be attributed to the community's temporary lack of a minister. The children from this marriage were baptised in the French church between 1588 and 1596.[95] The baptisms of the sons of another couple married outside the French Church were recorded in the church's register, suggesting that the couple were reconciled with the church.[96] However, there is no further reference in the *Registre* to the three other such marriages. Pierre Thieudet obtained a marriage licence in order to marry Elizabeth Clement of Dibden in 1609, but there is no reference to the marriage in the records of the French church.[97]

Although language was a significant barrier between the townspeople and the refugees, it has been suggested that it could also provide an indicator of the gradual integration of the French community.[98] This can be examined through the language used in wills, although wills can be problematic as they are not always written by the testator; Walerand Thevelin, for example, occasionally acted as a scribe. The wills of Jane Sohier [Jehanne de Caignoncle] (1569), Francois Bourgayse (1583) and Georgette Loys (1583) were all written in French.[99] The will of Anthoine Jurion (1578) was translated from French by John Vovert in Southampton while Dionysius le Blanq translated into English the will of Robert Cousin in 1584. It is interesting to note that the will of Gilles Seulin for which Walerand Thevelin had acted as the amanuensis in 1583 survives in the records of the Prerogative Court of Canterbury in English without any note that it had been translated.[100] Later wills tended to be written in English, although the wills of Jean Rochefort (1606) and Robert le Page (1612) were both written in French. Rochefort had only joined the French Church in December 1594. The will of Mathieu Sohier, one of the initial settlers in Southampton, was also written in French in 1593 after he had migrated to London.[101] Perhaps the use of French was more common in a large community such as existed at London, than in Southampton.

There is no sure standard by which the gradual integration of the French community can be measured. Intermarriage with the host community and the continued use of the French language can provide at best only rough indications of the process. The refugees did forge links with their host community

---

[94] *Registre*, pp. 88, 89, 91, 92.

[95] See above p. 118. Samuel Hersent and Susanne Sellier were married on 25 January, 1585. Hersent had been admitted to the Lord's Supper in April 1579. Their four children were baptised in the French church. *Registre*, pp. 15, 47, 49, 50, 52, 88.

[96] Timothée Mesnier of Jersey married Marguerite Markes of Winchester in 1601. He had been admitted to the Lord's Supper in 1592. Their children Timothée and Philippe were baptised in the French church. *Registre*, pp. 24, 54, 92.

[97] *Hampshire Marriage Licences, 1607–1640*, ed. A.J. Willis, (London, 1957–60), p. 12.

[98] James, 'Geographical Origins and Mobility', p. 353; A. Spicer, 'A process of gradual assimilation: the exile community in Southampton, 1567–1635', *HSP*, 26 (1995–), p. 187.

[99] HRO, Wills 1569/B/81–84, 1583/B/12, 1583/B/13.

[100] PRO, PCC Prob. 11/67 Robert Cousin, Prob. 11/88 Gilles Seulin; HRO Wills 1578/B/53.

[101] PRO, PCC Prob. 11/106 Mathieu Sohier; HRO, Wills 1606/B/46, 1612/A/58; *Registre*, p. 25.

partly through their obligation to train apprentices in the skills of the 'new draperies' as well as through developing business contacts. Integration was however an inevitably slow and uncertain process while the refugees were perceived as a distinct group in the town and while they in turn viewed their exile as being temporary and nursed the hope that they might return to the continent. As the influx of newcomers gradually declined and the number of the first generation exiles dwindled, attitudes changed. It became inevitable that they would become integrated into their host community and the entry of men of refugee stock into the burgess ranks of the town is perhaps the clearest sense of their arrival. The burial of Judith de la Motte, a first generation exile and the widow of a minister, in the parish church of St. John is indicative of this gradual integration.[102] By the 1630s the process of integration had proceeded so far that when the French Church was visited in 1635, only six of the sixteen fathers of families who attended the church were considered to be aliens.[103]

---

[102] *Registre*, p. 114.
[103] PRO, SP16/291/66.

CONCLUSION

In March 1604, the first synod of all the French-speaking and Dutch churches in England was held in London. The synod met:

> *Pource que les Freres des Eglises étrangeres des deus langues avisé de presenter requête a sa Majesté, pour confirmation de la liberté de laquelle ils ont joui jusques a present, en ont eté déconseillez et détournez par ceus sans lesquels ils n'eussent rien sceu obtenir, Atendu que les dites Eglises sont en possession de leurs libertez sans molestes ni empêchement quelconque, Pourtant ont les dits Freres resolu par commun avis de requerir ce qu'on conoîtra d'Amis Bourgeois et ayans vois en Parlement de vieller pour le bien de nos Eglises, et nous donner avis de ce qui se metroit en avant a leur prejudice, pour chercher remede au contraire.*

The meeting was attended by ministers and elders from the London churches, the Norwich churches, Canterbury, Colchester and Sandwich. The interests of the Southampton and Maidstone churches were represented by an elder from Sandwich.[1] While the delegates looked forward expectantly to the new reign and a Calvinist king, the conditions in Europe, which had led many of them to seek exile, had changed markedly. Philip II was dead and a newly formed confederation – the United Provinces – was emerging in the Northern Netherlands; in France, the religious wars had seemingly come to an end with the Edict of Nantes and the grant of religious freedom to the Huguenots. The dislocation of the Thirty Years War and the policies of Louis XIII and Richelieu, which were to cause more French Protestant exiles to seek refuge in England, as well as the creation of new communities associated with the draining of the Fens, still lay in the future. The synod therefore provides a convenient point from which to survey the exile churches in England and to consider the significance of the Southampton church.

With the exception of London, all of the exile churches in England had been established during Elizabeth's reign and even the London churches were refounded on her accession.[2] A number of these churches are however conspicuous by their absence from the synod: Rye (founded *c.*1562), Stamford (1567), King's Lynn (1570), Dover (*c.*1571), Winchelsea (*c.*1572), Ipswich

---

[1] *Actes des Colloques*, p. 46.

[2] For recent general surveys of the exile churches, see R.D. Gwynn, *Huguenot Heritage. The history and contribution of the Huguenots in Britain*, (London, 1985); B. Cottret, *The Huguenots in England. Immigration and Settlement, c. 1550–1700*, (Cambridge, 1991); M. Greengrass, 'Protestant Exiles and their Assimilation in Early Modern England', *Immigrants and Minorities*, 4 (1985), 68–81.

(*c.*1573), Thetford (*c.*1573) and Halstead (1577). For the most part these churches had ceased to exist by 1604. They disappeared as the refugees gradually returned to the continent as the European situation improved. The churches at Yarmouth and Dover were already on the point of collapse by 1576, and even the communities at Norwich and Maidstone were experiencing difficulties.[3]

The communities established during Elizabeth's reign differed markedly in their character. The size of the community and the social composition and degree of coherence of the original settlers all had an important effect upon them. The host community could also influence their character. The size of the host population, the attitudes of the authorities and of the local inhabitants towards the strangers (these could of course change over time), and the economic conditions and opportunities which existed for the refugees were all important factors. The stability of the communities was a further determinant.

A significant distinction can be made between the churches which were represented in 1604 and the more transitory communities. Those which survived had been essentially 'planted' settlements. They were established with the consent and support of the municipal authorities and central government, with specific terms governing the size of the community, their relations with the local inhabitants and the skills or new techniques that they were expected to introduce.[4] A similar pattern can be seen in the Empire where settlements were established in small territorial towns under the control of a feudal lord or in cities such as Frankfurt or Hamburg. However there were no *Exulantenstädte*, newly-founded refugee towns, established in England during Elizabeth's reign; the Glastonbury community set up by Protector Somerset may have been equivalent to this type of community.[5] These English 'planted' communities can be contrasted with those, such as Dover and Rye, which developed pell-mell as a result of their geographical proximity to the continent, as refugees fled from war and persecution. The authorities far from encouraging these communities were often anxious about the large numbers of settlers.[6]

It should not however be considered that official approval and encouragement was in fact any guarantee of success; as Schilling has pointed out 'good political and religious conditions could not outweigh disadvantageous econ-

[3] Pettegree, *Foreign Protestant Communities*, pp. 256–57.
[4] See above pp. 22–34 passim; *CPR, Elizabeth*, II, p. 236, III, pp. 209–10, IV, pp. 39–40; Pettegree, *Foreign Protestant Communities*, p. 263; Backhouse, 'The Strangers at Work in Sandwich', 74–75; Cross, *History of the Walloon & Huguenot Church at Canterbury*, pp. 14–16; N. Goose, 'The "Dutch" in Colchester: the Economic Influence of an Immigrant Community in the Sixteenth and Seventeenth Centuries', *Immigrants and Minorities*, 1 (1982), 266; Moens, *The Walloons and their Church at Norwich*, pp. 17–18; V. Morant, 'The settlement of Protestant Refugees in Maidstone during the sixteenth century', *Ec.H.R.*, Second Series, 4 (1951–52), 210–14.
[5] H. Schilling, 'Innovation through Migration: The Settlements of Calvinistic Netherlanders in Sixteenth- and Seventeenth-Century Central and Western Europe', *Social History*, 16 (1983), 16–19, 20–25; Pettegree, *Foreign Protestant Communities*, p. 43.
[6] Hardy, 'Foreign Refugees at Rye', 575–76; G.H. Overend, 'Strangers at Dover', *HSP*, 3 (1888–91), 116–17.

omic, transportation and financial facilities'.[7] Permission was given in 1576 for a substantial community to be established under the Queen's licence at Halstead which initially flourished but collapsed in less than four years because of the opposition of the local inhabitants.[8]

In a sense, such broad distinctions are artificial because most of the 'planted' communities also attracted refugees from the continent. The Sandwich community was created by letters patent in 1561, with the members of the community being carefully selected by the Dutch church in London, the Archbishop of Canterbury, the Bishop of London and the Lord Warden of the Cinque Ports. However exiles from the Southern Netherlands had earlier settled in the town and the geographical proximity of Sandwich to the continent meant that many fled there in the wake of the Troubles.[9] A similar pattern can be seen at Norwich and Colchester, where formally established communities expanded due to their geographical proximity to the continent. A sizeable alien community had already developed in London for commercial reasons, many years before letters patent were granted to John à Lasco for the establishment of the exile churches. Some of these aliens were attracted to the exile churches, as were other later refugees.[10] The Southampton community was established by Walloon refugees but besides attracting refugees from the persecution in France, Channel Islanders who had settled in the town or visited for commercial reasons, also worshipped at the church.[11]

Although these communities included a number of diverse groups, in some settlements there was an influential core of refugees. At Southampton, the founder members of the community formed a particularly cohesive group. The refugees originated from Valenciennes and had established familial and business ties between themselves, as well as with some Tournai and Antwerp Calvinists, before the group migrated to the town. A smaller, but less cohesive group migrated from Armentières. The later settlers in Southampton from northern France did not form such a closely-knit group. This pattern of migration from particular towns can be seen in other exile communities. Refugees from Valenciennes were also prominent at Frankfurt and at Canterbury. A number of those who settled at Norwich had originated from Ieper; the Maastricht church moved *en masse* to Aachen in 1567, clothworkers from Hondschoote migrated to Leiden. Many of those who were recorded in Rye in 1572 had fled from Dieppe, a slightly smaller number from Rouen.[12] A more regional migration can be seen in the exiles from the Pays de Caux who settled in Southampton and those from the Westkwartier at Sandwich.[13]

---

[7] Schilling, 'Innovation through Migration', 18.
[8] Hardy, 'Foreign Settlers at Colchester and Halstead', *HSP*, 12 (1919–24), 9.
[9] Backhouse, 'The Strangers at Work in Sandwich', 74–75.
[10] Pettegree, *Foreign Protestant Communities*, pp. 9–17, 77–79.
[11] See above pp. 2–21.
[12] H. Meinert, (ed.), *Das Protokolbuch der Niederlandischen Reformierten Gemeinde zu Frankfurt am Main (1570–1581)*, (Frankfurt, 1977), p. 15; Cross, *History of the Walloon & Huguenot Church at Canterbury*, pp. 24–25; Pettegree, *Emden and the Dutch Revolt*, p. 246; Hardy, 'Foreign Refugees at Rye', 568–75.
[13] See above pp. 15–16; Backhouse, 'The Strangers at Work in Sandwich', 75.

These regional influences endured in these exile communities. While the attentions of the Flemish or Dutch churches and their communities were inevitably directed towards the Netherlands, this was also true of some of the provincial French-speaking communities. They supported the Reformed churches in the Netherlands with funds and ministers and later they looked to these churches for advice and ministers for their own churches.[14] This is certainly the case with the Southampton church, in spite of its relative proximity to France and the fact that the refugees had more frequent commercial links with France than the Netherlands. The reason for this seems to have been the dominant influence of the original settlers in Southampton from the Walloon areas and the fact that until the early seventeenth century the church was served by Walloon ministers. A similar pattern can be seen at Canterbury. The dominance of refugees from France at Rye inclined that community to look predominantly towards France; the London French church seems to have had a more mixed aspect, but it too was served by French ministers during this period.[15]

These Walloon and French distinctions survived in Southampton for a long time. At first this was no doubt due to the domination of the close-knit Walloon oligarchy. Arnoul le Clercq and Mathieu Sohier were not only the leading refugee merchants but they also played an important rôle in the religious life of the community as members of the consistory. Although the Walloon influence was weakened by their departure and the influx of French refugees, it still persisted.[16] The distinction between the Walloon and French refugees was most clearly identified in the community's marriage patterns.[17]

The Southampton community was potentially one of the largest 'planted' communities to be established in England. Initially it was expected to be similar in size to the Sandwich settlement, but during the negotiations it was agreed that up to forty households would be permitted to settle in the town. In this context the term household referred to a working-unit in which a master employed a certain number of workmen and thus does not include women and children. In Southampton permission was given for up to twelve men per household. Cecil was therefore granting permission for up to 360 *adult men* to settle in Southampton with their families.[18] Permission had only been granted for no more than twenty-five households to settle at Sandwich, thirty at Norwich and thirty at Maidstone.[19] The Southampton community never seems to have fulfilled its potential. Unfortunately accurate figures do not survive for the size of the Southampton community before 1596 but an impression of its size, compared with other exile communities, can be gleaned from Table VI. The Southampton community seems to have been smaller than communities

---

[14] See above p. 129; Spicer, ' "A Faythful Pastor in the Churches" ', pp. 202–4.
[15] Spicer, ' "A Faythful Pastor in the Churches" ', pp. 197, 203.
[16] See above, pp. 52, 105.
[17] See above p. 154.
[18] See above pp. 31–32, 79–80.
[19] *CPR, Elizabeth*, II, p. 361, III, pp. 209–10, IV, pp. 39–40.

Table VI – The size of exile communities in England

Founded	Community	Size	
1550	London	1568	6,704 strangers
		1571	4,269 strangers
		1571	4,631 strangers
		1573	7,143 strangers
		1593	7,113 strangers
1561	Sandwich	1561	406 strangers
		1571	1,900 Flemings & 300 Walloons
		1574	2,400 Flemings & 500 Walloons
c. 1562	Rye	1569	83 men
		1572	641 strangers
1565	Norwich	1568	339 Walloons & 1,132 Flemings
		1569	2,825 strangers
		1571	3,900 strangers
		1583	4,678 strangers
1565	Colchester	1565	11 households, 55 people
		1571	185 strangers (177 Dutch)
		1573	431 'Dutchmen'
		1586	1,297 (incl. 500+ born in realm)
1567	Southampton	1584	186 Communicants
		1596	297 aliens
1567	Stamford	—	
1568	Gt. Yarmouth	1571	390 strangers
1570	Kings Lynn	1571	67 men & 159 women, children & servants
c. 1571	Dover	1571	64 men, 76 women & 137 children
c. 1572	Winchelsea	—	
c. 1573	Ipswich	1568	31 male 'aliens'
		1576	39 male 'aliens'
c. 1573	Thetford	—	
1575	Canterbury	1582	1,679 in congregation
		1591	2,760 in congregation
		1593	3,013 in congregation
1576	Halstead	—	

Sources: PRO, SP12/78/9–10, 13, 19; SRO, SC3/1/1, f. 254v; *Registre*, p. 19; *Returns of Strangers in the Metropolis*, pp. 73–76; P. Denis, 'Bibliographie de l'histoire démographique des réfugiés flamands et wallons en Angleterre (1558–1625)', *Bulletin de la Société d'histoire du Protestantisme Belge*, 6 (1974), 98–110; M. F. Backhouse, 'The Flemish and Walloon communities at Sandwich during the reign of Elizabeth I (1561–1603)', (unpublished Ph. D. thesis, University of Southampton, 1992), pp. 40–41, 50; Esser, *Niederländische Exulanten im England*, p. 49; Hardy, 'Foreign Refugees at Rye', 567–74; Goose, 'The "Dutch" in Colchester', 263; Oakley, 'The Canterbury Walloon Congregation', pp. 62–63; V. B. Redstone, 'The Dutch and Huguenot Settlements at Ipswich', *HSP*, 12 (1917–23), 184–85, 200–1.

such as Rye and Dover which grew rapidly with the sudden influx of refugees.

Some communities were too small to be viable. The cost of maintaining a minister as well as looking after the welfare of the sick and poor placed a heavy burden upon the exile communities. The Winchelsea community probably grew rapidly with the arrival of French refugees but as these returned to the continent, the community quickly subsided. This may explain the migration from Winchelsea to Canterbury in 1574.[20] The small size of the Rye community was given as the reason for the financial difficulties experienced in 1583. All of the communities were affected by the exodus of refugees to the continent but 'planted' settlements such as Norwich and Southampton do not appear to have begun to experience financial difficulties until the early seventeenth century.[21] The Southampton community although small when compared with communities such as Norwich and Canterbury remained active until the early seventeenth century; the church did not request assistance from the colloquy until 1610. In fact, the community in its early years was sufficiently wealthy to contribute to the poor relief of Sandwich and Canterbury.[22] We can only speculate but it would seem that the wealth of several key members, the refugee merchants, sufficed to sustain the church.

The limited size of the Southampton community also seems to have had its advantages. The settlement did not overwhelm its host community as was the case in some communities; at Sandwich, the strangers accounted for about half of the town's total population and at Canterbury it seems to have been at least a third.[23] The limited size of the community meant that there was less competition for employment and may partly explain why Southampton seems to have been relatively free of the petty jealousies, complaints, xenophobic self-interest and even violence which afflicted certain other communities. It was the hostility of the native population which apparently caused the collapse of the Halstead community.[24] The refugees there were accused of increasing the rents, causing overcrowding and food shortages. In Norwich, the overcrowding by refugees and their alleged dirty habits were blamed as being the cause of the outbreak of plague in 1578–79. There were disturbances in London directed against strangers in 1563 and 1595.[25] In Sandwich the hostility towards the stranger community took the form of vigorous social and economic discrimination, with draconian measures being introduced and enforced by the municipal authorities. However the hostility at Sandwich was not solely due to the size of the stranger community, it was linked with the town's declining economic

---

[20] De Schickler, *Les Eglises du Refuge*, I, p. 302; Cross, *History of the Walloon & Huguenot Church at Canterbury*, pp.17–18.

[21] Spicer, ' "A Faythful Pastor in the Churches" ', pp. 206–7.

[22] See above p. 113.

[23] The population of Canterbury was about 9,000 between 1591 and 1600, at this time the size of the Canterbury congregation was between 1,656 and 3,312 people. Backhouse, 'The Strangers at Work in Sandwich', 78; Oakley, 'The Canterbury Walloon Congregation', pp. 62–63.

[24] Hardy, 'Foreign Settlers at Colchester and Halstead', 195–96.

[25] Pettegree, *Foreign Protestant Communities*, pp. 283, 284–86, 294–95; Backhouse, 'Strangers at Work in Sandwich', 87.

prosperity.[26] Although the commercial activities of the Southampton community were also restrained by civic regulations, the Corporation does not seem have been as harsh as the Sandwich authorities. The Southampton refugees were privileged in the temporary restriction of customs duties; elsewhere they remained subject to the laws of the land which restricted the freedoms of the refugees and charged them higher rates of taxation.[27]

These settlements were expected to be innovative and to reinvigorate the local economy.[28] Writing about the stranger communities in the Empire, Schilling commented that the innovative impact of the refugees was greater than that of other migrant groups because of the confessional differentiation between the exiles and their hosts. The Protestant Netherlanders settled in towns which predominantly had developed well-defined Lutheran characteristics by the 1560s. This meant that the refugees were confessionally isolated and created distinctive communities, which encouraged industriousness and innovation.[29] A similar confessional differentiation can be seen initially in a town as religiously conservative as Southampton.[30] But the process of confessionalisation was only beginning in Elizabethan England in the 1560s, whereas it was well-advanced in the German towns. The Elizabethan Religious Settlement had only recently restored Protestant worship in England and many of the refugees, it should be remembered, were but very recent converts and were themselves still adjusting to the Calvinist faith. At first the doctrinal and liturgical differences between the Walloons and the nascent Protestantism of the town parish churches would not have seemed that significant. In these early years it was language and culture, rather than religion, which set the exile communities apart from the host community.

The exile communities in England were encouraged by the government for economic motives. While the skills of the 'new draperies' were not unknown before the Calvinist diaspora, the refugees were actively involved in the production and development of these textiles.[31] The economic contribution made by the communities was recognised by contemporaries. Ironically the inhabitants of Halstead petitioned the Privy Council in 1589 for the re-establishment of the Dutch community because of the increase in poverty after their departure. The benefits brought about by the refugees were also recognised by the authorities in London, Norwich and Colchester, as well as by central government.[32] The refugees at Southampton may not have been as dynamic as in the textile centres of East Anglia, but they certainly contributed to the well being of the urban economy. The production of the 'new draperies' provided

[26] Backhouse, 'The Strangers at Work in Sandwich', 81–86.
[27] See above pp. 33, 140–42.
[28] See above pp. 23–24, 94.
[29] Schilling, 'Innovation through Migration', 32–33.
[30] See above pp. 97–99.
[31] See above pp. 71–91.
[32] Goose, 'The "Dutch" in Colchester', 269–70; Pettegree, *Foreign Protestant Communities*, p. 295.

employment in Southampton as well as establishing a new industry in the town.[33]

The refugee merchants played a significant rôle in the town's overseas trade. Although they could not compete with the wealthiest Southampton merchants, exiles such as Arnoul le Clercq, Mathieu Sohier and Jean le Mercier not only contributed to the town's established trade, they also opened up new areas of trade. These merchants dominated the exports of the 'new draperies' and developed markets for these cloths in Western France.[34]

1604 marks a turning-point for the Southampton community. The exiles had played an active role in the town's commercial life although by the early seventeenth century they no longer dominated the 'new draperies'. As in other communities, the process of assimilation and the return of exiles to the continent, served steadily to weaken the community. This decline accelerated after 1604, probably in part due to the impact of the plague epidemic of 1604 which resulted in more than 150 deaths.[35] In spite of the influx of refugees from the Ile de Ré in 1628, by 1635 there were only an estimated thirty-six members of the congregation.[36] The church had been experiencing financial difficulties since about 1610 and during the first half of the seventeenth century became increasingly dependent on the Threadneedle Street church for financial support.[37]

The weakness of the Southampton church was revealed by their response to the attacks made by Archbishop Laud upon the privileges of the foreign churches. Laud had a general policy to establish total religious conformity in the Anglican Church, and he regarded the quasi-independent 'stranger' churches as an anachronism which merely served to encourage the English Puritans. In April 1634, representatives of the exile churches of Kent (Canterbury, Sandwich and Maidstone) were summoned and questioned as to their liturgy, the number of their members who had been born in England and whether or not these members attended their parish church. A synod of all the exile churches was held in order to discuss Laud's attack upon their privileges. The Southampton church lacked the money to send a delegate to this meeting.[38]

In June 1635, the Archbishop's Vicar-General, Sir Nathaniel Brent, visited the French church in Southampton and questioned the minister, Daniel Sauvage. As in the case of the 'stranger' churches in Kent, he was questioned about the church's liturgy and how many members of the church were born in England. Of the fifteen heads of families who attended the church only six were

---

[33] See above, p. 89.
[34] See above, pp. 35–70.
[35] *Registre*, pp. 107–10.
[36] PRO, SP16/291/66; *Registre*, p. 35.
[37] See above, p. 112; *Actes des Colloques*, pp. 72, 82, 96, 116; *Calendar of the Letter Books of the French Church*, pp. 24, 43, 76, 79.
[38] *Actes des Colloques*, p. 68; Grell, *Dutch Calvinists*, pp. 224–48.

aliens, the remainder were natives of England. Brent therefore ordered these natives to attend their parish churches. The congregation briefly resisted but in October obeyed Brent's order.[39] Southampton was the only foreign church which submitted to Laud's attack upon their privileges.

The status quo was restored on Laud's downfall and Sauvage continued to serve the church until his death in 1655. By then the French church must have seemed like a relic from a by-gone age for it had lost much of its raison d'être. The community which it had been designed to serve had faded away as members drifted back to the continent or entered the local parish churches. There was little need for a separate church conducting services in the French language and the paucity of entries in the *Registre* are suggestive of a congregation in terminal decline. The sudden influx of French Huguenots, fleeing from the religious persecution of Louis XIV from the 1660s transformed the circumstances of the French church in Southampton.

It is perhaps ironic that the refugees, so keenly sought by the town in 1567 and who had made such an important contribution to the economy of the town, should have left so little to remind us of their passage. Even the street names such as French Street and Rochelle Lane recall the presence of the medieval French-speaking community. Few of those who today visit the French church at God's House will be aware that the first Calvinists in Southampton were not Huguenots but Walloon Netherlanders who hailed from the cities of Valenciennes and Tournai.

---

[39] PRO, SP16/291/66.

BIBLIOGRAPHY

Printed sources which are collections of documents or sources which have been significantly edited, are generally listed in the bibliography according to their editor. Where there are several titles by the same author, these are listed in chronological order.

Manuscript Sources:

Belgium:
Antwerp, Stadsarchief, Certificatieboeken.
Brussels, Archives Générales de Royaume, Chambre des Comptes 11, 1203, 19802.
   — Conseil des Troubles 6, 88, 104, 315A.

France:
Armentières, Archives Communales d'Armentières, FF40 Registre criminel d'Armentières.
   — FF84 Requête de Protestants.
La Rochelle, Archives Départementales de la Charente-Maritime, Notarial Archives.
Lille, Archives du Nord, Chambre des Comptes B12696–12704, B13190.
   — B20115 (Matières généalogiques 1355–1564).
Rouen, Archives Départementales de la Seine-Maritime, Series B Records of the Normandy Courts.
   — Series E Parish Registers (including Huguenot church's baptismal register).
   — Series G Parish Account Books.
   — Archives Communales de Rouen, B2–B4 Journaux des Echevins.
Valenciennes, Archives Communales de Valenciennes, CC146I Comptes des Massards 1565–66.
   — Bibliothèque Municipale, Manuscrits 809–818 Casimir de Sars, livres généalogiques.

The Netherlands:
Amsterdam, Bibliothèque Wallonne, Livre Synodal.
   — Index to the registers of the Walloon church at Middelburg.

United Kingdom:
Cambridge, University Library, MS Dd 3. 64 Petition of Le Sauvage to the Archbishop of Canterbury.

— MS Dd 11.43 Registre contenant les Actes des Colloques des Eglises de l'Isle de Jersey, 1577–1614.

Canterbury, City and Diocesan Record Office,U47/A1–3 Actes du Consistoire 1576–99.

— U47/B Elders' Accounts

— U47/D Account of money received and spent for students 1599–1601.

Guernsey, St.Peter Port, Islands Archives Service, Microfilm of Finch-Hatton Papers 312 (Northamptonshire Record Office).

— Greffe Archives.

Hatfield House, Hertfordshire, Salisbury MSS, CP64/37–38.

Jersey, St.Helier, Société Jersiaise, Papers of H.M.Godfray.

London, British Library, Cottonian MS, Vespasian F IX, XII.

— Egerton MS, 868: Delamotte Diary.

— Lansdowne MS, 161.

— French Protestant Church of London Archives, Soho Square, AC/MS 297, Ecclesiastical Discipline, 1578.

— AD/MS 3–4, Actes du Consistoire, 1578–1615.

— DC/MS 194, Deacons' Account Books, 1572–73.

— Guildhall Library, MS 9171, Commissary Court of London Wills.

— Corsini Correspondence 1567–1637 (Photocopies)

— Huguenot Library, MS/J 27, Sandwich French Church: Poor Relief Accounts, 1568–72.

— Public Record Office,

E179	Lay Subsidy Rolls.
E190/814–18	Port Books, Southampton.
HCA 13	High Court of Admiralty: Depositions.
Prob. 11	Prerogative Court of Canterbury: Registered Copy Wills.
REQ 2	Court of Requests: Proceedings.
RG4/4600	Register of the French Church, Southampton.
SP12, 15	State Papers Domestic.
SP70, 83	State Papers Foreign.
STAC 5	Court of Star Chamber: Proceedings.

Oxford, The Queen's College Archives, God's House Accounts.

Southampton, Civic Record Office,

D/FC	Papers concerning the French Church.
PR 4/2/1	Churchwardens Accounts, parish of St.Lawrence.
PR 7	Records of the parish of St.Michael.
SC2/6/5–6	Books of Instruments.
SC3/1/1	Book of Burgess Admissions.
SC3/5/1	Book of Free Commoners.
SC4/3	Counterpart leases by the Corporation.
SC5/1/42–47	Stewards' Book, 1557–67.
SC5/1/1–2	Book of Debts, 1534–1619.
SC5/3/1	Book of Fines, 1488–1594.
SC5/3/5–13	Mayoral Casualty Books.
SC5/4/64–88	Petty Customs Records, 1567–1601.

SC5/6/4–11   Cloth Hall Books, 1569–84.
SC5/7/1–6   Linen Hall Books, 1554–80.
SC5/17/1–30   Scavage lists, 1575–1625.
SC6/1/1–37   Court Leet Records, 1549–1620, including 'stall & art' payments.
SC7/1/10–14   Town and Piepowder Courts.
SC9/3/2, 4–7   Examination Books.
SC10/1/1–14   Poor Relief Assessments, 1552–1619.
SC13/2/1–10   Muster Books, 1544–1590.
SC14   Miscellaneous Tax Assessments.
TC Box 1/1   Town Clerks' Miscellaneous Boxes.

Winchester, Hampshire Record Office, Wills, Administrations and Inventories.

— 21M65, A1/30–31, Bishops' Registers.

— B1/27–34, Visitation Books.

— 37M73A/PRI, Titchfield Parish Registers.

Printed Sources:

Abjurations de Protestants faites à Bayeux; Guerre de religion, 1570–1573, ed. E. Anquetil, (Bayeux, n.d.).

Les Actes des Colloques des Eglises Françaises et des Synodes des Eglises Etrangères réfugiées en Angleterre 1581–1654, ed. A.C. Chamier, (HSQS, 2, 1890).

Actes du Consistoire de l'Eglise Française de Threadneedle Street, Londres. Vol. I, 1560–1565, ed. E. Johnston, (HSQS, 38, 1937).

Actes du Consistoire de l'Eglise Française de Threadneedle Street, Londres. Vol. II, 1571–1577, ed. A.M. Oakley, (HSQS, 48, 1969).

Acts and Proceedings of the General Assemblies of the Kirk of Scotland from the year MDLX, 3 vols. (Edinburgh, 1839–45).

Acts of the Privy Council of England, ed. J.R. Dasent, 32 vols. (London, 1890–1907).

The Admiralty Court Book of Southampton, 1566–1585, ed. E. Welch, (SRS, 13, 1968).

The Assembly Books of Southampton, ed. J.W. Horrocks, 4 vols. (PSRS 19, 21, 24, 25; 1917, 1920, 1924–25).

The Book of Examinations, 1601–1602, ed. R.C. Anderson, (PSRS, 26, 1926).

The Book of Examinations and Depositions, 1622–1644, ed. R.C. Anderson, 4 vols. (PSRS, 29, 31, 34, 36; 1929, 1931, 1934, 1936).

Books of Examinations and Depositions, 1570–1594, ed. G.H. Hamilton, (PSRS, 16, 1914).

Boucq, P.J. le, *Histoire des Troubles advenues à Valenciennes à cause des hérésies 1562–1579*, ed. A-P-L. de Robaulx de Soumoy, (Brussels, 1864).

Calendar of Letters and State Papers Relating to English Affairs, preserved principally in the Archives of Simancas, of the reign of Elizabeth, ed. M.A.S. Hume, 4 vols. (London, 1892–99).

Calendar of Patent Rolls, preserved in the Public Record Office, Edward IV, Edward V, Richard III, (London, 1901)

Calendar of Patent Rolls, preserved in the Public Record Office, Edward VI, 5 vols. (London, 1924–26).

Calendar of Patent Rolls, preserved in the Public Record Office, Elizabeth, (London, 1939–).

Calendar of Patent Rolls, preserved in the Public Record Office, Philip and Mary, 4 vols. (London, 1937–39).

A Calendar of Southampton Apprenticeship Registers, 1609–1740, compiled by A.J. Willis & ed. A.L. Merson, (SRS, 12, 1968).

Calendar of State Papers Domestic series, of the reigns of Edward VI, Mary, Elizabeth, ed. R. Lemon *et al.* (London, 1856–).

Calendar of State Papers Foreign Series of the Reign of Elizabeth, ed. J. Stevenson *et al.* (London, 1863–).

A Calendar of the Letter Books of the French Church of London from the Civil War to the Restoration, 1643–1659, ed. R.D. Gwynn, (HSQS, 54, 1979).

The Cartulary of God's House, Southampton, ed. J.M. Kaye, 2 vols. (SRS, 19–20, 1976).

The Cartulary of the Priory of St. Denys near Southampton, ed. E.O. Blake, 2 vols. (SRS, 24–25, 1981).

Cauchie, A., (ed.), 'Episodes de l'histoire religieuse de la ville d'Anvers durant le second semestre de l'année 1566 – Correspondance de Daniel di Bomalès avec François di Marchi', *Analectes pour servir à l'histoire ecclésiastique de la Belgique*, Second Series, 7 (1892), 20–60.

Central Hampshire Lay Subsidy Assessments, 1558–1603, ed. D.F. Vick, (Farnham, 1987).

The Charters of the Borough of Southampton, Vol.II 1484–1836, ed. H.W. Gidden, (PSRS, 9, 1910).

'Church Goods in Hampshire, A.D. 1549', trans. T. Craib, *PHFC*, 9 (1921–25), 92–98.

Court Leet Records, ed. F.J.C. Hearnshaw & D.M. Hearnshaw, (PSRS, 1,2,4; 1905–7).

Coussemaker, E. de, *Troubles religieux du XVIe siècle dans la Flandre Maritime 1560–1570*, 4 vols. (Bruges, 1876).

Crespin, J., *Histoire des Martyrs persecutez et mis à mort pour la verite de l'Evangile, depuis le temps des apostres iusques à present (1619)*, ed. D. Benoit, 3 vols. (Toulouse, 1885–89).

Daval, G. & Daval, J., *Histoire de la Reformation à Dieppe 1557–1657*, ed. E. Lesens, 2 vols. (Rouen, 1878).

Delteil, F., (ed.), 'Lettres de l'Eglise de Saint-Lo', *BSHPF*, 117 (1971), 84–87.

Diegerick, I.L.A., *Archives d'Ypres. Documents du XVIe siècle, faisant suite à l'inventaire des chartes . . .*, 4 vols. (Bruges, 1874–77).

Duke, A.C., Lewis, G., & Pettegree, A., (ed.), *Calvinism in Europe 1540–1610. A collection of documents*, (Manchester, 1992).

Essen, L. van der, 'Episodes de l'histoire religieuse et commerciale d'Anvers dans la seconde moitié du XVIe siècle, *Bulletin de la Commission Royale d'Histoire*, 80 (1911), 321–62.

Essen, L. van der, 'Les progrès du Luthéranisme et du Calvinisme dans le monde commercial d'Anvers et l'espionnage politique du marchand Philippe Dauxy, agent secret de Marguerite de Parme, en 1566–1567', *Vierteljahrsch-rift für Sozial- und Wirtschaftsgeschichte*, 12 (1914), 152–234.

Gallars, N. des, *Forma Politiae ecclesiasticae nuper institutae Londini in coetu Gallorum*, (London, 1561).

Gallars, N. des, *Forme de police ecclesiastique instituée à Londres en l'Eglise des François*, ([London], 1561).

Geisendorf, P-F., *Livre des habitants de Genève*, 2 vols. (Geneva, 1957–63).

A God's House Miscellany, ed. J.M. Kaye, (SRS, 27, 1984).

Gouberville, Gilles de, *Le journal du Sire de Gouberville*, ed. Abbé Tollemer, (Société des Antiquaires de Normandie, Caen, 1892).

Grosart, A.B., (ed.), *The Spending of the money of Robert Nowell of Reade Hall, Lancashire: Brother of Dean Alexander Nowell*, (Manchester, 1877).

Halkin, L-E. & Moreau, G., 'Le procès de Paul Chevalier à Lille et Tournai en 1564', *Bulletin de la Commission Royale d'Histoire*, 131 (1965), 1–74.

The Hampshire Lay Subsidy Rolls, 1586, ed. C.R. Davey, (Hampshire Record Series, 4, 1981).

Hampshire Marriage Licences, 1607–1640, ed. A.J. Willis, (London, 1957–60).

Hessels, J.H., (ed.), *Ecclesiae Londino-Batavae Archivum*, 3 vols. (Cambridge, 1887–97).

HMC, *Calendar of the Manuscripts of the Most Hon. Marquess of Salisbury K.G. preserved at Hatfield House, Hertfordshire*, 24 vols. (London, 1883–1976).

HMC, *The Manuscripts of Rye and Hereford Corporations; Capt. Loder-Symonds, Mr. E.R. Wodehouse, M.P., and others*, (London, 1892).

Kervyn de Lettenhove, J.M.B.C., *Relations politiques des Pays-Bas et de l'Angle-terre, sous le règne de Philippe II*, 11 vols. (Brussels, 1882–1900).

Kossmann, E.H., & Mellink, A.F., *Texts concerning the Revolt of the Netherlands*, (Cambridge, 1974).

Laughton, J.K., (ed.), *State Papers relating to the Defeat of the Spanish Armada Anno 1588*, (Navy Records Society, 1–2, 1894).

Letters of Denization and Acts of Naturalization for Aliens in England, 1509–1603, ed. W. Page, (HSQS, 8, 1893).

Letters of Denization and Acts of Naturalization for Aliens in England and Ireland, 1603–1700, ed. W.A. Shaw, (HSQS, 18, 1911).

Letters of the Fifteenth and Sixteenth Centuries from the Archives of Southampton, ed. R.C. Anderson, (PSRS, 22, 1921–22).

List and Analysis of State Papers, Foreign Series, Elizabeth I, ed. R.B. Wernham, (London, 1964–).

Livre Synodal contenant les Articles résolues dans les Synodes des Eglises Wallonnes des Pays-Bas, 2 vols. (The Hague, 1896).

Meinert, H., (ed.), *Das Protokolbuch der Niederlandischen Reformierten Gemeinde zu Frankfurt am Main (1570–1581)*, (Frankfurt, 1977).

The Minute Book of the French Church at Southampton,1702–1939, ed. E. Welch, (SRS, 23, 1979).

The Miscellaneous Papers of Captain Thomas Stockwell, ed. J. Rutherford, 2 vols. (PSRS, 32–33, 1932–33).

Moens, W.J.C., *The Walloons and their Church at Norwich: their History and Register, 1565–1832*, (HSQS, 1, 1887–88).

Mothe-Fénélon, B. de la, *Correspondance diplomatique de Bertrand de Salignac de la Mothe-Fénélon, Ambassadeur de France en Angleterre de 1568 à 1575*, ed. A. Teulet, 7 vols. (Paris-London, 1838–40).

Nichols, J.G., (ed.), *Narratives of the Days of the Reformation*, (Camden Society, 77, 1859).

Nieuw Nederlandsch Biografisch Woordenboek, ed. P.C. Molhuysen & P.J. Blok, 10 vols. (Leiden, 1911–37).

The Oak Book of Southampton, ed. P. Studer, (PSRS, 10–11, 1910–11).

Paillard, C., *Histoire des Troubles religieux de Valenciennes 1560–1567*, 4 vols. (Brussels, 1874–76).

Paillard, C., 'Les Grands Prêches Calvinistes de Valenciennes', *BSHPF*, 26 (1877), 33–43, 73–90, 121–33.

Paillard, C., (ed.), 'Papiers d'état & documents inédits pour servir à l'histoire de Valenciennes pendant les années 1566 et 1567', *Mémoires Historiques sur l'arrondissement de Valenciennes*, 5–6 (1878–79).

Paillard, C., *Une page de l'histoire religieuse des Pays-Bas. Le procès de Pierre Brully*, (1878).

Paillard, C., 'Interrogatoires Politiques de Guy de Bray', *BSHPF*, 28 (1879), 59–67.

Paillard, C., 'Interrogatoires Politiques de Pérégrin de la Grange', *BSHPF*, 28 (1879), 224–33.

The Port and Trade of Early Elizabethan London Documents, ed. B. Dietz, (London Record Society, 8, 1972).

Quick, J., *Synodicon in Gallia Reformata: or the Acts, Decisions, Decrees and canons of those Famous National Councils of the Reformed Churches in France*, 2 vols. (London, 1692).

Rahlenbeck, C., 'Les chanteries de Valenciennes. Episodes de l'histoire du seizième siècle', *Bulletin de la Commission de l'Histoire des Eglises Wallonnes*, First Series, 3 (1888), 121–88.

Recueil des Ordonnances des Pays-Bas (Deuxième série – 1506–1700), ed. C. Laurent et al., (Brussels, 1893–).

Recveil des Lettres & Mandemens du Roy enuoyées en sa Court de Parlement de Rouen, (Paris, 1569).

Register of the Attestations or Certificates of Membership, Confessions of Guilt, Certificates of Marriages, Betrothals, Publications of Banns &c, preserved in the Dutch Reformed Church, Austin Friars, London 1568 to 1872, ed. J.H. Hessels, (Amsterdam-London, 1892).

Register of the Minister Elders and Deacons of the Christian Congregation of St. Andrews . . . 1559–1600, ed. D. Hay Fleming, (Publications of the Scottish History Society, 4, 7; 1889, 1890).

The Registers of the French Church of Threadneedle Street, London, 1600–1639, ed. W.J.C. Moens, (HSQS, 9, 1896).

The Registers of the Walloon or Strangers' Church in Canterbury, ed. R. Hovenden, 3 Parts, (HSQS, 5, 1891–98).

Registre des Baptesmes, Mariages & Mortz, et Jeusnes de l'Eglise Wallonne ... établie à Southampton, ed. H.M. Godfray, (HSQS, 4, 1890).

Registres de la Compagnie des Pasteurs de Genève, ed. J-F. Bergier *et al.*, (Geneva, 1962–).

Returns of Aliens dwelling in the City and Suburbs of London, ed. R.E.G. Kirk & E.F. Kirk, 4 Parts, (HSQS, 10, 1900–8).

Returns of Strangers in the Metropolis 1593, 1627, 1635, 1639. A Study of an Active Minority, ed. I. Scouloudi, (HSQS, 57, 1985).

Schelven, A.A. van, 'Verklikkers-rapporten over Antwerpen in het laatste kwartaal van 1566', *Bijdragen en mededeelingen van het historisch genootschap*, 50 (1929), 238–320.

Select Pleas in the Court of Admiralty, Vol.II High Court of Admiralty (A.D. 1547–1602), ed. R.G. Marsden, (Selden Society, 11, 1897).

Slyngisbie, W., 'Relation of the Voyage to Cadiz, 1596', ed. J.S. Corbett, in J.K. Laughton, (ed.), *The Naval Miscellany*, (Navy Records Society, 20, 1902), pp. 23–92.

Smit, H.J., (ed.), *Bronnen tot de geschiedenis van den handel met Engeland, Schotland en Ierland*, 2 vols. (Rijks Geschiedkundige Publicatiën, 9, 1950).

The Southampton Mayor's Book of 1606–1608, ed. W.J. Connor, (SRS, 21, 1978).

Southampton Probate Inventories, 1447–1575, ed. E. Roberts & K. Parker, 2 vols. (SRS, 34–35, 1992).

The Southampton Terrier of 1454, ed. L.A. Burgess, (SRS, 15, 1976).

The Spanish Company, ed. P. Croft, (London Record Society, 9, 1973).

Speed, J., *The Theatre of the Empire of Great Britaine*, (London, 1611).

Speed, J., *The History & Antiquity of Southampton*, ed. E.R. Aubrey, (PSRS, 8, 1909).

Stadsarchief Antwerpen, *Antwerpse Poortersboeken 1533–1608*, 3 vols. (Antwerp, 1977).

Statutes of the Realm ... (1101–1713), ed. A. Luders *et al.*, 12 vols. (London, 1810–28).

A Supplement to Dr. W.A. Shaw's Letters of Denization and Acts of Naturalisation, ed. W. & S. Minet, (HSQS, 35, 1932).

The Third Book of Remembrance of Southampton 1514–1602, ed. A.L. Merson *et al.*, 4 vols. (SRS, 2, 3, 8, 22; 1952, 1955, 1965, 1979)

Tudor Royal Proclamations, ed. P.L. Hughes & J.F. Larkin, 3 vols. (New Haven-London, 1964–69).

Verheyden, A.L.E., 'Une correspondance inédite adressée par des familles protestantes des Pays-Bas à leurs coreligionnaires d'Angleterre (11 novembre 1569–25 février 1570), *Bulletin de la Commission Royale d'Histoire*, 120 (1955), 95–257.

Wernham, R.B., (ed.), *The Expedition of Sir John Norris and Sir Francis Drake to Spain and Portugal, 1589*, (Navy Records Society, 127, 1988).

The Zurich Letters, ed. H. Robinson, (Cambridge, 1842).

The Zurich Letters, (Second Series), ed. H. Robinson, (Cambridge, 1845).

Secondary Sources:

Agnew, D.C.A., *Protestant Exiles from France in the reign of Louis XIV*, ([Edinburgh], 1866).

Allin, P.F.D., 'Medieval Southampton and its Jews', *Transactions of the Jewish Historical Society of England*, 23 (1970–71), 87–95.

Alumni Cantabrigienses. A biographical list of all known students, graduates and holders of office at the University of Cambridge, from the earliest times to 1900. Pt.I From the earliest times to 1751, compiled by J. Venn & J.A. Venn, 4 vols. (Cambridge, 1922–27).

Alumni Oxonienses: The Members of the University of Oxford, 1500–1714, ed. J. Foster, 4 vols. (Oxford, 1891).

Andrews, K.R., *Elizabethan Privateering. English Privateering during the Spanish War, 1585–1603*, (Cambridge, 1964).

Appleby, J.C., 'Neutrality, Trade and Privateering, 1500–1689', in A.G. Jamieson, (ed.), *A People of the Sea. The Maritime History of the Channel Islands*, (London, 1986), pp. 59–105.

Armorial Général de la France. Registre premier (-sixième), ed. L.P. d'Hozier, 6 vols. (Paris, 1738–68).

Armorial Général de France de d'Hozier. Complément. Notice Généalogique sur la famille Sohier de Vermandois, (Paris, 1879).

Atkinson, E.G., 'The Cardinal of Châtillon in England, 1568–1571', *HSP*, 3 (1888–91), 172–285.

Backhouse, M.F., 'The Official Start of Armed Resistance in the Low Countries: Boeschepe 12 July 1562', *Archiv für Reformationsgeschichte*, 71 (1980), 198–226.

Backhouse, M.F., 'De Vlaamse vluchtelingenkerk in Sandwich in 1563. Twee manuscripten uit het British Museum', *Bulletin de la Commission Royale d'Histoire*, 147 (1981), 75–113.

Backhouse, M.F., 'De Vlaamse vluchtelingenkerk in Sandwich in 1573. Een derde manuscript uit het British Museum', *Bulletin de la Commission Royale d'Histoire*, 148 (1982), 229–67.

Backhouse, M.F., 'Guerilla War and Banditry in the Sixteenth Century: the Wood Beggars in the Westkwartier of Flanders (1567–1568)', *Archiv für Reformationsgeschichte*, 74 (1983), 232–56.

Backhouse, M.F., 'The Strangers at Work in Sandwich: Native Envy of an Industrious Minority 1561–1603', *Immigrants and Minorities*, 10 (1991), 70–99.

Backhouse, M.F., *The Flemish and Walloon Communities at Sandwich during the Reign of Elizabeth I (1561–1603)*, (Brussels, 1995).

Balleine, G.R., *A Biographical Dictionary of Jersey*, (London, 1948).

Barbier, F., 'L'imprimerie, la Réforme et l'Allemagne: le cas de Nicolas Bassé, Valenciennois', *Valentiana*, 12 (1993), 9–16.

Barrett Lennard, T., 'Glass-making at Knole, Kent', *The Antiquary*, 41 (1905), 127–29.

Barry, J., (ed.), *The Tudor and Stuart Town. A Reader in English Urban History 1530–1688*, (London, 1990).

Benedict, P., 'Heurs et malheurs d'un gros bourg drapant. Note sur la population de Darnétal aux XVIᵉ et XVIIᵉ siècles', *Annales de Normandie*, 28 (1978), 195–205.

Benedict, P., *Rouen during the Wars of Religion*, (Cambridge, 1981).

Benedict, P., 'Rouen's Foreign Trade during the Era of the Religious Wars (1560–1600)', *The Journal of European Economic History*, 13 (1984), 29–74.

Bernard, G., et al., *Les Familles Protestantes en France XVIᵉ siècle-1792. Guides des recherches biographiques et généalogiques*, (Paris, 1987).

Beuzart, 'La Réforme dans les environs de Lille, spécialement à Armentières, en 1566 d'après un document inédit', *BSHPF*, 78 (1929), 42–60.

Beuzart, P., *La répression à Valenciennes après les troubles religieux de 1566*, (Paris, 1930).

Bisson, S.W., 'The Minute Book of the Jersey Colloquy, 1577–1614', *Société Jersiaise. Bulletin Annual*, 22 (1977–80), 310–17.

Black, J.B., 'Queen Elizabeth, the Sea Beggars, and the Capture of Brille, 1572', *English Historical Review*, 46 (1931), 30–47.

Bor, P., *Oorsprongk, begin, en vervolgh der Nederlandsche oorlogen*, 4 vols. (Amsterdam, 1679–84).

Boumans, R., 'Le dépeuplement d'Anvers dans le dernier quart du XVIᵉ siècle', *Revue du Nord*, 29 (1947), 181–94.

Bowden, P.J., *The Wool Trade in Tudor and Stuart England*, (London, 1962).

Bratchel, M.E., 'Alien merchant colonies in sixteenth-century England: community organisation and social mores', *Journal of Medieval and Renaissance Studies*, 14 (1984), 39–62.

Brenner, R., *Merchants and Revolution. Commercial Change, Political Conflict, and London's Overseas Traders, 1550–1653*, (Cambridge, 1993).

Briels, J., 'De Emigratie uit de Zuidelijke Nederlanden Omstreeks 1540–1621/30' in *Opstand en Pacificatie in de Lage Landen. Bijdrage tot de studie van Pacificatie van Gent*, (Ghent, 1976), pp. 184–220.

Briels, J., *Zuid-Nederlanders in de Republiek 1572–1630. Een demografische en cultuurhistorische studie*, (Sint-Niklaas, n.d.).

Brulez, W., 'De diaspora der Antwerpse kooplui op het einde van de 16e eeuw', *Bijdragen voor de geschiedenis der Nederlanden*, 15 (1959–60), 279–306.

Burn, J.S., *The History of the French, Walloon, Dutch and other Foreign Protestant refugees settled in England*, (London, 1846).

Camden, W., *The History of the most Renowned and Victorious Princess Elizabeth, late Queen of England*, (London, 1675).

Carpentier, J.B., *La Véritable origine de la très-ancienne et très-illustre maison de Sohier*, (Leiden, 1661).

Cauvin, M., 'Dernière Expédition de Montgomery dans le Cotentin (1574)', *BSHPF*, 104 (1958), 201–7.

Cauvin, M. 'Le Protestantisme dans le Cotentin, XVIᵉ, XVIIᵉ, XVIIIᵉ, XIXᵉ & XXᵉ siècles', *BSHPF*, 112 (1966), 365–88; 113 (1967), 66–86, 347–70,

473–80; 114 (1968), 114–18, 433–44; 115 (1969), 79–92; 116 (1970), 57–
84, 268–83, 428–36, 598–613; 117 (1971), 69–84.

Clark, E.G., 'Glass-making in Lorraine', *Journal of the Society of Glass Technology*, 15 (1931), 107–19.

Clark, P. & Slack, P., (ed.), *Crisis and Order in English Towns, 1500–1700*, (London, 1972).

Clark, P., 'The migrant in Kentish towns, 1580–1640', in P. Clark & P. Slack, (ed.), *Crisis and Order in English Towns, 1500–1700*, (London, 1972), pp. 117–63.

Clark, P., 'A Crisis Contained? The Condition of English Towns in the 1590s', in P. Clark, (ed.), *The European Crisis of the 1590s. Essays in Comparative History*, (London, 1985), pp. 44–66.

Coleman, D.C., 'The Early British Paper Industry and the Huguenots', *HSP*, 19 (1952–58), 210–25.

Coleman, D.C, 'An Innovation and its Diffusion: the "New Draperies" ', *Ec.H.R.*, Second Series, 22 (1969), 417–29.

Collinson, P., *Archbishop Grindal, 1519–1583. The Struggle for a Reformed Church*, (London, 1979).

Collinson, P., *The Religion of Protestants. The Church in English Society, 1559–1625*, (Oxford, 1982).

Collinson, P., 'Calvinism with an Anglican Face: The Stranger Churches in Early Elizabethan London and their Superintendent', in *idem, Godly People. Essays on English Protestantism and Puritanism*, (London, 1983), pp. 213–44.

Collinson, P., 'The Elizabethan Puritans and the Foreign Reformed Churches in London', in *idem, Godly People. Essays on English Protestantism and Puritanism*, (London, 1983), pp. 245–72.

Collinson, P., 'The Protestant Town', in *idem, The Birthpangs of Protestant England. Religious and Cultural Change in the Sixteenth and Seventeenth Centuries*, (Basingstoke, 1988), pp. 28–59.

Coornaert, E., *Un centre industriel d'autrefois. La draperie-sayetterie d'Hondschoote (XIVe – XVIIIe siècles)*, (Paris, 1930).

Coornaert, E., 'Draperies rurales, draperies urbaines. L'évolution de l'industrie flamande au moyen age et au XVIe siècle', *Revue Belge de philologie et d'histoire*, 28 (1950), 59–96.

Coornaert, E., *Les Français et le commerce international à Anvers. Fin du XVe – XVIe siècle*, 2 vols. (Paris, 1961).

Corfield, P., 'Urban Development in England and Wales in the sixteenth and seventeenth centuries', in J. Barry, (ed.), *The Tudor and Stuart Town. A Reader in English Urban History 1530–1688*, (London, 1990), pp. 35–62.

Cottret, B., *Terre d'exil. L'Angleterre et ses réfugiés français et wallons, de la Réforme à la Révocation de l'Edit de Nantes, 1500–1700*, (Paris, 1985).

Cottret, B., *The Huguenots in England. Immigration and Settlement, c. 1550–1700*, (Cambridge, 1991).

Courbet, D., 'Les Protestants à Valenciennes entre 1520 et 1545', *Valentiana*, 12 (1993), 17–24.

Craeybeckx, J., *Un grand commerce d'importation: Les vins de France aux anciens Pays-Bas (XIIIᵉ – XVIᵉ siècle)*, (Paris, 1958).

Crawford, O.G.S., 'Mead Hole and Shoesflete', *PHFC*, 17 (1949–52), 112–15.

Crew, P.M., *Calvinist Preaching and Iconoclasm in the Netherlands, 1544–1569*, (Cambridge, 1978).

Cross, F.W., *History of the Walloon & Huguenot Church at Canterbury*, (HSQS, 15, 1898).

Cunningham, W., *Alien Immigrants to England*, (Second edition, New York, 1969).

Davies, J.S., *A History of Southampton*, (Southampton, 1883).

Decavele, J., *De Dageraad van de Reformatie in Vlaanderen (1520–1565)*, 2 vols. (Brussels, 1975).

Delafosse, M., 'Les Corsaires Protestants à La Rochelle (1570–1577)', *Bibliothèque de l'Ecole des Chartes*, 121 (1963), 187–217.

Demeulenaere-Douyère, C., 'Les espagnols et la Société Rouennaise au XVIᵉ siècle', *Etudes Normandes*, 3 (1981), 75–81.

Denis, P., 'Disciplines of Huguenot Churches in England: A Handlist', *HSP*, 22 (1970–76), 353–355.

Denis, P., 'Bibliographie de l'histoire démographique des réfugiés flamands et wallons en Angleterre (1558–1625), *Bulletin de la Société d'Histoire du Protestantisme Belge*, 6 (1974), 61–80, 97–124.

Denis, P., ' "Discipline" in the English Huguenot Churches of the Reformation: a Legacy or a Novelty?', *HSP*, 23 (1977–82), 166–72.

Denis, P., *Les Eglises d'étrangers en Pays Rhénans (1538–1564)*, (Paris, 1984).

Denis, P., 'Pour une histoire économique et sociale des réfugiés wallons et flamands à Norwich au XVIᵉ siècle: Travaux récents et sources inexplorées', *Analectes et Bibliothèques de Belgique*, 46, 472–88.

Dent, C.M., *Protestant Reformers in Elizabethan Oxford*, (Oxford, 1983).

Deursen, A.T. van, *Plain Lives in a Golden Age. Popular culture, religion and society in seventeenth-century Holland*, (Cambridge, 1991).

Deyon, S. & Lottin, A., *Les 'Casseurs' de l'été 1566. L'iconoclasme dans le Nord de la France*, (Paris, 1981).

Dictionaire des Familles Françaises anciennes ou notable à la fin du XIXe siècle, (Evreux, 1904).

Dictionary of National Biography, ed. L. Stephen & S. Lee, 21 vols. (Oxford, 1917).

Dietz, B., 'The Huguenot and English Corsairs during the Third Civil War in France, 1568 to 1570', *HSP*, 19 (1952–58), 278–94.

Dietz, B., 'Overseas trade and metropolitan growth', in A.L.Beier & R. Finlay, (ed.), *London 1500–1700. The making of the metropolis*, (London, 1986), pp. 115–40.

Douyère, C., 'Les marchands étrangers à Rouen au XVIᵉ siècle', *Revue des Sociétés Savantes de Haute-Normandie, Lettres et Sciences Humaines*, 69 (1973), 23–61; 73 (1974), 27–61.

Duke, A.C., *Reformation and Revolt in the Low Countries*, (London, 1990).

DuPlessis, R.S., *Lille and the Dutch Revolt. Urban Stability in an Era of Revolution 1500–1582*, (Cambridge, 1991).

Dupont, G., *Histoire du Cotentin et de ses îles*, 4 vols. (Caen, 1870–85).

Dyer, A., 'Growth and Decay in English Towns 1500–1700', *Urban History Yearbook*, 1979, 60–72.

Eagleston, A.J., 'The Quarrel between the Ministers and the Civil Power, 1581–5', *La Société Guernesiaise. Reports and Transactions*, 12 (1933–36), 480–90.

Eagleston, A.J., 'Guernsey under Sir Thomas Leighton (1570–1610)', *La Société Guernesiaise. Reports and Transactions*, 13 (1937–45), 72–108.

Eagleston, A.J., *The Channel Islands under Tudor Government, 1485–1642*, (Cambridge, 1949).

Esser, R., 'Social Concern and Calvinistic Duty: The Norwich Strangers' Community', in *Het Beloofde Land. Acht opstellen over werken, geloven en vluchten tijdens de XVIe en XVIIe eeuw*, (Dikkebus-Ieper, 1992), pp. 172–84.

Esser, R., *Niederländische Exulanten im England des 16. und frühen 17. Jahrhunderts*, (Berlin, 1996).

Fanu, W.R. le, 'Huguenot Refugee Doctors in England', *HSP*, 19 (1952–58), 113–27.

Fines, J., *A Biographical Register of Early English Protestants and others opposed to the Roman Catholic Church 1525–1558*, (n.p., 1981).

Fisher, F.J., 'Commercial trends and policy in sixteenth-century England', *Ec.H.R.*, 10 (1939–40), 95–117.

Fox, R., & Lewis, E., *William Overton and Glassmaking in Buriton*, (Petersfield, 1982).

French, M.J., 'Privateering and the Revolt of the Netherlands: The *Watergeuzen* or Sea Beggars in Portsmouth, Gosport and the Isle of Wight 1570–71', *PHFC*, 47 (1991), 171–80.

Fréville, E. de, *Mémoire sur le commerce maritime de Rouen*, 2 vols. (Paris-Rouen, 1857).

Fritze, R.H., 'The role of the family and religion in the local politics of Early Elizabethan England: The case of Hampshire in the 1560s', *The Historical Journal*, 25 (1982), 267–87.

Fritze, R.H., ' "A Rare Example of Godlyness Amongst Gentlemen": The Role of the Kingsmill and Gifford families in Promoting the Reformation in Hampshire', in P. Lake & M. Dowling, (ed.), *Protestantism and the National Church in Sixteenth Century England*, (London, 1987), pp. 144–61.

Frondeville, H. de, *Les conseillers du Parlement de Normandie au seizième siècle (1499–1594)*, (Paris-Rouen, 1960).

Garrett, C.H., *The Marian Exiles. A Study in the Origins of Elizabethan Puritanism*, (Cambridge, 1938).

Gilmont, J.F., 'Premières éditions françaises de la *Confessio belgica* (1561–1562)', *Quaerendo*, 2 (1972), 173–81.

Godfrey, E.S., *The Development of English Glassmaking 1560–1640*, (Oxford, 1975).

Goose, N., 'Household size and structure in early Stuart Cambridge', *Social History*, 5 (1980), 347–85.

Goose, N., 'The "Dutch" in Colchester: the Economic Influence of an Immigrant Community in the Sixteenth and Seventeenth Centuries', *Immigrants and Minorities*, 1 (1982), 261–80.

Gosselin, 'Simple Notes sur les Imprimeurs et Libraires Rouennais', *Glânes Historiques Normandes a Travers les XVe, XVIe, XVIIe et XVIIIe siècles. Documents inédits*, (Extraits de la Revue de la Normandie, 1869), 53–175.

Gould, J.D., 'The Crisis in the Export Trade, 1586–1587', *English Historical Review*, 71 (1956), 212–22.

Grave, J.W. de, 'Notes on the Register of the Walloon Church of Southampton and on the Churches of the Channel Islands', *HSP*, 5 (1894–96), 125–78.

Grazebrook, H.S., *Collections for a Genealogy of the Noble Families of Henzey, Tyttery, and Tyzack*, (Stourbridge, 1877).

Gray, I.R., *Huguenot Manuscripts: A descriptive catalogue of the remaining manuscripts in the Huguenot Library*, (HSQS, 56, 1983).

Greengrass, M., 'Protestant Exiles and their Assimilation in Early Modern England', *Immigrants and Minorities*, 4 (1985), 68–81.

Grell, O.P., *Dutch Calvinists in Early Stuart London. The Dutch Church in Austin Friars, 1603–1642*, (Leiden, 1989).

Grell, O.P., Israel, J.I., Tyacke, N., (ed.), *From Persecution to Toleration. The Glorious Revolution and Religion in England*, (Oxford, 1991).

Grell, O.P., 'Merchants and ministers: the foundations of international Calvinism', in A. Pettegree, A.Duke & G. Lewis, (ed.), *Calvinism in Europe 1540–1620*, (Cambridge 1994), pp. 254–73.

Gwynn, R.D., 'Disciplines of Huguenot Churches in England: The Need for Further Research', *HSP*, 22 (1970–76), 590–93.

Gwynn, R.D., *Huguenot Heritage. The history and contribution of the Huguenots in Britain*, (London, 1985).

Haag, E. & Haag, E., (ed.), *La France Protestante*, First edition, 10 vols. (Paris, 1846–58); Second edition, 6 vols. (Paris, 1877–88).

Haigh, C., *English Reformations. Religion, Politics, and Society under the Tudors*, (Oxford, 1993).

Hardy, W.J., 'Foreign Settlers at Colchester and Halstead', *HSP*, 2 (1887–88), 182–196.

Hardy, W.J., 'Foreign Refugees at Rye', *HSP*, 2 (1887–88), 406–27, 567–87.

Hasler, P.W., (ed.), *The History of Parliament. The House of Commons 1558–1603*, 3 vols. (London, 1981).

Hocquet, A., *Tournai et le Tournaisis au XVIe siècle au point de vue politique et social*, (Brussels, 1906).

Horridge, W., 'Documents relating to the Lorraine Glassmakers in North Staffordshire, with some notes thereon', *Glass Notes*, 15 (1955), 26–33.

Houlbrooke, R.A., *Church Courts and the People during the English Reformation 1520–1570*, (Oxford, 1979).

Hutton, R., 'The local impact of the Tudor Reformations', in C. Haigh, (ed.), *The English Reformation Revised*, (Cambridge, 1987), pp. 114–38.

James, T.B., *Southampton Sources: 1086–1900*, (SRS, 26, 1983).

James, T.B., 'Southampton and Spain in the Sixteenth Century: A survey of sources for links with the Iberian peninsula to 1588', in C.M. Gerrard & A. Gutiérrez, (ed)., *Spanish Medieval Ceramics in Spain and the British Isles*, (British Archaeological Reports (International Series), 610, 1995), pp. 41–49.

Janssen, H.Q., *Kerkhervorming in Vlaanderen*, 2 vols. (Arnhem, 1868).

Jones, J.D., 'The Hampshire Beacon Plot of 1586', *PHFC*, 25 (1968), 105–18.

Kell, E., 'On the Discovery of a Glass Factory at Buckholt', *The Journal of the British Archaeological Association*, 17 (1861), 55–58.

Kenyon, G.H., *The Glass Industry of the Weald*, (Leicester, 1967).

Kerling. N.J.M., 'Aliens in the County of Norfolk, 1436–1485', *Norfolk Archaeology*, 33 (1962–65), 200–15.

Kernkamp, J.H., *De Handel op den vijand 1572–1609*, 2 vols. (Utrecht, 1913, 1934).

Kerridge, E., *Textile Manufactures in Early Modern England*, (Manchester, 1985).

Kingdon, R.M., *et al.*, 'Disciplines réformées du XVIᵉ siècle français: une découverte faite aux Etats-Unis', *BSHPF*, 130 (1984), 69–81.

Knetsch, F.R.J., 'Kerkordelijke bepalingen van de Nederlandse synoden "onder het kruis" (1563–64), vergeleken met die van de Franse (1559–1564)', in J. Fabius, A. Spaanse, J. Spaans, (ed.), *Feestbundel uitegeven ter gelegenheid van het 80 – jarig bestaan van het Kerkhistorisch Gezelschap S.S.S.*, (Leiden, 1982), pp. 29–44.

Lamet, M.S., 'French Protestants in a Position of Strength: The Early Years of the Reformation in Caen, 1558–1568', *Sixteenth Century Journal*, 9 (1978), 35–53.

Landurant, A., *Montgommery le régicide*, (Paris, 1988).

Langeraad, L.A. van, *Guido de Bray. Zijn leven en werken*, (Zierikzee, 1884).

Lapeyre, H., *Une Famille de Marchands, les Ruiz. Contribution à l'étude du commerce entre la France et l'Espagne au temps de Philippe II*, (Paris, 1955).

Lelièvre, M., 'La Réforme dans les îles de la Manche', *BSHPF*, 34 (1885), 4–18, 52–68, 97–109, 145–63.

Lesens, E., *Le Protestantisme dans le Pays de Caux*, ed. V. Madelaine, (Paris, 1906).

Lindeboom, J., *Austin Friars. History of the Dutch Reformed Church in London 1550–1950*, (The Hague, 1950).

Lloyd, H.A., *The Rouen Campaign 1590–1592. Politics, Warfare and the Early-Modern State*, (Oxford, 1973).

MacCaffrey, W.T., *Queen Elizabeth and the Making of Policy, 1572–1588*, (Princeton, 1981).

MacCaffrey, W.T., *Elizabeth I. War and Politics, 1588–1603*, (Princeton, 1992).

Magen, B., *Die Wallonengemeinde in Canterbury von ihrer Gründung bis zum Jahre 1635*, (Frankfurt, 1973).

Magen, B., 'The administration within the Walloon settlement in Canterbury, 1576–1599', *HSP*, 22 (1970–76), 307–17.

Mahieu, E., 'Le protestantisme à Mons des origines à 1575', *Annales du Cercle Archéologique de Mons*, 66 (1965–67), 129–247.

Marnef, G., 'The changing face of Calvinism in Antwerp, 1550–1585', in A. Pettegree, A. Duke & G. Lewis, (ed.), *Calvinism in Europe 1540–1620*, (Cambridge, 1994), pp. 143–59.

Marnef, G., *Antwerp in the Age of Reformation. Underground Protestantism in a Commercial Metropolis, 1550–1577*, (London, 1996).

Maulvault, A., 'La Réforme à Guernesey', *BSHPF*, 17 (1868), 254–56.

Mayhew, G., *Tudor Rye*, (Hove, 1987).

Meij, J.C.A. de, *De Watergeuzen en de Nederlanden 1568–1572*, (Amsterdam-London, 1972).

Merson, A.L., 'The History of Southampton: Southampton in the Sixteenth and Seventeenth Centuries', in F.J. Monkhouse, (ed.), *A Survey of Southampton and Its Region*, (Southampton, 1964), pp. 218–27.

Messervy, J.A., 'Listes des Recteurs de l'île de Jersey', *Société Jersiaise. Bulletin Annual*, 7 (1910–14), 75–98, 127–46, 265–88, 379–98.

Minns, G.W., 'The Slavonian Tombstone at North Stoneham. A Chapter in the History of the ancient Commerce of Southampton', *PHFC* 2 (1891–93), 356–64.

Moens, W.J.C., 'Discipline of the French Church of London, 1578', *HSP*, 2 (1887–88), 456–63.

Moens, W.J.C., 'The Walloon Settlement and the French Church at Southampton', *HSP*, 3 (1888–91), 53–76.

Moens, W.J.C., 'The Relief of the poor members of the French Churches in England', *HSP*, 5 (1894–96), 321–42.

Mollat, M., *Le commerce maritime de normand à la fin du moyen âge. Etude d'histoire économique et sociale*, (Paris, 1952).

Monter, E.W., *Studies in Genevan Government (1536–1605)*, (Geneva, 1964).

Monter, E.W., 'Historical Demography and Religious History in Sixteenth-Century Geneva', *Journal of Interdisciplinary History*, 9 (1979), 399–427.

Morant, V., 'The settlement of Protestant Refugees in Maidstone during the sixteenth century', *Ec.H.R.*, Second Series, 4 (1951–52), 210–14.

Moreau, G., *Histoire du Protestantisme à Tournai jusqu'à la veille de la Révolution des Pays-Bas*, (Paris, 1962).

Murdoch, T., (ed.), *The Quiet Conquest. The Huguenots 1685 to 1985. A Museum of London exhibition in association with the Huguenot Society, 15 May to 31 October, 1985*, (London, 1985).

Nijenhuis, W., *Adrianus Saravia (c. 1532–1613). Dutch Calvinist, first Reformed defender of the English episcopal church order on the basis of the ius divinum*, (Leiden, 1980).

Nortier, M., 'Les sources de l'histoire du protestantisme en Normandie à la Bibliothèque nationale', in *Protestants et Minorités religieuses en Normandie. Actes du 20ᵉ congrès des Sociétés historiques et archéologiques de Normandie*, (Rouen, 1987), pp. 31–48.

Norwood, F.A. *The Reformation Refugees as an Economic Force*, (Chicago, Illinois, 1942).

Norwood, F.A., 'The Strangers' "Model Churches" in Sixteenth-Century England', in F.H. Littell, (ed.), *Reformation Studies*, (Richmond, Va., 1962), pp. 181–96.

Oakley, A.M., 'The Canterbury Walloon Congregation from Elizabeth I to Laud', in I. Scouloudi, (ed.), *Huguenots in Britain and their French Background, 1550–1800. Contributions to the Historical Conference of the Huguenot Society of London, 24–25 September, 1985*, (Basingstoke, 1987), pp. 56–71.

Oakley, A.M., 'Archbishop Laud and the Walloons in Canterbury', in W.M. Jacobs & N. Yates, (ed.), *Crown and Mitre: Religion and Society in Northern Europe since the Reformation*, (Woodbridge, 1993), pp. 33–43.

Oberman, H.A., '*Europa afflicta*: The Reformation of the Refugees', *Archiv für Reformationsgeschichte*, 83 (1992), 91–111.

Ogier, D.M., 'The Authorship of Warburton's Treatise', *La Société Guernesiaise. Reports and Transactions*, 23 (1986–90), 871–77.

Ogier, D.M., *Reformation and Society in Guernsey*, (Woodbridge, 1996).

Olson, J.E., *Calvin and Social Welfare. Deacons and the Bourse française*, (London, 1989).

Overend, G.H., 'Strangers at Dover', *HSP*, 3 (1888–91), 91–171, 286–330.

Overend, G.H., 'Notes upon the Earlier History of the Manufacture of Paper in England', *HSP*, 8 (1905–8), 177–220.

Paillard, C., *Les Grands Prêches Calvinistes de Valenciennes 7 Juillet-18 Août 1566*, (Paris, 1877).

Paillard, C., 'Note sur Michielle de Caignoncle', *BSHPF*, 26 (1877), 554–63.

Pannier, J., 'Les Montgomery et leurs Eglises de Lorges et de Ducey (1562–1682)', *BSHPF*, 90 (1941), 291–97.

Parker, D., *The Making of French Absolutism*, (London, 1983).

Parker, G., *The Dutch Revolt*, (London, 1977).

Parker, G., *The Thirty Years' War*, (London, 1984).

Parquier, M.E. le, 'Le commerce maritime de Rouen dans la seconde moitié du XVIe siècle', *Bulletin de la Société libre d'Emulation du commerce et de l'industrie de la Seine-Inférieure*, (1926–27), 87–116.

Paul, J.E., 'Hampshire Recusants in the time of Elizabeth I, with special reference to Winchester', *PHFC*, 21 (1958–60), 61–81.

Pearl, V., 'Change and stability in seventeenth-century London', in J.Barry, (ed.), *The Tudor and Stuart Town. A Reader in English Urban History 1530–1688*, (London, 1990), pp. 139–65.

Pettegree, A., *Foreign Protestant Communities in Sixteenth-Century London*, (Oxford, 1986).

Pettegree, A., 'The Exile Churches and the Churches "Under the Cross": Antwerp and Emden During the Dutch Revolt', *Journal of Ecclesiastical History*, 38 (1987), 187–209.

Pettegree, A., *Emden and the Dutch Revolt. Exile and the Development of Reformed Protestantism*, (Oxford, 1992).

Pettegree, A., (ed.), *The Reformation of the Parishes. The ministry and the Reformation in town and country*, (Manchester, 1993).

Phythian-Adams, C., 'Urban Decay in Late Medieval England', in P. Abrams & E.A. Wrigley, (ed.), *Towns in Societies. Essays in Economic History and Historical Sociology*, (Cambridge, 1978), pp. 159–85.

Phythian-Adams, C.V., 'Dr Dyer's Urban Undulations', *Urban History Yearbook*, 1979, 73–76.

Platt, C., *Medieval Southampton. The port and trading community, AD 1000–1600*, (London, 1973).

Poole, R.L., *A History of the Huguenots of the Dispersion at the recall of the Edict of Nantes*, (London, 1880).

Portal, W.W., *Some Account of the Settlement of Refugees [l'Eglise Wallonne] at Southampton and of the Chapel of St. Julian, attached to the Hospital of God's House [Maison Dieu] in which they worshipped*, (Winchester, 1902).

Priestley, U., *The Fabric of Stuffs. The Norwich textile industry from 1565*, (Norwich, 1990).

Prims, F., *Beelden uit den cultuurstrijd der jaren 1577–1585*, (Antwerpensia, 15e reeks), (Antwerp, 1942).

Ramsay, G.D., 'The Distribution of the Cloth Industry in 1561–2', *English Historical Review*, 57 (1942), 361–69.

Ramsay, G.D., *The Wiltshire Woollen Industry in the Sixteenth and Seventeenth Centuries*, (London, 1943).

Ramsay, G.D., *The City of London in international politics at the accession of Elizabeth Tudor*, (Manchester, 1975).

Ramsay, G.D., *The Queen's Merchants and the Revolt of the Netherlands*, (Manchester, 1986).

Read, C., 'Queen Elizabeth's seizure of the Duke of Alva's pay-ships', *Journal of Modern History*, 5 (1933), 443–64.

Redstone, V.B., 'The Dutch and Huguenot Settlements at Ipswich', *HSP*, 12 (1917–23), 183–204.

Regnault, J-M., & Vermander, P., 'La crise iconoclaste de 1566 dans la région d'Armentières. Essai de description et d'interpretation', *Revue du Nord*, 59 (1977), 221–31.

Reulos, M., 'La Réforme et les relations entre la Normandie et l'Angleterre au cours de la seconde moitié du XVIᵉ siècle', *Revue des Sociétés Savantes Haute-Normandie, Lettres et Sciences Humaines*, 53 (1969), 37–40.

Reulos, M., 'Les débuts des Communautés réformées dans l'actuel département de la Manche (Cotentin et Avranchin)', *Revue du département de la Manche*, 24 (1982) numéro special, fasc. 93–95, 31–61.

Reynolds, B., 'Elizabethan Traders in Normandy', *Journal of Modern History*, 9 (1937), 289–303.

Richard, R., & Vatinel, D., 'Le Consistoire de l'Eglise réformée du Havre au XVIIᵉ siècle', *BSHPF*, 127 (1981), 1–77; 128 (1982), 283–362.

Roosbroeck, R. van, *Het Wonderjaar te Antwerpen 1566–1567. Inleiding tot de studie der godsdienstonlusten te Antwerpen van 1566 tot 1585*, (Antwerp, 1930).

Rosen, A., 'Winchester in transition, 1580–1700', in P. Clark, (ed.), *Country towns in pre-industrial England*, (Leicester, 1981), pp. 144–95.

Ruddock, A.A., 'Antonio Guidotti', *PHFC*, 15 (1941–43), 34–42.

Ruddock, A.A., 'The Merchants of Venice and their shipping in Southampton in the fifteenth and sixteenth centuries', *PHFC* 15 (1941–43), 274–91.

Ruddock, A.A., 'Alien Hosting in Southampton in the Fifteenth Century', *Ec.H.R.*, 16 (1946), 30–37.

Ruddock, A.A., 'Alien Merchants in Southampton in the Later Middle Ages', *English Historical Review*, 61 (1946), 1–17.

Ruddock, A.A., 'The Greyfriars in Southampton', *PHFC*, 16 (1944–47), 137–47.

Ruddock, A.A., 'London Capitalists and the Decline of Southampton in the early Tudor Period', *Ec.H.R.*, Second Series, 2 (1949–50), 137–51.

Ruddock, A.A., *Italian Merchants and Shipping in Southampton 1270–1600*, (SRS, 1, 1951).

Rushen, J., 'The Secret "Iron Tongs" of Midwifery', *The Historian*, 30 (1991), 12–14.

Russell, C.F., *A History of King Edward VI School, Southampton*, (Cambridge, 1940).

Salmon, J.H.M., *Society in Crisis. France in the Sixteenth Century*, (London, 1975).

Schama, S., *The Embarrassment of Riches. An Interpretation of Dutch Culture in the Golden Age*, (London, 1987).

Scheerder, J., 'Eenige nieuwe bijzonderheden betreffende het 3.000.000 goudguldens rekwest (1566)', in *Miscellanea Historica in honorem Leonis van der Essen*, (Brussels, 1947), pp. 559–66.

Schelven, A.A. van, 'Het verzoekschrift der drie millioen goud-guldens (October 1566)', *Bijdragen voor Vaderlandsche Geschiedenis en Oudheidkunde*, 6 No. 9 (1924–30), 1–42.

Schickler, F. de, *Les Eglises du Refuge en Angleterre*, 3 vols. (Paris, 1892).

Schilling, H., *Niederländische Exulanten im 16. Jahrhundert. Ihre Stellung im Sozialgefüge und im religiösen Leben deutscher und englischer Städte*, (Gütersloh, 1972).

Schilling, H., 'Innovation through Migration: The Settlements of Calvinistic Netherlanders in Sixteenth- and Seventeenth-Century Central and Western Europe', *Social History*, 16 (1983), 7–33.

Scott-Giles, C.W., (rev.), *Boutell's Heraldry*, (London, 1958).

Seward, D., 'The Devonshire cloth industry in the early seventeenth century' in R. Burt, (ed.), *Industry and Society in the South West*, (Exeter, 1970), pp. 29–50.

Smiles, S., *The Huguenots: their settlements, churches and industries in England and Ireland*, (Third edition, London, 1869).

Smith, R., *The Archives of the French Protestant Church of London*, (HSQS, 50, 1972).

[Sociéte de l'Histoire du Protestantisme Français], *Les Réformés à la fin du XVIᵉ siècle. Relevés de documents dans les fonds d'archives*, (Paris, n.d.).

Soil de Moriamé, E., 'L'église de Saint-Brice à Tournai', *Annales de la Société historique et archéologique de Tournai*, nouvelle série, 13 (1908), 73–638.

South, M.L., 'Epidemic Diseases, Soldiers and Prisoners of war in Southampton, 1550–1800', *PHFC*, 43 (1987), 185–96.

Southampton City Record Office, *Southampton in 1620 and the Mayflower. An Exhibition of Documents*, (Southampton, 1970).

Southampton City Record Office, *Southampton's Huguenot Heritage. An exhibition at Tudor House Museum*, (Southampton, 1985).

Spicer, A., 'Presbyterian Disorders: The State of Religion on Guernsey, 1582', *La Société Guernesiaise. Reports and Transactions*, 22 (1986–90), 638–42.

Spicer, A., 'The Sohiers of Valenciennes and Southampton: a Walloon family in the Diaspora', *HSP*, 25 (1989–93), 156–66.

Spicer, A., 'Valenciennes et Southampton: un nouvel éclairage sur leurs liens au XVIème siècle', *Valentiana*, 10 (1992), 33–44.

Spicer, A., 'Southampton, Sea Beggars and the Dutch Revolt, 1567–1573' in T. Hermans & R. Salverda, *From Revolt to Riches. Culture and History of the Low Countries 1500–1700*, (London, 1993), pp. 74–82.

Spicer, A., ' "A Faythful Pastor in the Churches": ministers in the French and Walloon communities in England, 1560–1620', in A. Pettegree, (ed.), *The Reformation of the Parishes. The ministry and the Reformation in town and country*, (Manchester, 1993), pp. 195–214.

Spicer, A., 'A process of gradual assimilation: the exile community in Southampton, 1567–1635', *HSP*, 26 (1995–), pp. 186–98.

Spicer, A., 'Poor relief and the exile communities', in B. Kümin, (ed.), *Reformations Old and New. Essays on the Socio-Economic Impact of Religious Change, c. 1470–1630*, (Aldershot, 1996), pp. 237–55.

Stelling-Michaud, S., (ed.), *Le Livre du Recteur de l'Académie de Genève (1559–1878)*, 6 vols. (Geneva, 1959–80).

Stone, L., 'Elizabethan Overseas Trade', *Ec.H.R.*, Second Series, 2 (1949–50), 30–58.

Sugden, J., *Sir Francis Drake*, (London, 1990).

Thielemans, M-R., *Bourgogne et Angleterre. Relations politiques et economiques entre les Pays-Bas Bourguignons et l'Angleterre 1435–1467*, (Brussels, 1966).

Thomas, J.H., 'Hampshire and the Company of White Paper Makers', *PHFC*, 26 (1969), 137–48.

Thrupp, S.L., 'Aliens in and around London in the Fifteenth Century', in A.E.J. Hollaender & W.Kellaway, (ed.), *Studies in London History presented to Philip Edmund Jones*, (London 1969), pp. 251–72.

Tittler, R., 'The Vitality of an Elizabethan Port: The Economy of Poole, c. 1550–1600', *Southern History*, 7 (1985), 95–118.

Trevor-Roper, H.R., 'Religion, the Reformation and Social Change' in *idem*, *Religion, the Reformation and Social Change and other Essays*, (London 1967), pp. 1–45.

Trocmé, E., 'L'Eglise Réformée de La Rochelle jusqu'en 1628', *BSHPF*, 99 (1952), 133–99.

Trocmé, E. & Delafosse, M., *Le Commerce Rochelais de la fin du XVᵉ siècle au début du XVIIᵉ*, (Paris, 1952).

Vane, C.M., 'The Walloon community in Norwich: the first hundred years', *HSP*, 24 (1983–88), 129–40.

Verheyden, A.L.E., *Le Conseil des Troubles. Liste des condamnés 1567–1573*, (Brussels, 1961).

The Victoria History of the Counties of England. Hampshire and the Isle of Wight, ed. H.A. Doubleday *et al.*, 5 vols. (London, 1900–12)

Wagenaar, J., *Vaderlandsche historie, vervattende de geschiedenissen der nu Vereenigde Nederlanden, inzonderheid die van Holland, van de vroegste tyden af*, 21 vols. (Amsterdam, 1749–59).

Weber, M., *The Protestant Ethic and the Spirit of Capitalism*, trans. T. Parsons, (London, 1930).

Wernham, R.B., *After the Armada. Elizabethan England and the Struggle for Western Europe 1588–1595*, (Oxford, 1984).

Whitlock, J.A., 'Domus Dei, or the Hospital of St. Julian, Southampton', *HSP*, 3 (1888–91), 42–52.

Willems-Closset, M-P., 'Le protestantisme à Lille jusqu'à la veille de la révolution des Pays-Bas (1521–1565)', *Revue du Nord*, 52 (1970), 199–216.

Williams, N.J., 'Two documents concerning the New Draperies', *Ec.H.R.*, Second Series, 4 (1951–52), 353–58.

Williams, N.J., *The Maritime Trade of the East Anglian Ports, 1550–1590*, (Oxford, 1988).

Wilson, C., *Queen Elizabeth and the Revolt of the Netherlands*, (London, 1970).

Winbolt, S.E., *Wealden Glass. The Surrey-Sussex Glass Industry, (A.D. 1226–1615)*, (Hove, 1933).

Woodward, D.M., 'Short Guides to records: Port Books', *History*, 55 (1970), 207–10.

Yeomans, D.K., *Comets. A Chronological History of Observation, Science, Myth and Folklore*, (New York, 1991).

Unpublished Theses:

Andrews, K.R., 'The Economic Aspects of Elizabethan Privateering', Ph.D. thesis, University of London, 1951.

Backhouse, M.F., 'The Flemish and Walloon Communities at Sandwich during the reign of Elizabeth I (1561–1603)', Ph.D. thesis, University of Southampton, 1992.

Clark, G.W., 'An Urban Study during the Revolt of the Netherlands: Valenciennes, 1540–1570', Ph.D. thesis, Columbia University, 1972.

Cluse, J. le, 'The Stranger Community and their Church in Southampton 1567–1712', dissertation, Portsmouth Polytechnic, 1988.

Denis, P., 'Les Eglises d'étrangers à Londres jusqu'à la mort de Calvin de l'église de Jean Lasco à l'établissement du calvinisme', mémoire de licence, Liège University, 1973–74.

Dietz, B., 'Privateering in North Western European Waters, 1568–1572', Ph.D. thesis, University of London, 1959.

Esser, R., 'Niederlandische Exulanten im England des späten 16. und frühren 17. Jahrhunderts die Norwicher Fremdengemeinden', Inaugural-Dissertation, Cologne University, 1993.

Fritze, R.H., 'Faith and Faction: Religious changes, national politics and the development of local factionalism in Hampshire, 1485–1570', Ph.D. thesis, Cambridge University, 1981.

Hodeigne, M., 'Le protestantisme à Valenciennes jusqu'à la veille de la Révolution des Pays-Bas', mémoire de licence, Université de Liège, 1966–67.

James, T.B., 'The Geographical Origins and Mobility of the Inhabitants of Southampton, 1400–1600', Ph.D. thesis, University of St. Andrews, 1977.

Jones, J.D., 'The Isle of Wight, 1555–1642', Ph.D. thesis, University of Southampton, 1978.

Lamb, D.F., 'The Seaborne Trade of Southampton in the first half of the seventeenth century', M.Phil. thesis, University of Southampton, 1972.

Marnef, G., 'Antwerpen in Reformatietijd. Ondergrondse protestantisme in een internationale handelsmetropool 1550–1577', thesis, Katholieke Universiteit Leuven, 1991.

Mildon, W.H., 'Puritanism in Hampshire and the Isle of Wight from the reign of Elizabeth to the Restoration', Ph.D. thesis, University of London, 1934.

Ogier, D.M., 'The Reformation and Society in Guernsey c.1500–1640', Ph.D. thesis, University of Warwick, 1993.

Regnault, J-M., & Vermander, P., 'Armentières au temps des troubles religieux du XVIe siècle, 1545–1574', mémoire de maîtrise, Université de Lille III, 1972.

Rothery, E.A., 'Poverty in Southampton, 1540 to 1560', dissertation Portsmouth Polytechnic, 1989.

Spicer, A., 'The French-speaking Reformed community and their Church in Southampton, 1567–c.1620', Ph.D. thesis, University of Southampton, 1994.

Thomas, J.L., (née Wiggs), 'The Seaborne Trade of Southampton in the second half of the sixteenth century', M.A. thesis, University of Southampton, 1955.

Unpublished Typescript:

Bartlett, A., 'Beaulieu in Tudor and Stuart Times. The End of the Abbey: The Wriothesleys 1500–1673', Cope Collection, Hartley Library, University of Southampton.

INDEX

LIST OF SUBSCRIBERS TO THE SERIES

Individual

Alexander, Miss M., M.A., 63 Common Lane, Titchfield, Fareham.
Bonnard, Mr B., The Twins, Le Petit Val, Alderney, Channel Isles.
Bunker, Mr B.A., 32 Redford Ave., Wallington, Surrey.
Butler, Ms C.B., 121 Bernard Street, Bitterne, Southampton.
Casson, M.C., 6 Wayside Green, Woodcote, Reading.
Chandler, J.H., B.A., Ph.D., Jupes School, East Knoyle, Salisbury.
Connor, W.J., Marigold Cottage, Galphay, Ripon, Yorks.
Cook, Mrs J., 7 Plaitford Walk, Southampton.
De Grouchy, P.J.W., 1 Khartoum Road, Southampton.
Diaper, Mr C., 36 Kellett Road, Southampton.
Douch, R., M.A., 46 Wilton Crescent, Southampton.
Douglas, Professor A.E., M.A., The University, Birmingham.
Emery-Wallis, F.A.J., D.L., Froddington, Craneswater Park, Southsea.
George, A., M.A., D.A.A., 33 West Road, Southampton.
Gibbons, Mrs D., 26 Bronte Way, Southampton.
Hammond, J.R.P., 236 Winchester Road, Southampton.
Harwood, Mrs E., 3 Lauriston Drive, Chandlers Ford, Southampton.
Hawes, T.L.M., 8 Keswick Road, Cringleford, Norwich.
Henton, J.C., 23 Welbeck Avenue, Southampton.
Hicks, Professor M., King Alfred's College, Winchester.
Hind, Ms. L., 21 Shaw Close, Andover, Hants.
Hodson, Professor F., B.Sc., Ph.D., F.G.S., The University, Southampton.
Hutton, Professor S.P., D.Eng., Ph.D., The University, Southampton.
James, Mrs D.K., 6 Morley College, The Outer Close, Winchester.
James, J.F., 3 Sylvan Close, Hordle, Lymington, Hants.
James, T.B., M.A., Ph.D., Sydenham Lodge, Cranham Road, Cheltenham, Glos.
Jones, Ms S., Ph.D., 20 Tennyson Road, Southampton.
Kaye, J.M., B.C.L., M.A., The Queen's College, Oxford.
Keene, D.J., D.Phil., 162 Erlanger Road, Telegraph Hill, London.
Key, D.M., 171 Cranbury Road, Eastleigh.
Lawton, Ms L., 23 Foyes Court, Shirley, Southampton.
Leonard, A.G.K., M.A., 10 Radway Road, Southampton.
Lewis, Ms E.A., B.A., 9 Hope View, Shipley, Bradford.
Lewis, Miss E.R., Museum Service, 75 Hyde Street, Winchester, Hants.
Mather, Mrs P.H., M.A., 3 Monks Road, Hyde, Winchester.
Morris, Rev. Professor C., M.A., F.R.Hist.S., 12 Bassett Crescent East, Southampton.
Morris, Mr M., 80 The Butts, Alton, Hants.
Morton, A.D., 32 Graham Road, Southampton.
Ogier, Mr D.M., Le Monnard D'Aval, St Andrews, Guernsey, Channel Isles.
Pain, J.H., 68 Summit Way, Southampton.
Pinhorn, M.A., B.A., F.S.G., Norman's Place, Newport, I.O.W.
Platt, Professor C.P.S., M.A., Ph.D., The University, Southampton.
Reuter, Professor T., M.A., D.Phil., F.R.Hist.S., The University, Southampton.

Riseborough, D., 24 Glenn Road, West End, Hants.
Rothery, Mrs E.A., 32 Hill Place, Bursledon, Southampton.
Ruddock, Miss A.A., B.A., Ph.D., F.R.Hist.S., Wren Cottage, 10 Heatherwood, Midhurst, Sussex.
Selby, Mrs V.A., 32 Oakley Road, Southampton.
Spicer, A., Ph.D., Stonyhurst College, Stonyhurst, Clitheroe, Lancs.
Stevens, Mr P., 6D Arthur Road, Southampton.
Stewart, Mrs S.C., 58 Upper St Helens Road, Hedge End, Southampton.
Sturman, C.J., 30 Broadbank, Louth, Lincs.
Thomson, Ms S.D., 51 Alfriston Gardens, Southampton.
Wagstaff, Professor J.M., Ph.D., The University, Southampton.
Welch, Dr C.E., 7487 Forest Turn, Lantzville, British Columbia, Canada.
White, A.J., 2 Swift Close, Winchester.
Woolgar, Mrs S.L., B.A., D.A.A., 16 Stinchar Drive, Chandlers Ford.

Institutions (Great Britain and Ireland)

Aberystwyth, National Library of Wales (copyright library).
Belfast, The Queen's University Library.
Birmingham, City Library.
Birmingham, University Library.
Bognor Regis College, West Sussex.
Brighton, University of Sussex Library.
Bristol, University Library.
Cambridge, University Library (copyright library).
Coventry, Warwick University Library.
Dublin, Trinity College Library (copyright library).
Edinburgh, National Library of Scotland (copyright library).
Edinburgh, University Library.
Exeter, University Library.
Glasgow, University Library.
Hull, Central Public Library.
Hull, University Library.
Leeds, Brotherton Library, University of Leeds.
Leicester, University Library.
Liverpool, University Library.
London, British Library (copyright library).
London, British Library of Political and Economic Science.
London, College of Arms.
London, Goldsmith's Librarian, University of London.
London, Guildhall Library.
London, Inner Temple Library.
London, Institute of Historical Research.
London, London Library.
London, Public Record Office.
London, Royal Historical Society.
London, Society of Antiquaries of London.
Manchester, University Library.
Newport, I.o.W., County Library.
Norwich, East Anglia University Library.
Nottingham, University Library.
Oxford, Bodleian Library (copyright library).
Oxford, The Queen's College Library.
Portsmouth, Central Public Library.
Portsmouth, Frewen Library, University of Portsmouth.

Reading, University Library.
St Helier, Jersey, Channel Isles, Société Jersiaise, Coutanche Library.
Sheffield, University Library.
Southampton, Central Library.
Southampton, Chamber of Commerce.
Southampton, Civic Record Office.
Southampton, King Edward VI School.
Southampton, La Sainte Union College of Higher Education.
Southampton, Tauntons Sixth Form College Library.
Southampton, St Joseph's Church.
Southampton, Southern Newspapers Ltd.
Southampton, Hartley Library.
Swansea, University College Library.
Wetherby, British Library – Document Supply Centre.
Winchester, City Library.
Winchester, Hampshire County Library.
Winchester, Hampshire Record Office.
Winchester, King Alfred's College of Higher Education.
York, University Library.

Institutions (Overseas)

AUSTRALIA

Adelaide, University Library.
Brisbane, Queensland University Library.
Canberra, Library (Chifley), Australian National University.
Melbourne, Victoria State University Library.
Perth, Western Australia University Library.

CANADA

Edmonton, Alberta University Library.
Kingston, Queen's University Library.
Toronto, University Library.

CHILE

Santiago, Sociedad Chilena de Historia y Geografia.

DENMARK

Copenhagen, Det Kongelige Bibliothek.

FRANCE

Paris, Bibliothèque de l'Université.

GERMANY

Göttingen, Niedersächsische Staats und Universitätsbibliothek.
Munich, Bayerische Staatsbibliothek.

ISRAEL

Jerusalem, Jewish National and University Library.

POLAND

Torun, Towrarzystwo Naukowe w Toruniu.
Warsaw, Institute of History.

PORTUGAL

Oporto, Biblioteca Pública Municipal.

SWEDEN

Uppsala, University Library.

UNITED STATES OF AMERICA

Albuquerque (N.M.), New Mexico University Library.
Ann Arbor (Mich.), Michigan University General Library.
Ann Arbor (Mich.), Michigan University Law Library.
Athens (Ga.), Georgia University Library.
Atlanta (Ga.), Woodruff Library, Emory University.
Austin (Tex.), Texas University Library.
Berkeley (Calif.), California University Library.
Cambridge (Mass.), Harvard College Library.
Cambridge (Mass.), Harvard University Law School Library.
Charlottesville (Virginia), Alderman Library University of Virginia.
Chicago (Ill.), Chicago University Library.
Chicago (Ill.), Newberry Library.
Cincinnati (Ohio), University Library.
Columbia (Mo.), Missouri University Library.
Dallas (Tex.), Dallas Public Library.
Durham (N.C.), Duke University Library.
Eugene (Oregon), Oregon University Library.
Iowa City (Iowa), Iowa State University Library.
Ithaca (N.Y.), Cornell University Library.
Los Angeles (Calif.), California University Research Library.
Madison (Wis.), Wisconsin University Library.
Minneapolis, Minnesota University Library.
Nashville (Tenn.), Vanderbilt University Library.
New Haven (Conn.), Yale University Library.
New York (N.Y.), Columbia University Library.

New York (N.Y.), Public Library.
Poughkeepsie (N.Y.), Vassar College Library.
Princeton (N.J.), Princeton University Library.
Providence (R.I.), John Hay Library, Brown University.
Rochester (N.Y.), Rochester University Library.
Salt Lake City (Utah), Genealogical Society.
San Marino (Calif.), Henry E. Huntington Library and Art Gallery.
Stanford (Calif.), Stanford University Library.
Stonybrook (N.Y.), State University of New York.
Tucson (Arizona), Arizona University Library.
Urbana (Ill.), Illinois University Library.
Washington (D.C.), Library of Congress.

THE SOUTHAMPTON RECORDS SERIES

XVIII. *A History of Southampton, 1700–1914. Volume III: Setbacks and Recoveries, 1868–1914*, by A. Temple Patterson (1975).

XIX–XX. *The Cartulary of God's House, Southampton*. Edited in two volumes, with an introduction, by J.M. Kaye (1976).

XXI. *The Southampton Mayor's Book of 1606–1608*. Edited, with an introduction, by W.J. Connor (1978).

XXII. *The Third Book of Remembrance of Southampton, 1514–1602*. Vol. IV (1590–1602). Edited, with an introduction, by T.B. James (1979).

XXIII. *Minute Book of the French Church*. Edited, with an introduction, by Edwin Welch (1980).

XXIV–XXV. *The St Denys Cartulary*. Edited in two volumes, with an introduction, by E.O. Blake (1981, 1982).

XXVI. *Southampton Sources: 1086–1900*. Edited, with an introduction, by T.B. James (1983).

XXVII. *A God's House Miscellany*. Edited, with an introduction, by J.M. Kaye (1984).

XXVIII. *The Brokage Books of Southampton for 1477–8 and 1527–8*. Edited by K.F. Stevens (1985). The Book of 1477–8 translated by T.E. Olding (1985).

XXIX. *Dilapidated Housing and Housing Policy in Southampton, 1890–1914*. Edited, with an introduction, by Martin Doughty (1986).

XXX. *Henry V and the Southampton Plot of 1415*, by T.B. Pugh (1987).

XXXI. *Minute Book of the Pavement Commissioners for Southampton 1770–1789*. Edited, with an introduction, by Jan Stovold (1990).

XXXII–XXXIII. *The Port Book of Southampton, 1509–10*. Edited in two volumes, with an introduction, by T.B. James (1990).

XXXIV–XXXV. *Southampton Probate Inventories 1447–1575*. Edited in two volumes, with an introduction, by Edward Roberts and Karen Parker (1992).

XXXVI. *The Southampton Port and Brokage Books, 1448–9*. Edited, with an introduction, by Elisabeth A. Lewis (1993).

XXXVII. *The Book of Examinations and Depositions Before the Mayor and Justices of Southampton 1648–1663*. Edited, with an introduction, by Sheila D. Thomson (1994).

XXXVIII. *The Southampton Steward's Book of 1492–93 and the Terrier of 1495*. Edited, with an introduction, by Anne Thick (1995).